Milnrow U.D.

Milnrow

B = BRIDGE STREET

NEW HEY STATION

Huddersfield Road

SHAW ROAD

NEWHEY ROAD

MILNROW ROAD

Newhey

DALE STREET NEWHEY

B

MILNROW STATION

River Beal

ROCHDALE ROAD

Firgrove

Canal

Newbold

Rochdale Canal

MILNROW ROAD

Crompton U.D.

High Crompton

Roch

Royton

MANCHESTER ROAD

SHAW

To Oldham

ROYTON STATION

Royton Depot

Dogford Rd

Fir Bank Road

High Barn St.

Thorp

ROAD OLDHAM

Middleton Rd.

OLDHAM ROAD

To Oldham

Summit

Springfield Lane

ROCHDALE ROAD

Royton U.D.

Thornham Old Road

Buersil Head

Buersil

Shaw Road

Ash Grove

ROAD OLDHAM

Platting Lane

Broad Lane

Frasel St.

Argyle St.

King's Road

Royds Road

Crawford Street

OLDHAM

ROAD

SPOTLAND ROAD

Mellor Street

Borough of Rochdale

Thornham New Road

Slattocks

Manchester Road

Castleton

CASTLETON STATION

Tows Lane

ROAD MANCHESTER

Rochdale Canal

Branch Canal

Norden U.D.

Bamford

Hooley Bridge

Bamford Road

Bury Road

River Roch

MANCHESTER ROAD

EAST BOLTON ROAD

Marland Old Road

Marland

Sudden

Primrose Hill Farm

Ryecroft House

Chadwick Lane

Green Lane

Borough of Heywood

Heywood

HEYWOOD STATION

MANCHESTER STREET

ROCHDALE ROAD

Aspinall St.

William Street (now Queens Park Road)

YORK ST

MP CHURCH ST

MARKET STREET

To Bury

SJ

D

Hopwood

WITHINGTON ST.

MANCHESTER ROAD

Middleton Road

Manchester Road

ROYTON DEPOT

DOGFORD ROAD

SCHOFIELD STREET

ROCHDALE ROAD

1. Standard Gauge Engine Shed.
2. Standard Gauge Car Shed.
3. Crew Rooms and Offices.
4. Narrow Gauge Car Shed.
5. Narrow Gauge Engine Shed.
6. Coke.

300 Feet
100 metres

Legend

tramway, 3'- 6" gauge
tramway, 4'- 8½" gauge
tramway, 3'- 6" and 4'- 8½" gauges
authorised tramway, 3'- 6" gauge, not built
authorised tramway, 3'- 6" and 4'- 8½" gauges, not built
other roads
railways
municipal boundaries

D = Heywood Depot (internal layout and arrangements not known)
MP = MARKET PLACE
SJ = St. James St.

SCALE EXAGGERATED AT LOOPS AND JUNCTIONS

1 mile
1000 yards
500
1 kilometre
0.5

£15

C000171295

R.A.Smith & A.P.Young
9/07- No.812

TRAMWAYS IN ROCHDALE

Steam, Electric and Metrolink

An early view of the town centre at the junction of Drake Street and Smith Street. Two 8-wheel bogie single deckers are the only vehicles to be seen. All the buildings have long since disappeared.
(MTMS)

Tony Young

January 2008

Published by Light Rail Transit Association
7 Ramsdale Court, Scarborough, YO11 2AP

ISBN
978-0-948106-34-7

Designed by Just My Type, Isle of Wight PO 37 6EA
Printed by Delmar Press Ltd, Nantwich, Cheshire CW5 5LS

TRAMWAYS IN ROCHDALE

Contents

Foreword

This book gives a detailed account of what must, in its thirty years of electric operation, have been one of the most remarkable yet little-known municipal tramway undertakings in Britain. There were no horse tramways and the company-owned steam tramways that preceded the municipal system have already been well documented. But apart from some fairly brief descriptions and the tantalizing glimpses in the Mitchell and Kenyon films, Rochdale's electric tramways have had to wait until now for a full presentation.

Ironically, the most revealing feature of Rochdale's tramways is the way they came to an end, almost precipitately, in 1930-32, only a few years after new cars had been bought and others fitted with top covers. Territory served by the undertaking was noticeably less populous than that of several of its neighbours; many routes had only three cars per hour, a situation in the Manchester area comparable only with the eastern extremities of the Stalybridge joint board. More than a third of Rochdale's fleet was bogie single decks that climbed at regular but infrequent intervals into neighbouring valleys.

As operating frequency is a major factor in track life, much of Rochdale's track lasted for thirty years instead of the more usual twenty at urban densities. So the system avoided the financial crisis of having to reconstruct track in the inflationary early 1920s, only to find that much of it required urgent reconstruction all at once in a time of trade depression. This, fuelled by the adverse attitude of the 1931 Royal Commission on Transport, the enthusiasm for buses of the neighbouring Manchester general manager R Stuart Pilcher, and the undesirability of raising a further tramway loan on top of the unexpired debt of earlier years, led almost inevitably to bus conversion.

Very little physically survives of the Rochdale tramways, although plans remain to extend the Manchester Metrolink into the town. There persists, however, just the possibility that the ex-Hull car at Heaton Park is on an ex-Rochdale truck. Meanwhile, let Tony Young transport you in his book to the past, a far country, and the tramways of one of its least-known dales.

Ian Yearsley

Transport journalist and historian.
President of the Tramway Museum Society 2007-08.

Preface

Tramways hold a fascination that is rarely equalled. Young and old, those who remember the first generation trams and those who only know the modern equivalents, find the movement of these giants of the highway on rails strangely appealing. Perhaps it is their clean, quiet movement in an otherwise polluted and noisy world; perhaps it is their friendly and reliable performance to take us about our daily tasks; perhaps it is some strange blend of nostalgia and science fiction.

I have to confess to being a lifelong tramway enthusiast, integrated with my career as a light rail consultant. I am enthusiastic about the way trams can provide us with clean, convenient, reliable, fully accessible transport for work, socialising, pleasure and recreation which no other form of transport seems to be able to achieve in our congested towns and cities. The fact that they can be equally at home running down the street, in a pedestrian area, along railway lines or through parks or tunnels makes them uniquely suited to serving homes, workplaces and town centres.

Such is the popularity of tramways that innumerable books have been written about systems long since abandoned and systems yet to start carrying passengers. But for some reason, Rochdale has been missed out, with two important exceptions. The steam tram era has been excellently documented by W.G.S. Hyde in his book 'The Manchester Bury Rochdale and Oldham Steam Tramway', published by The Transport Publishing Company, Glossop in 1979. The electric tramways were outlined in a booklet written by the late Clifford Taylor with many historic photographs, published by The Manchester Transport Museum Society (MTMS) in 1987. Cliff intended to write a definitive history of Rochdale trams but sadly died before he could complete the task. He collected a vast amount of information, now in the MTMS archives, which has proved an invaluable resource for this book. More recently Rochdale Tram Depot was covered in a book by T Clarkson.

These publications have been extremely helpful in preparing the text for this book. A third valuable resource is the three papers by H. G. Dibdin on Rochdale Corporation Tramways published in Tramway Review in 1978. These appear to be the only definitive historical reference to Rochdale's electric tramway era, although as the author freely admitted, there were some errors. Arthur Kirby's book on the Middleton Tramways, published in October 1976, describes in detail the tramways in what is now part of Rochdale Metropolitan Borough. Many other sources have been tapped including Rochdale Tramways Committee minutes, Rochdale Observer archives, the Tramway Museum Society archives at Crich and a host of publications listed in the bibliography.

Now trams are set to return to the streets of Rochdale after a gap of over seventy five years, albeit in a very different form and only over one kilometre (5/8 mile). We will never see the return of a network as it was in the early part of the last century. But we will be able to enjoy an effortless ride up Drake Street and remember that once upon a time, trams ran up there to all points south.

Note 1: where prices or costs are given in the text, the approximate value at current prices is given in brackets.
Note 2: where dates are given in dd.mm.yy format, the year refers to 19xx.

Front Cover
Artist Ashley Best's atmospheric painting depicts Rochdale Corporation 4-wheel double decker number 92 arriving at the Tramway Centre from Drake Street on a damp winter's evening. Manchester Corporation bogie car number 1040 waits to leave for Manchester High Street on the short lived joint route 17.

Back Cover
A classic Rochdale single deck tram built by Brush in 1906 with Brush bogies. It is seen in its later form with enclosed platforms which were added in the 1920's. (J. S. King).

Over a century later the next generation of single deck tram, built by Bombardier, will start delivery in 2009 and should reach Rochdale by 2011. (Bombardier Transportation).

Acknowledgements

Advice and encouragement to produce this book, and material to fill its pages, has come from many and varied sources. Dennis Gill, the author of a number of tramway books, first suggested the idea when he heard that I was moving to Rochdale as no-one had produced a history of its tramways. Dennis provided a lot of useful contacts and leads.

The late Cliff Taylor had intended to write a history and did produce a short booklet on Rochdale Trams but sadly did not live to see his ambition fulfilled. He did leave his collected historical material to the Manchester Tramway Museum Society (MTMS) at their Heaton Park Tramway and that has been invaluable as a reference source. The staff at Heaton Park have been very helpful in allowing access, particularly Geoff Hyde and Bob Hill. Eric Hall had researched committee minutes and other documentation and provided copies, as well as building excellent models of Rochdale trams. Information was also provided by Ian Yearsley, Peter Duncan and Roy Pickup.

Arthur Kirby has written a number of histories of tramways in the Manchester area including Oldham and Middleton. He collected material for a possible book on Rochdale and very kindly made it all available to me, including a full set of Tramways Committee minutes and some text which is incorporated in the early chapters.

Photographs have been donated by Eric Fielding, Ian Yearsley, Dillys and Graham Pearson of Littleborough Historical and Archaeological Society, Arthur Hodgson, Stanley King and others. The Tramway Museum Society, MTMS, Rochdale Observer and the Local Studies Centre, Touchstones Rochdale also provided photographs. The staff at Touchstones ably helped in finding files and archive material, as did Rosie Thacker and Glyn Wilton at Crich Tramway Village. (Where known, the source of the photograph is given in brackets but in many cases this is the collector not necessarily the photographer).

David Petrie kindly gave permission to use the extract from his father's unpublished historical notes which gives an eyewitness account of the tramways. Many other Rochdalians have given snippets of their experiences, or their parents' or grandparents', which add an important dimension to the story. Sadly some of the contributors have now died.

Permission to use the magnificent painting of Rochdale town centre on the cover was given by the artist, Ashley Best, who also provided technical details of Rochdale's popular single deck bogie trams. Philip Groves, who was born in Rochdale when trams were still running, provided information on rolling stock and checked the fleet list and text. Colin Reeve checked the sections covering buses.

Probably the only surviving original coat of arms from a Rochdale tram was kindly lent by Robert Ashworth to be photographed and colour checked.

An unenviable task was volunteered by Stanley King. He meticulously proof read the whole manuscript and made many relevant and helpful suggestions and comments and it is undoubtedly much the better for that.

Any book of this nature needs clear maps to support the text and Roger Smith, LRTA cartographer, has met this challenge with flying colours.

Finally sincere thanks must go the LRTA Publications Committee and their Chairman John Cadisch for accepting this book for publication and for expediting its production to meet tight timescales.

To all these contributors I offer my grateful thanks; without them this book could not have been written. Special thanks go to Janet Taplin who skilfully wove text and illustrations into a coherent whole and patiently dealt with the author's changes.

Tony Young
Rochdale
January 2008

1. Introduction

To many, the town of Rochdale may be unremarkable, just another industrial centre in the once great South Lancashire cotton belt. To others it is famous for the birth of the Co-operative movement and Gracie Fields, but not a lot more. Such simplifications belie a fascinating area with a wealth of history, culture and natural beauty that invites investigation. The Dale along the River Roch nestles in the western foothills of the Pennines, giving it a character quite different to other towns in Greater Manchester or beyond.

Although Rochdale was in many ways a child of the industrial revolution, its history goes back much further. After the Norman conquest Rochdale became part of the Salford hundred. A Saxon castle existed a millennium ago and a church dedicated to Saint Chad was recorded in 1194. At first it came under Lichfield Diocese, passing to Chester Diocese in 1541 and finally to Manchester Diocese in 1847. St. Chad's is Rochdale's parish church and still stands proudly overlooking the town centre, above the magnificent Town Hall. A charter to hold a weekly market and an annual fair was granted by King Henry III in 1240.

Trade in wool began around 1350. Cotton manufacture began much later in 1791 but in the early nineteenth century wool products were still the main output of the mills, notably flannel. However, cotton mills grew rapidly and became even larger than the woollen mills, aided by the new steam powered machinery, making textiles the leading industry in the town. As the industrial revolution gathered pace through the late eighteenth and early nineteenth centuries, mills and churches sprang up across the town, vying for attention: mills on workdays, church on Sundays. By the end of the nineteenth century business was prospering and the local economy buoyant. When the first electric trams ran in 1902, Rochdale was the third largest mill town in Lancashire (after Oldham and Bolton), with 2,422,000 spindles.

In 1881, before any trams ran, Rochdale's population was just under 69,000 but by the time electric trams began it had risen to over 83,000. By the early twenties it was nearing 93,000. Today it is over 200,000 but now includes many of the surrounding authorities which were then separate townships.

To many, Rochdale's tramways are as unremarkable as the town. They are long forgotten by all except the very elderly who still have fond memories. There are very few remains to be seen, with the notable exception of the original tramway offices where the smart red tiles above the main entrance doorway still proudly announce 'Tramway Offices'. It has long since ceased to be an operational public transport depot although it did continue to house buses until comparatively recently. Sadly, while trams from many systems have been rescued for preservation, all Rochdale's trams went to the breakers' yards.

And yet the tramways of Rochdale present a fascinating history with many unusual aspects. There were industrial tramways in the hills around Rochdale long before trams appeared on the streets. Horse trams never ran in Rochdale but steam trams started in 1883, followed by electric trams in 1902. The change of traction also involved changing the gauge, a feat which few operators would contemplate even today. Steam trams lasted only 22 years with even the electric network surviving for only 30 years - it vanished even more quickly than it had appeared. Amazingly, some trams were only four or five years old when the system was abandoned.

Most of the extensive local network was built in little more than three years which, ironically, is less time than it takes for GMPTE to put a Metrolink package out to tender! At their peak in 1928, Rochdale's trams carried over 27 million passengers, way above the total carried by today's Metrolink tram network. The Rochdale tramways once formed part of one of the largest tram networks in the world, stretching from the Pennines to the Irish Sea, from the Cheshire plains to deepest Lancashire, and embracing the North West's two great cities of Manchester and Liverpool.

There are four distinct forms of tramways that have, or hopefully will, serve Rochdale:

- Industrial tramways serving quarries and mines;
- Steam tramways;
- Electric tramways;
- Metrolink light rail.

Each is described in this book, within the limitations of available information and space. The steam tram era is included as background to the electric tramways but a more detailed history has been written by W.G.S.Hyde. (see bibliography).

There were three stages in the construction of Rochdale's electric tramway:

- new electric tramways in Rochdale;
- conversion of the steam tramways to electric traction;
- construction and operation of electric tramways in and for adjacent districts.

The first stage comprised routes to Bamford, Norden, Spotland and Firgrove; the second stage included routes to Whitworth, Littleborough, Thornham and Heywood and the last stage included extensions to Bacup, Summit (Littleborough), Milnrow and New Hey, and Castleton. Rochdale operated trams on routes through the Urban Districts of Whitworth, Wardle, Littleborough, Milnrow and Norden and the Boroughs of Heywood and Bacup. It also operated on joint routes into the Boroughs of Oldham, Bury, Middleton and the City of Manchester.

2. Before the trams

Turnpikes and coaches

Roads date back to pre-Roman times and there were many packhorse tracks across the Pennine hills providing early trade routes. Some Roman remains can still be found over Blackstone Edge beyond Littleborough although their precise origin is disputed. But conditions were poor and progress slow and unreliable. Turnpike roads, precursors of the toll motorway, brought a new standard of construction and maintenance which encouraged regular coaching routes to be established.

Turnpike roads from Rochdale to Manchester and Burnley opened in 1754. A direct coach service from Rochdale to London began in 1777 taking five days for the somewhat hazardous journey. Soon regular coaches were operating between Manchester, Leeds and York via Rochdale. A local coach, the 'High Flyer', started in 1790 between Rochdale and Manchester, undercutting the fares on the Leeds mail coaches. They charged 4s inside or 2s outside (on the roof) compared with only 2s 6d or 1s 6d respectively on the local stage coach. Within about ten years the 'High Flyer' had been extended to Bradford, and possibly even Leeds, making it possible for Bradford cotton manufacturers (there were a few) to travel from Bradford to Manchester and back in a day. Sometime later a coach known as 'Neptune' ran from Rochdale to Liverpool via Bury, Bolton and Wigan.

A new turnpike road between Rochdale and Manchester ran through Harpurhey and Blackley under a Turnpike Act of 1805, providing an alternative route to the old road through Crumpsall. Not much remains of the turnpike era but the Steanor Bottom Bar toll house for the 1824 Todmorden Turnpike (now A6033) still stands at the junction of Calderbrook Road and Todmorden Road, north of Summit on the northern fringe of the Borough and close to the post-1896 Yorkshire boundary.

Canals and railways

The earliest form of transport that was not road based was the canal. The Rochdale Canal opened in 1804, ten years after obtaining Parliamentary approval. It was the first Trans-Pennine canal, stretching 32 miles from the centre of Manchester to Sowerby Bridge in the West Riding. At Summit, between Littleborough and Walsden and the future north eastern limit of Rochdale's trams, it reached a height of 600 ft above sea level. A branch canal to Heywood was opened in 1834. Some passenger services were operated on the canals although their main role was to carry freight.

More than forty years before the first tram ran in Rochdale, and more than sixty years before the first electric tram ran, trains were running through Rochdale Station. The Manchester and Leeds Railway obtained an Act of Parliament in 1837, only seven years after the opening of the pioneering Liverpool and Manchester Railway, to build a railway from Manchester through Rochdale to the summit beyond Littleborough, continuing along the Calder Valley to Todmorden and Sowerby Bridge and then on towards Leeds. It opened in 1839 between Manchester and Littleborough, initially from a terminus in Oldham Road in Manchester.

Road charging is not new! Long before any trams ran around Rochdale, turnpike roads were built to speed horse drawn traffic between the towns. The toll house at Steanor Bottom Toll Bar on the Todmorden Turnpike can still be seen to the north of Summit. A scale of charges was made according to the type of animal or carriage. Horse drawn vehicles had to pay a toll of 6d (£1.68), not very different from current proposals for congestion charges.   (A P Young)

The section between Littleborough and Todmorden required completion of the formidable Summit tunnel. Construction began in 1838 but it was not completed until 1840, with the loss of 41 lives. At 2,885 yards (1.6 miles, 2.6 km) it was then the longest tunnel in Britain (some say the world). Trains began running through from Rochdale to Leeds in 1841 and the terminus moved to the now familiar Victoria Station in Manchester in 1844. Three years later in 1847 the Manchester & Leeds Railway became the Lancashire and Yorkshire Railway which was destined to be the dominant railway around Rochdale for the next seventy five years. Horse drawn coaches could not compete with railways and most were withdrawn.

Branch lines followed to Heywood in 1842, Middleton in 1857, Oldham via Milnrow in 1863 and Whitworth and Facit in 1870. Thus there were then twelve stations in what is now Rochdale Borough, all of which had opened before any tramway was built. Opening and closing dates are shown in Table 2.1.

The branch line between Rochdale and Bacup had a particularly long gestation. The Manchester and Leeds Railway obtained Parliamentary powers to build the line in 1846 but never started construction. It was left to its successor Lancashire and Yorkshire Railway to obtain powers for the section up the Whitworth Valley as far as Shawforth in 1862. It finally opened to Facit in 1870 but the last three and a half miles into Bacup did not open until 1881. That year Parliamentary Powers were granted for a steam tramway along the Whitworth Valley, threatening serious competition to the railway. Although the steam tramway would be much slower than the railway, it would be much more accessible as it ran along the road where most of the development was located. The railway was never a great commercial success although it did play an important role as a catalyst to the local economy of the valley.

Table 2.1 Railway station opening and closing dates in and around Rochdale.

Station	Opened	Closed	Railway at opening	Railway at closure	Notes
Bacup	01.10.1852	05.12.1966	L & Y	BR	(Lancs). 01.12.1881 on Rochdale line
Britannia	01.12.1881	02.04.1917	L & Y	L & Y	(Lancs).
Broadfield	13.09.1869	05.09.1970	L & Y	BR	
Broadley	01.11.1870	16.06.1947	L & Y	LMS	(Lancs).
Castleton	15.09.1839	open	M & L	na	Originally named 'Blue Pitts for Heywood'; renamed 'Blue Pitts' 17.04.1841; renamed 'Castleton' 1.11.1875.
Facit	01.11.1870	16.06.1947	L & Y	LMS	(Lancs).
Heywood	15.04.1841	05.10.1970	M & L	BR	Original station replaced 01.05.1848
Littleborough	04.06.1839	open	M & L	na	
Middleton	01.05.1857	07.09.1964	L & Y	BR	
Middleton Junction	31.03.1842	03.01.1966	M & L	BR	Originally named 'Oldham Junction'; Renamed 'Middleton' 11.08.1842; Renamed 'Middleton Junction' xx.05.1852.
Mills Hill	25.03.1985	open	BR	na	
Milnrow	02.11.1863	open	L & Y	na	
New Hey	02.11.1863	open	L & Y	na	
Rochdale	04.06.1839	open	M & L	na	Original station 520m east; Relocated 28.04.1889.
Shawclough & Healey	01.11.1870	16.06.1947	L & Y	LMS	Closed from 02.04.1917 to xx.07.1920.
Shawforth	01.12.1881	16.06.1947	L & Y	LMS	(Lancs).
Smithy Bridge	04.06.1839	open	M & L	na	Closed from 02.05.1960 to 19.08.1985.
Wardleworth	01.11.1870	16.06.1947	L & Y	LMS	
Whitworth	01.11.1870	16.06.1947	L & Y	LMS	(Lancs).

M & L   Manchester and Leeds Railway (became Lancashire & Yorkshire Railway on 9 July 1847).
L & Y   Lancashire and Yorkshire (became part of London & North Western Railway on 1 January 1922).
LMS   London Midland & Scottish Railway (took over L&NWR on 1 January 1923).
BR   British Railways (took over all railways on 1 January 1948).
(Lancs)   Stations which are in Lancashire County Council area, not Rochdale MBC.

Horse drawn buses

The earliest form of urban public transport was the horse bus. The first horse buses in Britain are often credited to George Shillibeer who ran a route in London in 1829 but in fact John Greenwood ran a horse bus in Salford five years earlier in 1824. There were several departures a day between Pendleton and Market Street, Manchester at a flat fare of sixpence *(£1.30)*. Horse buses did not reach Rochdale for another thirty years with the earliest records indicating services from 1856 onwards.

A regular horse bus service began operating to Oldham on Christmas Day 1870 although an earlier service to Oldham had started on 26th August 1861 but probably did not survive beyond November 1863 when the Oldham railway opened. The fares were 5d *(£1.04)* inside and 4d *(83p)* outside. ('Outside' meant sitting on the roof.) Horse buses tended to operate between hotels, presumably because they were easily recognised locations, and passengers could fortify themselves for the journey to come, or recover from the one just completed. By the early seventies, horse drawn buses were running from several hotels in the centre of Rochdale:

- from the Spread Eagle Hotel, Cheetham Street, to Bacup 6 times a day;
- from the Roebuck Inn, Yorkshire Street, to Heywood and Bury 3 times a day;
- from White Hart Inn, St Mary's Gate to Smallbridge and Littleborough 3 times a day;
- from White Hart Inn, St Mary's Gate to Norden 3 times a day.

The Spread Eagle Hotel and the Roebuck Inn still exist.

The Heywood horse bus survived until 24th May 1887 when it succumbed to competition from the steam trams but the Norden horse bus, with no tram competition continued until the advent of electric trams. The Norden horse buses are recorded as costing 160 guineas *(£168)* each when new, *(£8,395)*, but when the three buses were sold in June 1902, having lost their customers to the bright new electric trams, they raised no more than £2 15s 0d *(£177)*, £4 15s 0d *(£306)* and £8 10s 0d *(£547)* each at auction.

Realising that horse bus days were numbered when work started on the electric tramway, Mr John Coupe of the Norden Coach Company applied for the position of Superintendent cleaner and occasional driver. His application was successful together with four of his colleagues.

Many towns and cities started their tramways with horse traction but hilly Rochdale progressed straight to steam and then electric. Although horses were used to pull most types of vehicle in the latter part of the nineteenth century including buses, they never pulled trams in Rochdale. Manchester's horse trams started in 1877 and reached Oldham in 1878. They ran for 19 years in Bolton, 21 years in Oldham and 26 years in Manchester but by 1900 most had been replaced by steam or electric trams.

Curiously, horse trams were briefly considered for Whitworth following the failure of the steam trams. In November 1891, four months after the last steam tram ran between Healey and Whitworth, a group of prominent local businessmen including some councillors formed a private company with a capital of £1,000 *(£62,000)* with the intention of operating horse cars. They proposed to purchase two second hand horse trams and hire the horses to operate a service between Whitworth and the cut-back steam tram terminus at Healey. Their scheme never got off the ground.

A three horse bus outside the Brown Cow Inn in Norden towards the end of the nineteenth century. (MTMS)

3. Industrial tramways in the hills.

Origins of the word 'tram'

Long before there were passenger carrying trams in Rochdale, tramway technology in a rather different form was being used to carry goods. The Pennine hills above Rochdale were rich sources of minerals, notably coal and stone. Transporting these heavy materials from the mines and quarries to roads or canals, and later railways, called for some ingenuity. One solution was the tramway, often fairly crude forms of railway powered by humans, horses, rope or steam, which eased the burden of getting the goods to market. The small trucks used in coal mines were sometimes called 'trams' and working them by hand was 'tramming'. Tramways were also used to move materials for construction of many of the dams built in the hills around the town to supply water for domestic and industrial use, and to feed the canals.

Information is not as well documented as for later tramways but remains can still be found in remoter places. It has to be admitted that the difference between a tramway and a railway in this context is somewhat blurred. The term 'tramway' was used in the eighteenth and early nineteenth centuries to describe some primitive forms of freight railway whereas the term 'tramroad' was first used around the turn of the eighteenth century to refer to railways laid with simple stone, wooden or iron rails for vehicles pushed manually or pulled by horses. Later, steam engines were used and rope hauled inclines were provided where gradients would be too steep for other forms of traction.

Early tramroads

A tramroad was marked on an 1848 map at Hogshead Colliery near Shawforth and an early chain hauled tramway was reportedly still working at Old Meadows drift mine near Bacup in the late nineteen sixties.

Another early tramroad connected the colliery at Hopwood Hall near Middleton with the canal basin in Heywood. Although the canal has long since disappeared, the line of the tramway can still be discerned as a tree lined embankment running northwards, to the east of A6046 Middleton Road. Tramroads linked the Rochdale Canal at Higher Boarshaw with nearby collieries and traces could still be seen in the sixties at the former wharf on the west side of the canal, next to the stone

bridge. Traces of a tramroad to a disused mine could be found at Higher Tunshill, close to Rochdale Way and south east of Hollingworth Lake.

The picturesque Ashworth valley was riddled with coal mines, many being drift mines cutting straight into the hillsides. Coal from the drift mines below Ashworth Hall was taken by tramway laid along the bank of Naden Brook to a weighbridge at Guelder Clough. Further west an aerial ropeway, sometimes termed 'aerial tramway', ran down from Wind Hill Pit to near Hardmans Mill at Deeply Vale, carrying coal from the pit across Ashworth Road, then dropping down the hill across a timber trellis bridge, through a narrow cutting and terminating at the foot of Deeply Hill. There were two four wheel wagons each carrying five 2½ cwt. tubs of coal. The gradient of the line allowed them to reach the valley by gravity but they had to be hauled back by a cable which was powered by a stationary steam engine at the pit. As the wagons passed over the road at the bottom, coal was tipped from the tubs into carts below. At the peak of production the wagons made over 22 journeys per day supplying coal to Deeply Vale Mills and to Longlands at Buckhurst. Some traces of the tramway are still visible.

A complex network of narrow gauge tramways and light railways existed in the Whitworth valley and across parts of Rooley Moor. Some included rope hauled inclined railways whose formations are still clearly visible, for example at Broadley and Facit. The course of the 3' 0" gauge line from

Quarry tramways abounded in the hills around Rochdale. Some were narrow gauge but Facit Quarry had a standard gauge system reached by a rope hauled incline from Facit L & Y Station. Steam loco 'Tam O Shanter', seen hauling a heavily loaded stone wagon, was built in 1890 by Manning Wardle and ran until about 1919.   *(MTMS)*

the top of the incline at Broadley is also visible with earthworks, bridge abutments and what appears to be the remains of an engine shed. It runs northwards for about a mile to the former Bagden quarries. Today this moorland setting is a haven of peace and tranquillity, but in its heyday a century ago it would have been a bustling hive of industrial activity.

A short tramway linked the Rochdale Canal near Summit in Littleborough with Sladen Mill Fold. There were a number of brickworks and coalmines in this area and narrow gauge tramways or railways were often used to move materials between pitheads or quarries and the canal or railway. A tramway linked Tetlows brickworks, behind Sladen Wood Mill at Summit, with coal and clay workings in Lydgate Clough.

There was also a tramway at Higher Slack, north of Watergrove Reservoir, climbing the hillside to the west of Higher Slack Brook. Much later, narrow gauge tramways or light railways were used extensively during the construction of Watergrove Reservoir, powered by steam, diesel and manpower. Although the idea of a reservoir was discussed by Rochdale Council in 1907, not long after electric trams began, work did not begin until 1930, not long before the Corporation trams finished. It was completed in 1938.

To the north west of Rochdale, high above Turn village, lies Scout Moor with a long history of stone quarrying. It is still worked today but the tramway which transported minerals into the fifties has long since been replaced by rubber tyred vehicles.

A narrow gauge tramway was used during the re-construction of Warland Reservoir, high up in the Pennine hills north of Littleborough. Originally built in 1801 to feed the Rochdale Canal, it was rebuilt in the twenties to supply drinking water to Rochdale. (Touchstones Rochdale)

Another view of the tramway at Warland. A similar narrow gauge system was used for the construction of Watergrove Reservoir to the north of Wardle. It was proposed in 1907 but construction did not begin until 1930 and it took eight years to complete. (Touchstones Rochdale)

4. The steam tram era.

A company tramway is born

The first passenger carrying tramways in Rochdale were promoted by Charles Philips of Bucklersbury in the City of London. The Manchester, Bury, Rochdale and Oldham Steam Tramways Company was formed in 1881 to construct and operate steam tramways in all these towns. It grew to become the largest single steam tramways company in Britain with over 30 miles (48 km) of track. Unfortunately it used two different gauges, standard 4ft 8½in and narrow gauge 3ft 6in, to meet differing local authority requirements so through running over the whole network was not possible. The Rochdale routes were all narrow gauge, connecting with standard gauge routes in Bury and Oldham. The network was thus in three separate sections with the majority, about 21 miles (34 km) being narrow gauge.

The tramway was authorised by the Rochdale Tramways Order 1881 and confirmed by the Tramways Orders Confirmation (No. 3) Act 1881. The following lines were authorised in Rochdale:

1. Town Hall Square, South Parade, Drake Street and Oldham Road terminating in Oldham Road 134 yards south of Broad Lane at Buersil. Total length one mile 937 yards of which one mile 312 yards was single track and 625 yards double track; Town Hall Square and South Parade were double track and there were seven passing loops at 33 yards, double at the termination.

2. Drake Street and Manchester Road, terminating in Manchester Road 112 yards south west of Law Street. Total length one mile 704 yards of which one mile 235 yards was single track and 469 yards double track; single track with six passing loops and 33 yards double at the termination.

3. South Parade and Rochdale Bridge. Total length 31 yards of which eleven yards was single track and 20 yards double track.

4. Rochdale Bridge, The Butts, Smith Street, Entwisle Road and Yorkshire Street terminating in Yorkshire Street 21 yards north east of Entwisle Road. Total length 1,629 yards of which 1,435 yards of single track and 194 yards of double track, four sections of double track.

5. Yorkshire Street from Cheetham Street to Whitworth Road. Total length 196 yards of which 130 yards was single track and 66 yards double track, one double track section.

6. Yorkshire Street from Whitworth Road to Entwisle Road. Total length 807 yards of which 675 yards was single track and 132 yards was double track and there were two passing loops.

7. Yorkshire Street and Halifax Road from Entwisle Road to Ashbrook. Total length 1,472 yards of which 1,153 yards was single track and 319 yards was double track and there were five double track sections.

8. Halifax Road from Ashbrook to the Ox and Plough Inn. Total length 1,188 yards of which 1,023 yards was single track and 165 yards was double track with two double track sections and 33 yards double at the termination.

9. A curve, from Yorkshire Street into Entwisle Road twenty yards of single track.

10. Whitworth Road from Yorkshire Street to a point 101 yards west of the Post Office at Ending. Total length one

A steam tram loco and open top trailer on the short route between Heywood and Hopwood. Originally opened in 1884 it was operated for a short time by Heywood Corporation Tramways, finally closing in 1905.

mile 1,222 yards of which one mile 617 yards was single track and 605 yards was double track, there were nine passing loops and 33 yards double at the termination.

The authorised tramways totalled seven miles 1,163 yards of track of which six miles 332 yards was to be single and one mile 834 yards double.

At the same time Philips was authorised to construct tramways in Bury under the Bury and District Tramways Order 1881, confirmed by the same Confirmation Act.

Further tramways in Bury and Rochdale were authorised by the Manchester, Bury, and Rochdale Tramways (extensions) Order 1882, confirmed by the Tramways Orders Confirmation (No.3) Act 1882. Tramways 1 - 5 were in Bury; the individual lines in Rochdale were:

6. Town Hall Square, The Esplanade and Manchester Road to a junction with tramway number two of the 1881 Order. Total length 961 yards of which 708 yards was single track and 253 yards was double track, the tracks were double at both ends of the tramway and at the Esplanade/Manchester Road junction.

6A. Town Hall Square 29 yards of single track.

7. Manchester Road 33 yards of double track being an extension of tramway number two of the 1881 Order.

7A. Manchester Road from the termination of tramway number 7 to the boundary with Castleton Urban District. Total length one mile 491 yards of which one mile 128 yards was single track and 363 yards double track; double track at the commencement and five passing loops.

8. Halifax Road from the Ox and Plough Inn to a point 31 yards east of Lodge Street, Littleborough. Total length one mile 206 yards of which 1,614 yards was

single track and 352 yards double track, double at the commencement with four passing loops.

9. Cheetham Street, St. Mary's Gate and Spotland Road to a point 18 yards east of Handley Street. Total length 1,056 yards of which 869 yards single track and 187 yards double, single at the commencement with three passing loops.

10. A continuation of tramway number 10 of the 1881 Order along Whitworth Road, Market Street (Whitworth), Market Street (Facit) and Market Street (Shawforth) and Rochdale Road to the boundary of Whitworth and Bacup. Total length three miles 1,646 yards of which three miles 672 yards single and 974 yards of double track, single at the commencement with fifteen passing loops.

11. A continuation of tramway number 10 along Rochdale Road, St. James' Street and Bridge Street, Bacup to a point 34 yards east of its junction with Newchurch Road. Total length one mile 992 yards of which one mile 596 yards was single track and 396 yards double track, single at the commencement with six passing loops.

Tramways 12 - 19 of the same Order authorised lines from Bacup to Rawtenstall. Tramways numbers 20 - 25 connected the Bury tramways at Heap Bridge to the Rochdale lines at the termination of tramway number 7, with a branch from Heywood Market Place to Hopwood. Tramway number 26 was an extension of tramway number one of the 1881 Order along Rochdale Road to Royton with a reversing triangle at its termination (tramways numbers 27 and 28). All the tramways so far mentioned were to be constructed to a gauge of three feet six inches, or such other wider gauge as might be required by the Board of Trade. Tramways numbers 29 to 31 were to be built to a gauge of 4 feet 8½ inches and were a continuation - after a gap of 28 yards - of tramway 27 towards Oldham.

Steam tram loco 82 is posed with its double deck trailer in Church Street Littleborough. The loco was built by Beyer Peacock in Manchester in 1885. The trailer is one of 32 built by Falcon Works in Loughborough between 1884 and 1886. The Littleborough route was the last steam tram service, closing in 1905 and spending its last few months under the control of Rochdale Corporation Tramways. (MTMS)

Street tramway works begin

Construction of the tramways in Rochdale began on 27th July 1882 and was inaugurated by the Mayor, Alderman Baron, and the Chairman of the Paving Committee, Alderman Tweedale, who ceremonially removed two paving stones at the junction of Drake Street and Oldham Road. A depot was constructed adjacent to Entwisle Road, alongside the sanitary works, and the lines along Oldham Road to Buersil and along Halifax Road to Littleborough were completed in April 1883. The official Board of Trade inspection took place on 26th April and the lines opened to the public on 7th May, 1883. The first tram left the Wellington Hotel for Buersil and then returned for the long through route to Littleborough.

Steam tram loco No. 49 is a Wilkinson type built by Black, Hawthorn and Company in 1884. It is towing open top double deck trailer No. 61 built by Falcon Works in Loughborough in 1884/85.

The Rochdale Observer reported:

"At a quarter past twelve on Monday afternoon the first tramcars for passengers were run on the length which has been completed between Buersil and Littleborough. Eleven o'clock was the time which had been fixed. A large crowd collected to watch the starting of the cars, one being dispatched from the Wellington Inn to Buersil and the other to Littleborough. The cars were filled. The one to Buersil accomplished the journey in about twenty minutes, but the one to Littleborough was a little less expeditious. Considerable difficulty was for a time experienced in getting up the Drake Street incline near the Wellington. Apart from these little hitches, which are inevitable in commencing to work a new scheme, the trams were fairly successful."

The Observer got their facts a bit muddled because it was the Buersil tram that had to negotiate the gradient on Drake Street, not the Littleborough tram. The Buersil car was heavily loaded and had to make several attempts to get up the hill.

The opening ceremony was followed by a banquet at the Reed Hotel where local dignitaries spoke in glowing terms of the company's future prospects and the benefits which would accrue to Rochdale.

A service along Whitworth Road to Healey commenced on the 1st November 1883. A through route to Bury via Sudden, Heywood and Heap Bridge, together with a branch from Heywood to Hopwood opened on 30th May, 1884; the Healey route was extended to Whitworth on 11th July, and to Facit on 3rd April 1885. The Buersil line was extended to Royton on 1st March 1885. Thus almost the entire steam tram network had been completed in less than three years. Passengers awaiting the arrival of trams in the Town Centre were first catered for on 24th May 1886 with the unveiling of the first passenger shelter.

One operational feature of steam trams was the need to provide reversing triangles or loops at terminals to allow the engine to run round its trailer. To minimise this manoeuvre, through routes were operated as far as possible between Royton and Littleborough or Facit.

The total fleet consisted of 91 tram locomotives and 81 trailer cars, of which 62 'locos' and 55 trailers were narrow gauge. Most locos were to the Wilkinson patent tramway engine design but built by three manufacturers, as shown in Table 4.1. The narrow gauge trailer cars are listed in Table 4.2

The engines were painted in brown lined out in black with white double edging, although some appeared in other liveries including green. The livery of the passenger cars was described as oak and white, lined out in black with double edging in white and was regarded as very smart. As time progressed the cars appeared in a more drab brown and cream or maroon and cream, probably coloured by the dirt and smoke from the engines. Most cars and some engines carried advertisements, particularly in later years.

Tramway company re-born

The authorised share capital of the operating company was £500,000 in 50,000 shares of £10 each and by 1884 £345,460 had been subscribed of which £308,895 had been paid up. In order to further the development of the tramways, the Manchester, Bury, Rochdale and Oldham Steam Tramways Act 1884, which received the Royal Assent on 28th July, authorised the dissolution of the Manchester, Bury, Rochdale and Oldham Steam Tramway Limited and the members became share holders in a new company, the Manchester, Bury, Rochdale and Oldham

Table 4.1.	Steam tramway locomotive fleet list (narrow gauge).		
Fleet number	Year in service	Locomotive type	Manufacturer
9 – 12	1883	Wilkinson	Thomas Green & Son
13 – 17	1883	Wilkinson	Wilkinson, Wigan
18 - 20	1883	Wilkinson	Thomas Green & Son
21 – 26	1883	Wilkinson	Beyer, Peacock and Company
27 – 34	1883	Wilkinson	Thomas Green & So
39 – 41	1884	Standard	Falcon Works, Loughborough
42 – 51	1884	Wilkinson	Black, Hawthorn & Company
60	1885	Wilkinson	Thomas Green & Son
61 – 62	1885	Wilkinson	Wilkinson, Wigan
63 – 82	1886	Wilkinson	Beyer, Peacock and Company
89 - 90	1886	Wilkinson	Wilkinson, Wigan

Note: 60 probably ex-South Staffs Tramway Company.

Table 4.2.	Steam tramway trailer car fleet list (narrow gauge).			
Fleet number	Year in service	Car type	Number of passengers	Manufacturer
17 - 26	1883	6-wheel double deck open top (1)	20 lower deck 16 upper deck (2)	George Starbuck & Co, Birkenhead
27	1889 ?	8-wheel single deck (3)	20 lower deck	George Starbuck & Co, Birkenhead
28 – 39	1883/84	8-wheel double deck open top	?	George Starbuck & Co, Birkenhead
40 – 64	1884/85	8-wheel double deck with top canopy	?	Falcon Works, Loughborough
75 - 81	1886	8-wheel double deck with top canopy	26 lower deck 26 upper deck	Falcon Works, Loughborough

Notes:
(1) converted to 8-wheel bogie cars in 1885.
(2) some rebuilt as 70 seater cars in 1899 with two bodies per car.
(3) originally built in 1883 as 6-wheel car.

STEAM TRAMS IN ROCHDALE

Steam loco No.80 with covered top trailer at Church Street terminus in Littleborough waits to depart for Royton. Holy Trinity parish church is in the background.

In the Entwisle Road depot, a driver and his crew have their steam tram engine steamed up and ready for the road.
(Arthur Hodgson)

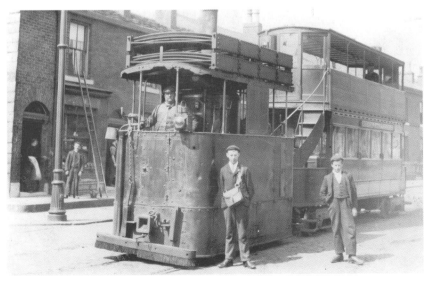

The crew of this unidentifiable steam tram loco and covered top trailer pose on Entwisle Road in Rochdale.

Steam Tramway Company. It took over all the assets and liabilities of the former company. The capital of the new company was £590,000 in £10 shares comprising of £350,000 "original" capital and £240,000 "additional" capital, shares being allotted to the shareholders of the original company in substitution for their existing shares. Additional capital was to be raised by the issue of not more than £240,000 in ordinary or preference shares as considered desirable. Amongst new tramways authorised was tramway number 9 in Church Street and Todmorden Road in Littleborough, a total of 473 yards of which 264 yards was single and 209 yards double track.

Further powers were conferred on the Steam Tramways Company by the Manchester, Bury, Rochdale and Oldham Steam Tramways Act 1887. Tramways 11 - 19 and the unconstructed portion of tramway number 10 of the 1882 Order, extending from the existing terminus in Market Street, Facit, were to form a separate undertaking of the company to be known as the Rossendale Valley Tramways (RVT). The company was to set apart £80,000 of its un-issued share capital for the construction of these tramways, the shares of which were to be separately registered and the share certificates distinguished as shares in the Rossendale Valley Tramways undertakings. In the event the MBRO was unable to finance the RVT and it became a separate undertaking with its own Act of 1888. Its steam tramway from Rawtenstall to Bacup proved to be one of the last built in Britain when it opened in 1889.

By autumn of 1887 the company was struggling and in serious debt. At some point the Healey to Facit section fell into disrepair and it was to be many years before trams returned to this part of the Whitworth valley route. Receivers were called in to restructure the finances and seek economies. Another new company was formed in 1888 under the title of the Bury, Rochdale and Oldham Steam Tramway

Company Limited. 'Manchester' was dropped from the title because by then there was no chance of ever running beyond Broughton into Manchester as The Manchester Carriage and Tramways Company had refused to allow steam trams to use its tracks.

The MBRO was a large unwieldy system extending from Higher Broughton on the northern fringes of Manchester through Bury and Heywood to Rochdale and Littleborough and from Rossendale to Oldham. The lines near Manchester were abandoned early by agreement with the local authorities and the Whitworth route was derelict by 1891. There were still 34 miles of single track including 12 miles in Rochdale. The lack of through running, caused by the existence of two gauges, no doubt affected the company's progress and profits were meagre.

In January 1897 the Directors of the steam tramways company considered the possibility of converting some local lines to electric traction, particularly the Littleborough route, as a means of increasing passenger revenue and decreasing running costs. Concerned that the Corporation might decide to exercise their compulsory purchase powers to acquire the lines when the company's protection expired in 1902, they tried to stave off municipal competition by asking the Corporation not to oppose the renewal of its running powers, promising that it would replace the 'evil smelling' steam trams on the Littleborough section, one of the main parts of the network, with electric trams. The Corporation refused the bait and company electrification was not pursued any further.

The following year on 2nd June 1898 Rochdale Council resolved to examine the possibility of acquiring the steam tramways under the provisions of the 1870 Tramways Act. Although steam trams were accepted as being better than nothing, the 'smoky and malodorous engines in the streets were looked upon as a nuisance'.

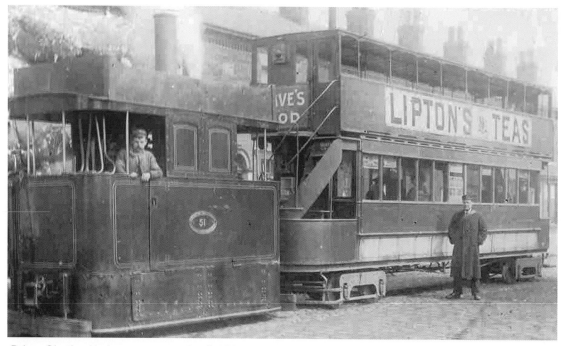

Driver Charles Hodgson prepares to pilot his steam tram loco No. 51 with double deck covered top trailer. Each driver always kept to his own engine; nobody else was allowed to drive it. (Arthur Hodgson)

Steam tramways in and around Rochdale

Opening and closing dates - Page 1

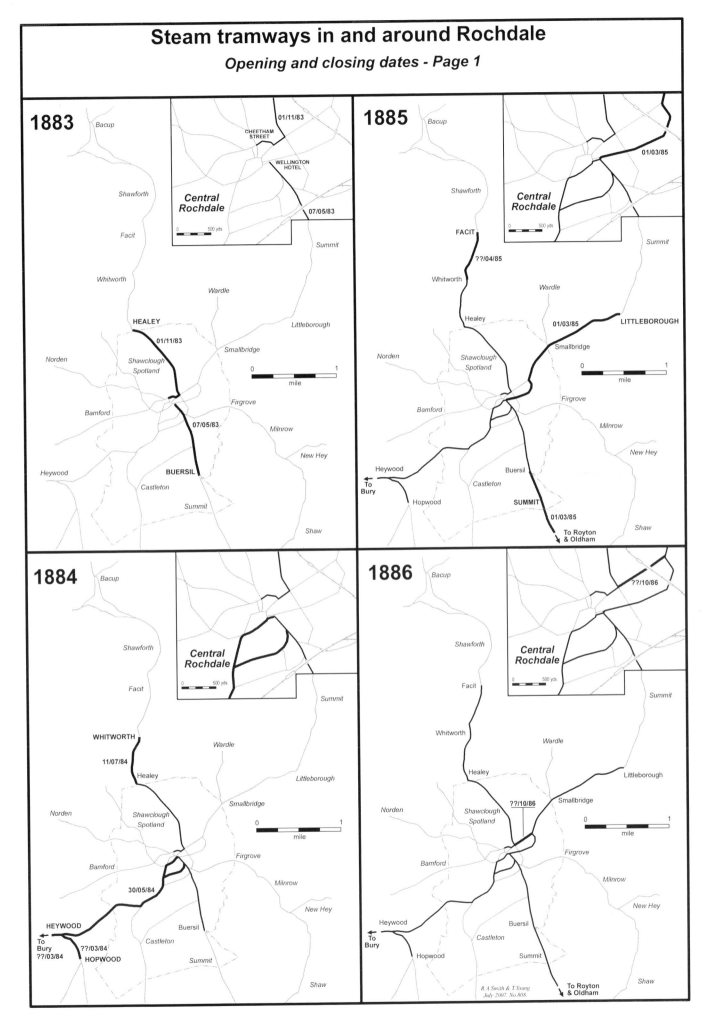

Steam tramways in and around Rochdale
Opening and closing dates - Page 2

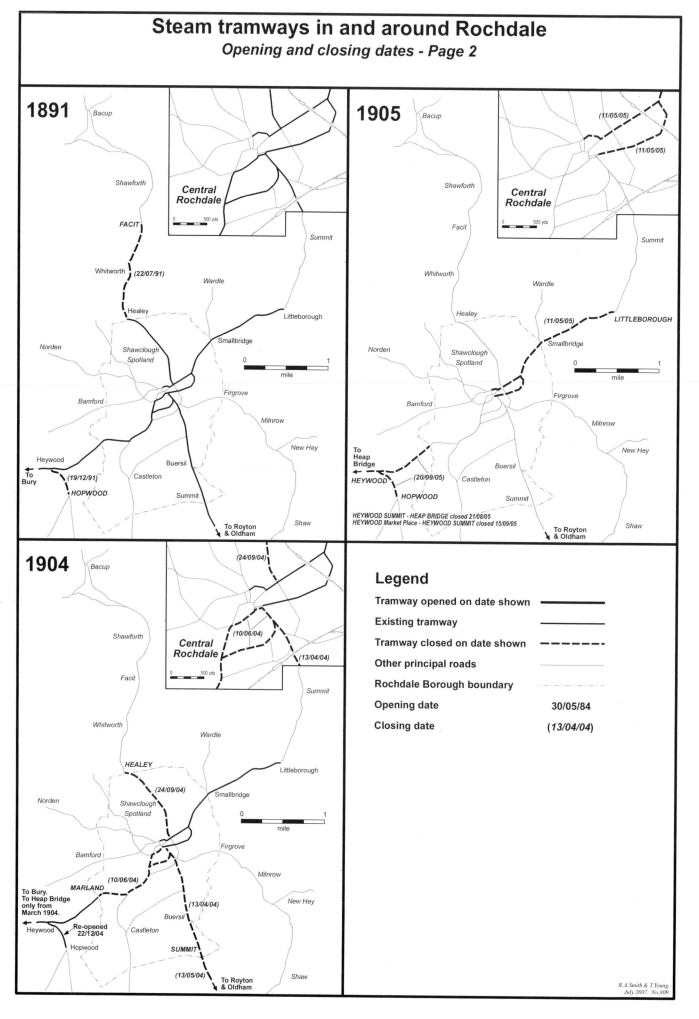

1891

FACIT

Whitworth *(22/07/91)*

← To Bury

(19/12/91)

HOPWOOD

Central Rochdale

1905

(11/05/05)

(11/05/05)

Central Rochdale

(11/05/05)

LITTLEBOROUGH

To Heap Bridge

HEYWOOD *(20/09/05)*

HOPWOOD

HEYWOOD SUMMIT - HEAP BRIDGE closed 21/08/05
HEYWOOD Market Place - HEYWOOD SUMMIT closed 15/09/05

To Royton & Oldham

1904

Central Rochdale

(24/09/04)

(10/06/04)

(13/04/04)

HEALEY

(24/09/04)

To Bury.
To Heap Bridge only from March 1904.

MARLAND

(10/06/04)

Heywood

Re-opened 22/12/04

Hopwood

(13/04/04)

SUMMIT

(13/05/04)

To Royton & Oldham

Legend

Tramway opened on date shown	▬▬▬▬
Existing tramway	────
Tramway closed on date shown	▬ ▬ ▬ ▬
Other principal roads	────
Rochdale Borough boundary	─·─·─
Opening date	30/05/84
Closing date	*(13/04/04)*

R.A.Smith & T.Young.
July 2007. No.809

5. A new century approaches

MR. S. S. PLATT, M.INST.C.E.,
Borough Engineer.

Samuel Sidney Platt, M.Inst.C.E. was Rochdale's forward thinking Borough Engineer from 1881 to 1918. He strongly advocated electric traction and oversaw the construction of all the tramways within the Borough.

Mr Platt's seminal paper

In the last days of the nineteenth century it was clear that radical changes to the transport scene were approaching. Rochdale was fortunate in having the services of an enlightened and far sighted Borough Surveyor, Mr. Samuel Sydney Platt, M.Inst.C.E.. who had been appointed on 6th October 1881 and continued in post until succeeded by Henry Yarwood in September 1918.

On 18th March 1898, Mr Platt read a paper to the Rochdale Literary and Scientific Society entitled 'Tramway Traction', illustrated by lantern slides in which he revealed that he had made a careful and exhaustive study of the advantages and disadvantages of all the types of urban transport then available, particularly the various forms of traction for tramways. Convinced that the days of horse haulage were numbered, he reviewed possible new modes. There were no horse trams in Rochdale although some horse buses could still be found.

Steam tramways were, he said, convenient, cheap and reliable, but their objectionable steam, smoke and fumes, the dust and noise all conspired to make them a nuisance to passengers, other road users and people living along the roads. A system invented by M. Serpollet to reduce these adverse effects had not appealed to English engineers although it was widely used in Paris. In 21st Century terms, this was an early example of adverse environmental impacts influencing transport developments.

Among alternatives to steam Mr Platt described:

- gas haulage – the most common was the Luhrig system which was cheap and, unlike electric trams, required no overhead apparatus or conduit. But it had an objectionable smell, high noise and vibrations levels and difficulty ascending steep gradients. It was considered to be only experimental;

- oil haulage – the Connelly system had similar objections to the gas system;

- compressed air – some systems had tried this method but had not achieved much success;

- battery or accumulator cars – no overhead wires or conduits were needed, and existing track could be used, but the cars were very heavy and accumulators were unreliable. Maintenance and repair costs were high and constant re-charging was needed creating unpleasant smells and risk to passengers' clothing. They had been tried in Birmingham but were not a financial success;

- combined accumulator and overhead wires – Hanover in Germany had developed a hybrid system using accumulators in the city centre and overhead wires elsewhere. They planned to convert the whole system to accumulator cars. Deputations from Leeds, Glasgow, Sheffield, Birmingham, Liverpool and Douglas had not been impressed and did not recommend them;

- external electric power supply – power supplied from a power station and passed through overhead wires or conduit in the middle or side of the track. Either poles and wires had to be provided or the existing track had to be rebuilt;

- underground cable haulage – a continuously moving wire rope was carried in a brick, iron or concrete tube below the track between the tram rails, maintaining its position by passing over small pulleys fixed in the tube at intervals. Motive power was provided by a stationary engine at the terminus or some intermediate position. A cable grip device fitted underneath the cars connected to the cable through a slot about 3/4 in. wide in the top of the buried tube.

Mr Platt considered the cable system relevant because it could operate at speeds between 6 m.p.h. and 9 m.p.h. on severe gradients without any difficulty. A special advantage was that descending a steep gradient the car could only travel at the speed of the cable, a feature that would have prevented runaway accidents on John Street. Furthermore it did not require overhead wires, it was safe and always travelled at a regular speed, was quiet, clean and did not create any unpleasant smells.

Conversely, the disadvantages were that if time was lost it could not be regained as the speed of the tram was limited to the speed of the cable. It could not be reversed, and more ironwork was needed in the street than was desirable. Power failures or cable breakages would immobilise the trams. Capital cost was about twice that for ordinary tramway track. Construction created major disruption to road traffic and interference with sewers, drains, gas and water mains, telegraph and telephone wires and cables. (Electricity cables were not mentioned as none had then been laid).

The few cable hauled systems built in Britain had not been a financial success. Cable trams were cheaper only at service frequencies of two or three minutes or less, otherwise overhead electric traction was cheaper and no routes in Rochdale would have justified such high frequencies.

Electric traction favoured

Passing on to the technical aspects of electric traction, Mr Platt explained that the cars could be double or single deck and could haul trailers. The latest cars had reversible 'garden seats' upstairs (or 'outside' as it was called then); interior lighting was electric, either in series from the overhead supply or from a small storage battery at one end of the car.

Acknowledging a major objection in the need for poles and overhead wires which spoiled the appearance of the street, Mr Platt showed examples of well designed overhead with neat appearance which added to the ornamentation of the street. He quoted Bristol, Dover, Leeds and Dublin where the overhead was claimed to be very elegant and people had soon got used to it. Various types of overhead supports were available including single or double bracket arms and span wires. Rosettes attached to buildings in place of poles planted in the pavements prevented obstruction of footpaths and roadways and were much preferred by shopkeepers. Where poles were unavoidable, they could also be used for electric street lighting, replacing the separate gas lights. (Joint use of poles for street lights and traction is still debated with today's light rail systems, while use of rosettes has still not been fully exploited, demonstrating Mr Platt's farsightedness).

At that time many telephone and telegraph wires were placed overhead and protective measures had to be taken to ensure that they were protected from any contact with the traction voltage and from breaking if the trolley pole came off the wire. Guard wires were therefore strung wherever necessary to meet the stringent requirements of the legal protection afforded by the enabling Parliamentary Acts and the eagle eye of the Board of Trade inspectors. Fortunately, it was expected that most telephone and telegraph wires in Rochdale would be replaced underground in the near future, a situation we take for granted today.

Compared with all other forms of electric traction, the main advantages of the overhead system were its cheapness, simplicity and ease of maintenance. Conversion could be rapid and Mr Platt quoted Rouen, France, where a horse system was converted to electric overhead in about ten months.

The conduit system of electricity supply avoided the visual intrusion of overhead wires but it was very expensive, between 40% and 50% more than overhead. It also required major re-construction of the streets with consequent disruption to traffic. Mr Platt also cited the problems with maintenance, danger to other road users from the slot in the track, the difficulty in keeping the conduit clean and maintaining satisfactory insulation, and the liability for stoppage through storms. An alternative version was the stud contact collection

system which did not require a slot, but there was a danger of a horse being electrocuted if the delicate apparatus failed and a stud remained live after a tram had passed.

Mr Platt gave comparative operating costs for different systems:

- steam trams: 10d to 1s 2d per mile, equivalent to 63 to 90% of receipts;
- cable trams: 5½d to 6d per mile, equivalent to 45 to 50% of receipts;
- electric accumulators: 117% of receipts;
- overhead electric: 5½d per mile, 50% of receipts.

He stressed how rapidly electric traction was being adopted by municipalities and in nearly every case it was on the overhead wire system. Other advantages of electric overhead systems were:

- cars could move with the speed of traffic, slowly or quickly;
- cars could reverse;
- in case of accident, only the section immediately affected was taken out of use;
- every car would be available for use in case of emergency instead of being dependent on the number of horses or locomotives;
- much less space was taken up than by horse or steam trams;
- less interference with other traffic;
- greater cleanliness of cars and streets.

The last three advantages also applied to cable trams.

In concluding Mr Platt stated:

"In cities or towns with a large suburban population, improved facilities of communication had brought the residential suburbs much nearer the centre in point of time. If people could live further away from the centre of the town, building operations would be developed and land would accordingly increase in value. Over-crowding would decrease and public health be improved. This had been exemplified at Bristol which was visited by a Rochdale delegation twelve months ago. It was manifest from all the experience of other places that taking all the circumstances into account, electric traction was the only method within the range of consideration calculated to satisfactorily meet local necessities."

Mr Platt's persuasive discourse aroused loud applause. Asked to specify what system he considered best for Rochdale, Mr Platt emphatically recommended the overhead system. In his vote of thanks, Mr S. Turner said the address was very opportune as the Council were just on the point of considering the introduction of electric traction. The overhead trolley system was likely to be adopted as it was cheap and by no means an eyesore. Seconding the vote, Councillor Dunning, who five years later became chairman of the Tramways Committee, agreed that the overhead system was the one for Rochdale. Electric trams "would not knock the roads about so much as the present heavy cars". Support for overhead electric traction was unanimous.

6. First steps towards a municipal tramway

Municipal tramways committee formed

The earlier attempt by the steam tram company to electrify the Littleborough route had prompted the Corporation to set up a Tramways Sub-Committee in 1898. At first, the Sub-Committee opposed plans for municipalisation of the tramways but it soon changed its policy to proposed unanimously the establishment of electric tramways as soon as possible.

A late proposal for a company-built electric tramway from the Drake and Gorham Traction Syndicate Limited for light railways in Rochdale with connections to surrounding districts was considered by the Tramways Sub-Committee but was firmly rejected by its parent Paving and Sewering Committee on 29th March 1899. The Committee then proceeded to consider several matters relating to the proposed municipal electric tramways, recommending that the gauge be the standard 4ft 8½ins rather than the 3ft 6ins of the steam tramway, even though it would involve the reconstruction of all the existing tracks.

This was a wise move as most adjacent tramways were standard gauge and through running to Oldham, Bury and eventually Manchester would be possible. Tramways to this gauge would be laid along the existing routes to the Borough boundaries on the Manchester, Oldham, Halifax and Whitworth Roads. Additional tramways would be built to the Borough boundaries on Milnrow, Edenfield, Rooley Moor and Bury Roads, these routes never having had steam trams. Connections would be included along John Street and Molesworth Street and round by the Station between Drake Street and Manchester Road via High Level Road, as shown on plans which were submitted by the Borough Surveyor. In the event, the Molesworth Street route was never built.

Following a request from the Town Clerk of Heywood for Rochdale to consider running trams into Heywood, it was resolved that the Town Clerk write to all the Urban District Councils in the area, seeking their views on the proposed Bill to enable them to extend and work standard gauge tramways to the Borough boundary. In November 1899 Littleborough, Castleton, Norden and Royton had indicated that they would not object to Rochdale cars running in their areas. Conversely, Wardle wanted better terms while Whitworth declined altogether. The Rochdale Observer of 16th November commented "Our Whitworth neighbours will soon regret their decision. A local authority can pursue no more

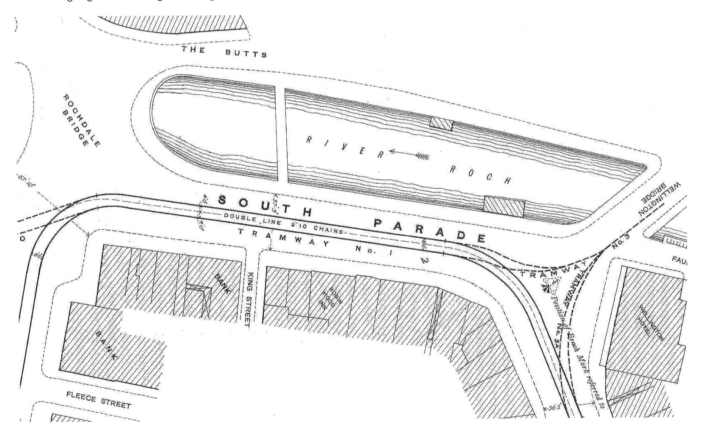

The original plans for electric tramways in the town centre envisaged a track layout similar to the steam tramway along South Parade. The river was then still open between Rochdale Bridge and Wellington Bridge but work to cover it over began in May 1903 to create the tramway centre with its one way anticlockwise circulation. The resulting wide space spanning between The Butts and South Parade became known as Broadway. This track layout showing parts of Tramway Numbers 1, 3 and 3A was never built. Curiously, this plan prepared by the Borough Engineer, Sidney Platt, is dated 17 July 1903, after work had already started on the river covering.
(MTMS)

Table 6.1 Tramways authorised by the Rochdale Corporation Act, 1900.

Tramway. No	Road (s)	Section	Length (single track) (miles, furlongs chains)	Length (double track) (miles, furlongs chains)	Total length (miles, furlongs, chains)
1	South Parade Drake Street Oldham Road	Town Hall Square to Borough boundary	1m 0f 0.15ch (1,613m)	0m 6f 3.95ch (1287m)	1m 6f 4.10ch (2,900m)
2	Drake Street Manchester Rd	Kenion St to Borough boundary	0m 4f 1.28ch (831m)	0m 7f 2.60ch (1,461m)	1m 3f 3.88ch (2,292m)
3	Smith Street Entwisle Road Halifax Road	South Parade to Borough boundary	1m 1f 7.41ch (1,960m)	0m 4f 0.77ch (821m)	1m 5f 8.18ch (2,781m)
3A	Drake Street	Faulkner Street to South Parade	0	0m 0f 1.82ch (37m)	0m 0f 1.82ch (37m)
3B	Entwisle Road	George Street to Depot entrance	0.65ch (13m)	0	0.65ch (13m)
3C	Entwisle Road	George Street to Depot entrance	0.65ch (13m)	0	0.65ch (13m)
3D	Yorkshire Street	Entwisle Road junction	1.20c (24m)	0	1.20ch (24m)
4	Cheetham Street Yorkshire Street	Redcross Street to Entwisle Road	0m 4f 7ch (946m)	6ch (121m)	0m 5f 3ch (1,067m)
5	Whitworth Road	John Street to Borough boundary	1m 2f 9.85ch (2,211m)	0m 2f 7.50ch (553m)	1m 5f 7.35ch (2,764m)
5A	Yorkshire Street	Yorkshire Street to Whitworth Road connection	0.91ch (18m)	0	0.91ch (18m)
6	Whitworth Road Spotland Road Edenfield Road	Rope Street to Borough boundary	1m 2f 1.37ch (2,040m)	0m 3f 8ch (765m)	1m 5f 9.37ch (2,805m)
7	Rooley Moor Road	Leech's Place to Woodlands Rd (Spotland Bridge)	0m 2f 7.87ch (561m)	8.58ch (173m)	0m 3f 6.45ch (734m)
8	Esplanade Dane Street Bridge Street Mellor Street Spotland Road	Manchester Road to Leech's Place (Spotland Bridge)	0m 4f 2.55ch (856m)	0m 1f 7.25ch (347m)	0m 5f 9.80ch (1,203m)
9	Bury Road	Bridge Street to Borough boundary	0m 5f 1.37ch (1,034m)	0m 1f 2.80ch (257m)	0m 6f 4.17ch (1,291m)
10	Esplanade Manchester Rd	Town Hall Square to Drake Street	0	0m 4f 4.22ch (890m)	0m 4f 4.22ch (890m)
11	Tweedale Street ? ?	Drake Street to Manchester Road	0m 5f 0.64ch (1,019m)	6.50ch (131m)	0m 5f 7.14ch (1,150m)
12	High Level Road	Oldham Road to Station Road	0m 1f 6.45ch (331m)	0	0m 1f 6.45ch (331m)
13	Milnrow Road	Oldham Road to Borough boundary	0m 7f 0.92ch (1,427m)	0m 1f 8.10ch (364m)	1m 0f 9.02ch (1,791m)

Tramway No	Road (s)	Section	Length (single track) (miles, furlongs chains)	Length (double track) (miles, furlongs chains)	Total length (miles, furlongs, chains)
14	John Street Molesworth St Wood Street	Yorkshire Street to Oldham Road	0m 3f 7.68ch (758m)	9.50ch (191m)	0m 4f 7.17ch (949m)
14A	Whitworth Road John Street	Junction connection	1.12ch (23m)	0	1.12ch (23m)
14B	Wood Street Oldham Road	Junction connection	1.05ch (21m)	0	1.05ch (21m)
15	'new street' Lord Street Blackwater St St Mary's Gate Spotland Road	Esplanade to Hudson Street	0m 1f 5.37ch (309m)	0m 1f 2.50ch (252m)	0m 2f 7.87ch (561m)
	Totals in Rochdale Borough		9m 7f 4.99ch (15,989m)	4m 6f 0.59ch (7,655m)	14m5f 5.58ch (23,644m)
16	Oldham Road (Castleton) boundary	Borough boundary to Royton Borough	0m 5f 4.30ch (1,093m)	9ch (181m)	0m 6f 3.30ch (1,274m)
17	Manchester Rd (Castleton) Bury Road (now Bolton Road)	Borough boundary to Heywood Borough boundary	0m 5f 6.31ch (1,133m)	0m 1f 8.25ch (367m)	0m 7f 4.56ch (1,500m)
	Totals in Castleton		1m 3f 0.61ch (2,225m)	0m 2f 7.25ch (548m)	1m 5f 7.86ch (2,773m)
18	Edenfield Road (Norden)	Borough boundary to Church View	0m 6f 3.55ch (1,279m)	0m 1f 2ch (241m)	0m 7f 5.55ch (1,520m)
19	Whitworth Road Market Street (Whitworth)	Borough boundary to Ending Rake	8.75ch (176m)	3.75ch (75m)	0m 1f 2.50ch (251m)
20	Halifax Road (Wardle)	Borough boundary to Littleborough Borough boundary	0m 4f 4.91ch (904m)	9ch (181m)	0m 5f 3.91ch (1,085m)
	Grand totals		12m 6f 2.81ch (20,572m)	5m 3f 2.59ch (8,700m)	18m1f 5.40ch (29,272m)

Note: 1 chain   = 66 feet = 20.117 m.
1 furlong = 220 yards = 201.168 m.
1 mile   = 1,760 yards = 1,609 m.
10 chains = 1 furlong.   8 furlongs = 1 mile.

short-sighted policy than to deprive its district of facilities of cheap and frequent communication with the outside world."

Parliamentary Bill approved

A special Council meeting was held on 15th February 1900 to give consent to the promotion of a Parliamentary Bill in the present Session seeking powers to construct and operate tramways in the Borough of Rochdale and also in the Urban Districts of Castleton, Norden, Wardle and Whitworth. The Bill would include all the necessary powers to take over the steam tramways and convert them for electric operation, and the powers to generate electric energy for the tramway and for general supply. The former Bridge Mills site on Dane Street was earmarked for the power station. Powers were also to be sought to cover part of the River Roch, a move that would radically change the centre of Rochdale. A Town's Meeting on 22nd March 1900 duly endorsed the application.

Victorian officialdom was prompt and decisive. Within five months (on 6th August) the Rochdale Corporation Act had received Royal Assent for the construction and operation of tramways within the Borough (Tramways Nos. 1 to 15) and outside the Borough (Tramways Nos. 16 to 20). The full list is shown in Table 6.1 below. Eighty four years later, GMPTE's first Metrolink Bill in 1984 took nearly four years to obtain Royal Assent, for a relatively short section of tramway.

Temporary restrictions were placed on some tramways:

- Tramway No. 8 could not be constructed between Bury Road and Spotland Road until the new road (Mellor Street) had been constructed;

- Tramway No.13 could not be laid beyond the Rochdale Canal bridge until the bridge had been widened to a width of 12 yds *(11m)*;

- Tramway No. 14 could not be constructed between Milnrow Road and Oldham Road until Wood Street had been widened;

- Tramway No. 15 could not be constructed unless the new bridge over the River Roch between the Esplanade and Theatre Street was built and the intended new street between Theatre Street and Lord Street.

The Powers to construct these sections were limited to two years after completion of the conditional works and the Powers for the remaining tramways were limited to five years. Authority to construct Mellor Street had been obtained long before the tramways under the Improvement Act of 1872 but had been allowed to lapse following disagreements over the route.

The Act also enabled the Council to borrow £145,000 *(£9.05m)* for tramway construction and £98,000 *(£6.11m)* for other tramway purposes while a further sum was authorised for purchase of the steam tramway undertaking and £71,400 *(£4.45m)* for the necessary street works.

As well as the tramway proposals, various road improvements were agreed to facilitate tramway construction:

a) the covering of the river from Rochdale Bridge to Wellington Bridge, eliminating the old iron footbridge;

b) the making of a new street 15 yards *(13.7m)* wide from Bury Road to Spotland Bridge (Mellor Street);

c) a new street in continuation of Blackwater Street from Lord Street across the Manor Estate to the Esplanade. (Newgate).

Progressively, many of the main roads were widened when the tramways were built as there had to be at least 9ft. 6 ins. *(2.9m)* between the outer rail and the kerb on double track sections.

Tramways Committee fully fledged

The Tramways Committee first met on 23 November 1900 and appointed Councillor Duncan as its chairman. Previously it had been a Sub-Committee of the gloriously named 'Paving, Sewering and Scavenging Committee', generally known as 'The Paving Etc. Committee'! Their first decisions were to open negotiations with the Middleton Light Railway Company with a view to acquiring or leasing the tramway between Sudden and Castleton; inviting Mr E.M. Lacey of Queen Anne's Gate in London to meet the Committee to discuss his terms for acting as Electrical Engineer for the tramways in the Borough; and appointing the Borough Surveyor, Mr Samuel Sydney Platt, to be the Engineer for the laying of the permanent way for the tramways.

Sudden was at that time the Rochdale boundary, the route between Sudden and Castleton lying within the Urban District of Castleton. Although the tramway had been authorised by the Middleton Light Railways Order, 1898 as far as Silk Street at Sudden, the company was named the "Middleton Electric Traction Company Limited", not the Middleton Light Railway Company.

Maintaining the vigorous pace already set, when the Committee met only three days later, after the weekend, Mr Lacey duly attended the meeting and was appointed as Electrical Engineer for the Corporation Tramways. It was also agreed that all the local authorities interested in taking over the ailing Bury, Rochdale and Oldham Tramway Company should meet to discuss the arrangements for its acquisition. At the December meeting, the Town Clerk reported that he had written to the other Local Authorities about the acquisition of the company. He had obtained also obtained a copy of the plan for the proposed Littleborough Tramway Provisional Order which conferred powers to construct electric tramways within the Urban District of Littleborough.

Also, the Town Clerk had met three representatives of the British Electric Traction Company (B.E.T.) who owned the Middleton Company and who were seeking running powers over the Rochdale tracks between Sudden and Rochdale in exchange for the Corporation purchasing or leasing the tracks which B.E.T. owned within the former Urban District of Castleton. Castleton had become part of the Borough of Rochdale in 1900. The Committee asked the Town Clerk and Borough Surveyor to ascertain what arrangements Manchester, Oldham, Middleton and Chadderton were making with the Company. It was subsequently decided that the Company's request for running powers in Rochdale should not be accepted;

instead they would be willing to enter negotiations with the Company to acquire their powers for running tramways between Sudden and Castleton. Unfortunately the talks ended in stalemate and for the next twenty years passengers wanting to make through journeys between the towns found themselves penalised by authorities and companies who guarded their borders jealously.

Also before the Committee was a request from the Gas and Electricity Committee for information as to how much power the tramway would need. The question was referred, quite understandably, to Mr Lacey. The draft agreement for Mr Lacey's services was tabled at the same meeting and agreed. An unsolicited offer from the Lancashire Electric Power Company to provide electricity for the tramway was firmly declined – Rochdale Corporation would supply Rochdale's needs.

Steam tramway acquisition progresses

The future of The Bury, Rochdale and Oldham Tramway Company was considered at a conference of Local Authorities was held on 21st January 1901. It was agreed that it was desirable for a joint arrangement to be made, or joint arbitration, to determine the terms of the acquisition of the Company's undertaking, the share of the purchase money and the costs incurred by each Local Authority. The Council asked the Tramways Committee to take the necessary action, noting that the desirability or otherwise of acquisition before the expiration of powers of the Company should be considered. The Tramways Committee met later that day to report that the Conference was to seek a joint arrangement if possible with the Company as previously proposed. Final agreement depended the issue of the varying periods of expiration of powers. A further meeting was planned for 18th February in Rochdale Town Hall. Agreement appeared feasible and suggested dates for the acquisition were 31st July and 31st December 1902.

At that meeting Bury Council decided to withdraw from the Conference and it was left to the Mayor of Rochdale and the Town Clerks of Rochdale and Heywood to seek a meeting with the Company to see what terms they would accept to dispose of the portion of their undertaking lying to the east of Heywood Market Place.

When the Tramways Committee met on January 21st, the Chairman was deputed, with Councillors Dunning and Walker, to meet representatives of Bury and Heywood Corporations to negotiate the future of tramways in their districts. Their deliberations were reported at the meeting on 4th February, 1901 where the following proposals were recommended:

1. The term to be for 21 years.

2. Rochdale to purchase from the Tramway Company the lines in Heywood, from the boundary at Marland to Heywood Market Place (St. Luke's Church).

3. Heywood to reconstruct track to a gauge of 4ft. 8½in.to the satisfaction of the Rochdale Corporation.

4. Rochdale to be credited in the cost of reconstruction with the value of any setts or other materials in the present track used or disposed of by Heywood Corporation.

5. Rochdale to pay Heywood 10% on the cost of reconstruction (as referred to in Nos. 3 and 4) to meet Heywood's contribution for interest, sinking fund and maintenance.

6. Heywood to maintain in good condition to the satisfaction of the Rochdale Corporation the tramway tracks in this section in the Borough of Heywood.

7. Rochdale to provide and lay the electrical equipment, and supply the electrical energy.

8. At the end of 21 years, failing a renewal of the agreement between Heywood and Rochdale, Heywood to take over from Rochdale at a valuation the said electrical equipment.

9. Rochdale to maintain as frequent a service between Heywood and Rochdale as at present and not to charge higher prices in Heywood than the fares generally charged in the Borough of Rochdale.

These terms were agreed.

Boundary issues continued to dominate proceedings when Bury Rural District Council (which covered the rural areas around Bury, not to be confused with Bury Borough Council which covered the town itself) asked if the Bury Road route which was to terminate at the Dog and Partridge Inn could be extended along Bury Old Road as far as War Office Road in Bamford. The request was declined on the reasonable grounds that at that time most of Bury Road ran through fields with very few potential customers for a tramway. A similar request from 125 inhabitants of Bamford was also refused. For the next thirty years, trams trundled up Bury Road displaying the name 'Bamford' on their destination indicators but stopped about a mile short of the village.

Tramway construction begins; negotiations continue

Construction of the first sections of tramway began during 1901. A ceremony to lay the first rail, in Norden, was performed by the Chairman of the Norden Urban District Council Tramways Committee, Councillor R. A. L. Hutchinson, on 13th June. The whole Tramways Committee of Rochdale were invited to lunch in Norden to celebrate. A similar ceremony followed at Cutgate, just inside the Rochdale boundary on the Norden route, by the Rochdale Tramways Committee Chairman, Councillor Duncan.

The Norden route began from a terminus in Blackwater Street in the town centre and thence via St Mary's Gate, Spotland Road, Spotland Bridge and Edenfield Road to a terminus in Norden at Industry Street, just short of St Paul's parish church. At Spotland Bridge, the Spotland route diverged from the Norden route, continuing up Rooley Moor Road to a terminus at the White Lion (*no longer a public house; opposite present day Woolpack*), referred to as Spotland Fold. The Bury Road route commenced at a temporary terminus in Dane Street, opposite the present ASDA supermarket, and then along Bridge Street (*now Mellor Street*) and Bury Road to the Cemetery Gates. Construction of the Bury Road route started shortly after the Norden and Spotland routes.

Another conference was arranged for 9th December 1901 between the local authorities interested in taking over the Company's tram route to the east of Heywood, and the Directors of the Bury, Rochdale and Oldham tramway Company. The outcome was to seek a valuation of the undertaking to the east of Heywood Market Place, Mr. James More Junr. of George Street, Edinburgh being subsequently appointed as valuer, possibly on the basis that a Scottish valuer might be reasonably unbiased!. Mr More was authorised to fix the amount to be paid to the company by each authority.

When the steam tram lines were constructed in the early eighties they cost £17,000 per mile *(£923,800)*, including equipment. They were acquired by the later company in 1889 for £4,500 per mile *(£294,400)*. The arbitrator's award in 1902 was surprisingly high at £5,500 per mile *(£353,900)* even though the permanent way, rolling stock and plant had deteriorated during the intervening years. There were loud complaints that the authorities had mishandled their case, allowing the company's directors to hire the best witnesses and over-valuing the undertaking. The cost of constructing the new electric tramway was put at £10,000 per mile *(£643,500)*.

By this time, the staff of the steam tramways company were distinctly fearful for their jobs and a letter from the Amalgamated Association of Tramway, Hackney Carriage Employees and Horsemen in General, (an evocative title in itself!) requested that a deputation be allowed to meet the Committee with three requests:

1. That at the expiration of the Tramway Company's lease, the men be taken over in a body.

2. That when the Norden and subsequent routes were opened, they be taken over as required, according to seniority.

3. That men receiving the maximum rate of wages under the Company be placed as "first-class" under the Corporation.

Although not unfavourably disposed towards this request the Committee did not consider it appropriate to receive a deputation until April 28th.

The Committee on June 17th confirmed the appointment of Mr W.E.Preston of Bury as Timekeeper and Clerk at 30/- per week (£1 10s, *£93.60).*

When the steam tramway closed some staff transferred to the new tramway. Driving electric trams demanded different skills but it was much quieter and cleaner, even if still open to the elements.
(Rochdale Observer)

7. Study visits

Learning from other tramways

In recent years, it has been a feature of all new light rail systems that study visits have been made to operating tramway and light rail systems to learn more about their engineering and operational features and the design of all aspects of the system including rolling stock. In the nineteen eighties and early nineties, visits had to be made to European cities or even North America because there were no light rail systems in Britain and there were other technologies such as guided buses, guided light transit (GLT) or trolleybuses which did not exist in Britain.

Similar trails had been blazed at the turn of the nineteenth century. On 7th January 1901, the Chairman announced that he together with Councillor Dunning and the Borough Surveyor would visit such places as they thought fit where tramways had been laid, and would report on types of rails in use.

Subsequently the Committee resolved to inspect various tram designs used in different parts of the country, following Mr Lacey's proposals for car designs. They inspected tram factories in Preston, Birkenhead and Loughborough, as explained in more detail in Chapter 15.

Electrification of tramways, and construction of new tramways, was proceeding at breakneck speed right across the country, and the Second International Tramways and Light Railways Exhibition at the Agricultural Hall held on 1st and 2nd July 1902 in London enabled the Chairman, Borough Surveyor and Borough Electrical Engineer to see the latest products and services on offer.

A year later the Committee visited the Manchester works of the British Westinghouse Electric and Manufacturing Company and in September the British Electric Car Company in Trafford Park on 11th; Brush Electrical Engineering Company in Loughborough on 14th and Dick Kerr at Preston on 16th. These were in preparation for considering tenders for new trams.

Visits of a more specialised nature took place from time to time, for example in March 1904 when the Brakes Sub-Committee went to Bradford, Leeds, Halifax and Huddersfield to examine technical options.

In July 1904 the newly appointed Tramways Manager and Car Shed Superintendent travelled to the car sheds of other tramways in the area to see what equipment they would need. At Halifax they saw 'Raworth's System of Automatic Regenerative Control' in use on two newly acquired demi-cars.

Visits to manufacturers or other operators became commonplace. Sometimes they were only local, as in October 1909 when the Committee visited the tram route to Hathershaw in Oldham and then the Oldham Car Depot.

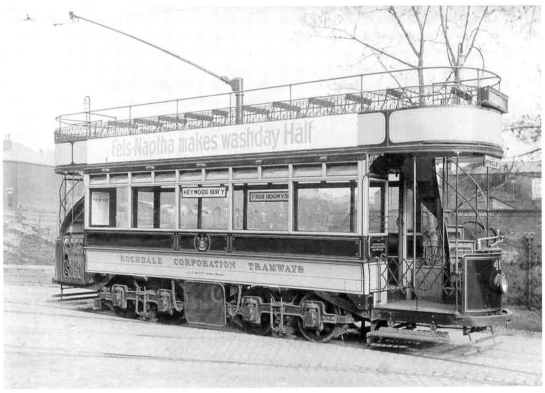

Brush built open top car No.45 with Brush equal wheel bogies is decked out for Heywood Boundary via Entwisle Road, a slightly fictitious route. It is seen when new in 1905 in the depot yard. (MTMS)

8. Opening of the first tram routes.

Bury Road trams start first

By the spring of 1902 the first of the new electric tramways were approaching completion and the Chairman and Councillors Dunning and Redfern were appointed as a Sub-Committee to progress the opening of the Bury Road route. The Bury Road and Norden routes had been constructed simultaneously but Bury Road was finished first. As the new Mellor Street was still under construction, the two routes were not yet connected and each had to have their own temporary car shed.

Thursday 22nd May 1902 was set aside for the formal opening date, with public opening on Whit Friday, 23rd May. The Board of Trade were asked to inspect the route on 15th, 16th or 19th May, indicating that the Committee had every confidence that approval would be forthcoming. Major Druitt, R.E., and Mr A.P.Trotter confirmed that the inspection would take place on 15th May, Major Druitt covering the trackworks and Mr Trotter the electrical equipment.

Tram stops were not envisaged as it was agreed that the cars would stop for passengers anywhere as required to pick up or set down.

MR. C. C. ATCHISON, A.M.I.E.E.,
Borough Electrical Engineer.

The Borough Electrical Engineer, Mr C. C. Atchison, A.M.I.E.E., was appointed as temporary superintendent to operate the tramway.

May 22 1902 and Car No 1, closely followed by No.3, is ready to be the first tram on Rochdale's first electric tram route. The temporary terminus is on Dale Street (near the current entrance to ASDA). The Mayor and Mayoress and Councillor Duncan (Chairman of the Tramways Committee) and Mrs Duncan are standing on the platform of No.1. (Eric Fielding)

Rochdale's first tram on Rochdale's first tram route. Single deck bogie combination car No. 1 stands at the Cemetery terminus on the Bury Road route. The three man crew, driver, conductor and trolley boy, show off their smart uniforms. This terminus only lasted about a year as the route was extended the short distance down the hill to the Dog and Partridge pub. (Eric Fielding)

COUNCILLOR W. H. DUNCAN,
Chairman Tramways Committee.

Councillor W. H. Duncan was elected the first Chairman of The Tramways Committee and served from 1900 to 1903.

A host of administrative details were then agreed. Mr C.C. Atchison, who had been appointed Electrical Engineer in October 1900 when the new electricity works opened on Dane Street,, was to act temporarily as Superintendent and was to acquire record sheets and way sheets as well as rubber gloves or gauntlets and mackintoshes. Meanwhile the Borough Surveyor was to obtain samples of uniforms with prices by the next meeting. He did so, obtaining samples from Messrs. Pearson, Huggins & Company of London.

Recruitment was delegated to the Chairman and Mr Atchison. Two drivers and two conductors, with suitable experience, and two cleaners for the cars were required. The cleaners were to be trained to act as driver and conductor, one of them being Mr James Ledgard of 1, Monmouth Street, Rochdale. Three drivers were considered, one each from Bolton, Failsworth and Halifax and three potential conductors, all from Stockport. The two drivers appointed were Mr J Venting of 106 Auburn Street, Daubhill, Bolton and Mr. Arthur Devitt of 12 Birks Hall Terrace, Penton Lane, Halifax. The conductors were Mr Joseph Jones of 45 Travis Brow, Heaton Norris, Stockport and Mr. Joseph Hardy of 66, Great Portwood Street, Stockport. Mr James Ledgard was confirmed as cleaner. Wages for a 60 hour week were 6d per hour for drivers, 5d per hour for conductors and 4$^{1}/_{2}$d per hour for the cleaner. *(£1.61, £1.34 and £1.07 respectively).* For any future appointments the rates would be 5$^{3}/_{4}$d, 5$^{1}/_{4}$d and 4$^{1}/_{2}$d per hour respectively, rising to 6d, 5$^{1}/_{2}$d and 4$^{3}/_{4}$d after six months and to 6$^{1}/_{4}$d, 5$^{3}/_{4}$2d and 5d after twelve months.

Rules and regulations and licensing of the electric cars, drivers and conductors were next considered. The 'Rochdale Corporation Tramways Rules and Regulations for Officers and Servants' were produced in hardback booklet form to become the bible for all employees.

The proposed timetable envisaged a 20 minute service in the 'forenoon' and as frequently as possible in the afternoons on weekdays whilst the last cars would leave the town end at 11.00 pm. On Sundays cars would run as required from 12.00 noon until 10.00 pm although this was revised to 2.00 pm to 10.00 pm.

Major Druitt's report was sent to the Board of Trade on 17th May, only two days after his inspection, (another remarkable achievement by today's standards). It covered the whole of the Bury Road route, from the junction of Manchester Road and Dane Street via Bridge Street (now Mellor Street) and Bury Road to the terminus at the Cemetery Gates. He imposed 8 mph speed limits on Dane Street and Bridge Street, 4 mph round the corner on Bridge Street into Bury Road, and 10 mph on Bury Road. Surprisingly, in view of the long gradient on Bury Road, no compulsory stop was required.

Concerns were raised regarding the steps and braking systems on the trams (see 'Rolling Stock') and other technical details, but Major Druitt finished his report with the satisfying words "Subject to remarks re cars, and any requirements in Mr Trotter's report, I can recommend the Board of Trade to sanction the use of the above-described tramways for passenger traffic". The last hurdle to opening Rochdale's electric tramways had been cleared.

Illustrating the standard Tramways uniform, Conductor Edwin Hornby poses in 1914 at the age of 27. The heavy material and high collar were welcome in winter but rather warm in summer. *(Photo courtesy of Touchstones Rochdale)*

COUNCILLOR S. TURNER,
The Mayor.

Councillor S. Turner was Mayor of Rochdale when the tramway opened in 1902. He had earlier strongly supported Sidney Platt in his advocacy of electric traction.

The official opening

Arrangements for the opening of Rochdale's first electric tram route on 22nd May 1902, from Dane Street to the Cemetery Gates on Bury Road, were almost complete. Members of the Council, the Engineers and the Contractors were to meet at the Town Hall at 11.30am and then join the first car at the top of Dane Street. The Mayoress and Mrs Duncan, wife of the Committee Chairman, would drive the first cars. Afterwards the polished tram controller handle was presented to Mrs Duncan and it can still be seen today in the Touchstones local museum.

Dane Street was as close as the electric trams could get to the Town Hall. The presence of steam trams still running along the Esplanade and up Manchester Road prevented the electric trams from reaching the Town Hall, so that the Official party had to board them in Dane Street. With them were the Mayor of Bury together with representatives from Heywood Corporation and the Urban District Councils of Littleborough, Wardle, Royton and Norden. Advertisements were placed in the press to publicise the running of electric cars on 22nd, 23rd and 24th May.

The Municipal Journal in May 1902 commented approvingly that:

"Councillor Duncan has taken a deep and practical interest in the working out of the scheme and has proved himself to be a strong, able and resourceful head of his Committee. Mr E.M.Lacey of London has been consulting engineer from the first, and has been specially retained during the construction of the lines to advise on the electrical service and equipment generally. The Borough Surveyor, Mr S. S. Platt, whose long and valuable service to the Corporation has given him its complete confidence, has undertaken the duties of engineer for the permanent way. He has been fortunate in securing the services of Mr. W. Marshall who has had many years experience in the construction of tramways in various parts of the world. In the engineering department Mr Platt's right hand man has been Mr. J. S. D. Moffet who has had the details of tramways at his fingers' end. For the present the superintendent is Mr. C.C.Atchison, the electrical engineer."

Rochdale Corporation's tram route to Bury Road was not in fact the first to open in the Borough. Two months earlier on 28th March 1902 the Middleton Electric Traction Company, a British Electric Traction (BET) subsidiary company, had opened its route from Sudden along Manchester Road via Castleton to Middleton. Through running from Sudden into Rochdale centre was prevented by the antipathy between the Corporation and the Company and was not achieved for another 23 years.

The Norden route opens

Plans were then put in hand to open the Norden route as soon as practicable although it was physically separate from the Bury Road route. The connecting tracks along the new Mellor Street were nor completed so Rochdale had in effect two separate tram routes, each having its own temporary car shed.

The wide awake Secretary of Norden Agricultural Society enquired when the trams would start, as their Show was on 19th July and they would like to advertise the trams on their placards. The Town Clerk assured him that cars were expected to be running by that date from a terminus at the bottom of Blackwater Street. In fact it opened on 19th June.

Timetables for the Norden and Spotland routes were specified as:

Lord Street to Spotland Bridge:	1/4 hr service;
Lord Street to Norden:	1/2 hr service.
Lord Street to Spotland Fold:	1/2 hr service.

Lord Street no longer exists but formerly connected what is now Newgate and Yorkshire Street. The tram route ran down Blackwater Street, also no longer there, to a temporary terminus at Lord Street. Workmen's cars would leave Blackwater Street for Spotland Fold at 5.30 a.m. while ordinary cars would leave for Norden at 7.30 a.m. and for Spotland Fold at 7.45 a.m.

To cope with the expanding system 7 drivers, 7 conductors and 1 cleaner were recruited. Driver J. Venting and conductor Joseph Jones were made up to Inspectors. The Borough Electrical Engineer was to order uniforms and tickets and punches for the new staff. At the end of May 1902 it was agreed that all Tramway employees would wear the same type of cap that was being worn by the drivers.

The Board of Trade responded slightly frostily to the Committee's request for a date for the inspection of the Norden and Spotland routes in that before they made the necessary arrangements, they would need to be assured that the lines and electrical equipment were actually ready for their inspection. Perhaps they had had some bad experiences in being asked to inspect too soon. The Town Clerk was directed to inform the Board immediately on completion, hoping to keep to the original date of 18th June or as soon as possible thereafter.

Things moved fast and the inspection took place only eight days later on 17th June when the Mayor, the Chairman and six other Committee members met Major Druitt at the junction of Blackwater Street and Lord Street. The Norden section was inspected first. At the Borough boundary at Cutgate they were met by the Norden delegation including the Chairman, Surveyor, and Clerk to Norden Urban District Council who gratifyingly told the Inspector that they had no representations to make on behalf of their Council. Returning from Norden, Major Druitt inspected the Spotland section along Rooley Moor Road. His Report was again completed within three days - perhaps he wrote it on the train back to Whitehall. He specified speed limits on the Norden route:

Spotland Road: Hudson Street
  to Hinchcliffe Street: 8mph;

Hinchcliffe Street to Spotland Bridge: 4mph downwards,
                                    8mph upwards;

Edenfield Road: whole route: 10mph
Edenfield Street to Spotland Bridge: 4mph downwards;

Rooley Moor Road: whole route: 8mph;
Edenfield Street to Spotland Bridge: 4mph downwards.

Compulsory stops were required on downward journeys on Spotland Road before crossing Hinchcliffe Street, in Edenfield Road before crossing Edenfield Street and in Rooley Moor Road before crossing Edenfield Street. The cars on these routes were to be fitted with slipper brakes and were prohibited from stopping to pick up passengers on the sharp ascending gradients in Edenfield Road, Rooley Moor Road and Spotland Road unless some form of run-back protection was fitted. *[Details of Board of Trade inspections for the remaining parts of the network are set out in the Chapter on Tramway Trackwork].*

As neither the Norden or Post Office representatives had offered any adverse comments, Major Druitt recommended approval of the Norden and Spotland routes for passenger operation. Passenger service had already begun on the Norden route on 19th June and the Spotland route opened on 21st July. It was estimated that newly opened sections had cost about £10,000 per mile *(£643,500)* to construct including permanent way, overhead equipment, cars and all other costs. The total route length was just over 5 miles with 6½ miles of track. The cost of track and bonding was £40,000 giving a cost per mile of just over £6,000. As the Parliamentary estimate was £6,300 per track mile, it was well within budget.

From July all services to Norden, Rooley Moor Road and Bury Road were timed to leave 10 minutes later including the Workmen's journeys. On Sundays the Norden service started 9.10 and ran hourly until 2.10 p.m. and then half hourly until 10.10 p.m. The Bury Road service was increased to every 10 minutes on weekdays after 1.30 p.m. and after 2 p.m. on Sundays. Visits to Rochdale Cemetery on Sunday afternoons boosted the revenue.

Rochdale's first recorded 'Special Car' was booked to convey the officials and exhibits for the Norden Agricultural Show on 19th July 1902. The Tramway Department insisted that the Show promoters should pay the cost of a full tram in each direction, thus ensuring that private hire would be a lucrative business. The charge for special cars was later revised to two thirds of the full capacity for the distance travelled.

The Board of Trade Certificates which authorised the Bury Road, Norden and Spotland routes for passenger operation together with the Order sanctioning use of electrical power

above)
Detail from picture left.
(Touchstones Rochdale)

below) An early view of Spotland Bridge with four wheel open top Brush car No.13 to Norden waiting for a similar car to depart for Spotland. All the buildings in this photograph can still be seen but there is rather more road traffic now! The tracks from Mellor Street to the left joined the tracks from Spotland Road from the right for a short distance but the overhead lines were kept separate.   *(MTMS)*

were sent to the Town Clerk on 1st August 1902. By then all these routes were already running and the Bury Road route had been in operation for over two months. Clearly they were not too concerned about getting the paperwork first.

Rochdale folk quickly learned that the new tram routes provided a gateway to fresh air and healthy exercise, as advertised in a guide to the Norden area:

"Rochdale's prettiest, healthiest and most restful suburb. From a residential point of view, the most valuable asset of the district is the bracing air. Knowl Hill is within a comfortable three-quarter hour walk from the tram terminus on Bury Road (sic.). The UDC had several acres of land at Woodgate on the south side of Bury Road, just beyond the electric car terminus and the Cemetery, ripe for building purposes, a penny stage from town, on a 20 minute service, ten minutes in the summer and on Saturdays."

In fact it was the Norden route, not Bury Road which gave access to Knowl Hill.

Norden remained a separate Urban District until absorbed into Rochdale in 1933.

SPOTLAND SCENES

Tram No. 17, a Brush 4 wheel balcony car of 1903, waits at the Spotland terminus on Rooley Moor Road.
(Rochdale Observer)

Car No. 1, Rochdale's first tram, stands at the terminus of the Spotland route on Rooley Moor Road. The White Lion on the right has long since ceased to be a pub and the buildings either side demolished but the Woolpack almost opposite is still there.

Long skirts on the pavement and a plentiful supply of horse manure in the road. Car 4 heads for town from Spotland along Rooley Moor Road.
(Eric Fielding)

EDENFIELD ROAD SCENES

Rochdale's second tram route was to Norden. Open top 4-wheel Preston built car No.7 of 1902 has Edenfield Road to itself as it rounds the bend at Passmonds. Today this is one of Rochdale's busiest main roads. (Ian Yearsley)

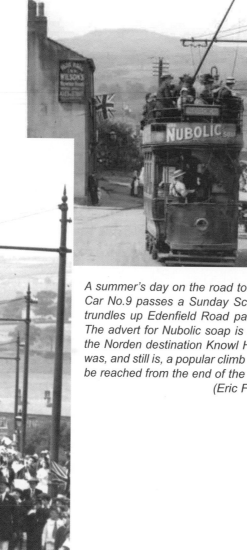

A summer's day on the road to Norden. Well loaded Car No.9 passes a Sunday School procession as it trundles up Edenfield Road past the Blue Ball pub. The advert for Nubolic soap is more prominent than the Norden destination Knowl Hill in the background was, and still is, a popular climb for walkers and could be reached from the end of the tram route.

(Eric Fielding, Ian Yearsley)

DRAKE STREET SCENES

Car No. 10 was the first of twenty 4-wheel open top cars from Brush. It was almost new when seen climbing Drake Street, then Rochdale's premier shopping street. The only other traffic was horse drawn.
(Eric Fielding)

Open top Brush 4-wheeler No. 21 climbs up Drake Street which is almost devoid of any other traffic.   (Eric Fielding)

An early view of the foot of Drake Street. Straw boaters and a crowded top deck on Oldham tram No. 49 suggest a warm summer's day. The joint service with Oldham Corporation ran from Norden to Hathershaw for ten years between 1906 and 1916.   (Eric Fielding)

Drake Street is busy with shoppers as English Electric enclosed double decker No.82 of 1925 approaches Broadway. A Brush single decker is following it down the gradient. Pedestrians wander about the road in the absence of motor traffic.

BROADWAY SCENES

The Tramway centre in its early days in 1905 with a solitary 4-wheel carat the island, bound for Norden, In the foreground the remains of narrow gauge steam track can be seen left of the standard gauge electric track (Eric Fielding, Collectorcard Croydon)

The covering of the River Roch has been completed and the trams are running but the buildings which formed the Tramway Centre have yet to be built.   (Eric Fielding)

Another view of the Tramway Centre at Broadway in its early form shows the anti-clockwise routing with two 1905 Brush bogie cars. No. 40 on the left is preparing to depart for Heywood. There are remarkably few traction poles given the complex overhead, unlike today's Piccadilly Gardens in Manchester. Moreover they fitted gas lamps to traction poles which would never be permitted now. The shelter was replaced with a more impressive building in 1907.

9. Steam trams struggle on while electric trams expand.

Steam tram company acquired

Major Druitt was back in Rochdale on 5th August 1902 to inspect the remaining steam tram routes following an application from the Bury, Rochdale and Oldham Tramway to renew their licence for steam power, which was about to expire. Their powers had been granted under the Rochdale Tramway Order of 1881 for a period of 21 years, expiring about 11th or 12th August 1902. The Committee promptly decided that the steam tramways should be acquired by the Corporation and instructed the Town Clerk to do whatever was necessary to bring this about. The Board of Trade duly approved Major Druitt's recommendation to extend the use of steam power for a further two years from 11th August.

Subsequently, in November the Board of Trade informed the Town Clerk that they had approved the Corporation serving notice on the Tramway Company to sell to the Corporation under the provisions of Section 43 of The Tramways Act 1870. This applied to all the tramways authorised by the Rochdale Tramways Act 1881 within the Borough of Rochdale. Notice was served on the Company on 27th November 1902.

For practical purposes, the steam era was doomed as soon as electric trams began to appear on Britain's streets. The final stages in the demise of Rochdale's steam trams began on 3rd September 1903 when Rochdale Corporation resolved to purchase the part of the Bury, Rochdale and Oldham Tramway within the County Borough boundary. They were exercising their powers under the 1870 Tramways Act and the Orders which authorised the tramways in 1882. The acquisition included "all lands, buildings, works, materials and plant of the said Company". Confirmation by the Board of Trade of the Corporation's proposed action was received and formal notice was duly served on the Company on 22nd December 1903.

Traffic receipts fluctuate

Passenger receipts for July 1902 were reported to the Committee in August:

Bury Road	£172	8s	4d	(£11,095)
Norden	£425	8s	6d	(£27,377)
Rooley Moor Road	£ 38	19s	4½d	(£2,508)
Total	£636	16s	2½d	(£40,980)

The total number of passengers carried was 101,663 giving an average fare of 1½d (40p).

The corresponding figures for August were:

Bury Road	£188	2s	3d	(£12,105)
Norden	£435	8s	6d	(£28,020)
Rooley Moor Road	£115	7s	2½d	(£7,424)
Total	£738	17s	11½d	(£47,549)

The total number of passengers carried was 120,250 giving an average fare of just under 1½d (40p). The patronage increase of 18% over the previous month showed a rapid but temporary rise and the November figures showed a marked drop in revenue and passengers:

Bury Road	£ 86	9s	7d	(£5,565)
Norden	£307	3s	6d	(£19,767)
Rooley Moor Road	£ 86	4s	10½d	(£5,550)
Contracts	£ 28	14s	0d	(£1,847)
Total	£508	11s	11½d	(£32,729)

Steam tramway employees pose with the last steam tram from Rochdale at the depot on Entwisle Road. The hand written caption puts the date as May 8 1905 but official records show the last steam tram ran on 11 May. *(LHAS)*

Steam tram loco and double deck trailer at Holy Trinity Church, Littleborough. The hand written caption puts the date as March 27 1905 but the last steam tram did not run until 11 May . (LHAS)

A busy scene at the foot of Drake Street. The steam tram route to Royton has been cut back to terminate at the Wellington Hotel while shiny new electric tram No. 10 makes its way from Kings Road on the Thornham section to Norden. This dates the photograph to between September 1904 and May 1905.

(John Ryan)

Narrow gauge steam tramway track is lifted to make way for new standard gauge electric track. The scene is Church Street in Littleborough between Eastwood Street and Hare Hill Road. The Queen's Hotel on the right, Seed Hill Buildings in the background, built in 1903, and some of the cottages are still there today, over a century later. The date was 1905.

All services had lost passengers, a total decrease of 32% to 81,277, excluding contract holders although contracts only represented 5% of the total revenue. It may be that the initial excitement had worn off or perhaps it was a seasonal effect. Nevertheless, receipts in December fell yet again, totalling £472 13s 3d. *(£30,417).*

As Christmas approached, the question arose as to what level of service to operate. It was decided to run a normal weekday service without workmen's cars. Christmas services have always been a bone of contention; at the present day no public transport operates on Christmas Day and there is very little on Boxing Day.

Another useful deadline for acquisition was approaching. Section 29 of the Rochdale Corporation Act 1900 allowed the Corporation to purchase the tramways within the Urban District of Wardle up to 31st December 1902. The Town Clerk was asked to extend the date to 31st December 1903, possibly because at the end of the financial year 1902/03 the tramways had incurred a deficit of £1,506 *(£92,982)*, to be made up from the rate fund. Fortunately, this early example of public transport subsidy was not an indication of things to come as the tramways were highly profitable for most of their existence.

Bye-laws, and better receipts

National legislation obliged every tramway system to have its bye-laws in respect of detailed day to day operational aspects. The Rochdale Corporation Tramways Bye-Laws were confirmed by the Council on 2nd July 1903 and authorised by the Board of Trade on 11th September. Copies were then exhibited on every car and in the depots.

The Bye-laws were also included in the Rochdale Corporation Tramways Rules and Regulations for Officers and Servants which set out all duties and responsibilities for drivers, conductors and other employees. A long list of offences risking dismissal included insubordination, slovenly habits, drinking on duty, smoking or reading newspapers in the cars, failure to report accidents, discourteous conduct towards passengers and running ahead of, or behind time. If the last applied to today's bus drivers, one wonders how many would survive!

Some frustration is evident at the slow progress in trams reaching the town centre. 'When will electric tramcars be running through the centre of Rochdale?' asked the Observer on 18 July 1903. 'The question is often put to us and today we give such answer as is now possible. There is every reason to believe that the new cars will be running on several important central routes before the end of October. By the agreement made with the Company, the local authorities will be able to stop the traffic on any portion of the lines whenever they choose after 31 July and then commence the reconstruction of the lines. The permanent way is already laid in Milnrow Road from the Railway Inn to near the Athletic Grounds and this is to be carried forward to Newbold Street, where it is expected the terminus will be.'

Receipts for July 1903 were reported to the Committee in August and showed an improvement over the July 1902 figures although Bury Road was still lower than the previous year:

Bury Road	£161	0s	9d	(£9,942)
Norden	£448	18s	3d	(£27,377)
Rooley Moor Road	£ 99	18s	2d	(£6,168)
Total	£709	17s	2¹/2d	(£43,827)
Contracts	£ 8	2s	0d	(£500)
Parcels	£ 3	7s	1¹/2d	(£207)
Special cars	£ 4	2s	4d	(£254)
Total	£725	8s	8d	(£44,789)

The total number of passengers carried was 121,409, an annual increase of 19%. Contracts and parcels contributed relatively modest sums.

The minor duties of the Tramways Committee was carried out by ad-hoc Sub-Committees which disappeared when their job was done. Some continued for long periods like the

Routes Sub-Committee which ran for a number of years but sometimes only met every two or three months although often more than half the Committee members attended. There were also the Brakes Sub-Committee, the Car-Shed Sub-Committee and the Traffic Sub-Committee to name but a few. Some were amalgamated, producing odd groupings such as 'The Traffic, Staffing and Car-Shed Sub-Committee'.

By the end of 1903 adjustments to levels of service were being made, reducing the weekday afternoon service on the Bury Road and Norden routes and a trial of a short working between Lord Street and Spotland Bridge. The short working was short lived and was abandoned in May 1904.

The first recorded resignation occurred in February 1904 when the Traffic Clerk, Mr. W. E. Preston, was appointed Senior Clerk in the Stockport Tramways Department. He had been one of the first tramway employees appointed in June 1902. Clearly, as tramways were expanding at a rapid rate throughout the country, expertise gained in early electric operations was a very marketable quality.

A comparison of traffic receipts between February 1903 and 1904 showed a modest increase in total revenue and passengers, although they were still well below the July 1903 figures, perhaps due partly to seasonal factors. Only contracts and parcels had increased significantly.

	February 1903				February 1904			
Bury Road	£ 71	4s	7d		£ 67	15s	6d	
Norden	£253	4s	9d		£253	8s	7d	
Rooley Moor Road	£ 80	0s	7¹/2d		£ 64	0s	8d	
Spotland Bridge	—				£ 18	15s	7d	
Total	£404	9s	11¹/2d		£404	0s	4d	
Contracts	£ 13	15s	0d		£ 26	12s	0d	
Parcels	£ 2	5s	1d		£ 4	2s	2d	
Total	£420	10s	0¹/2d	(£25,960)	£434	14s	6d (£27,340)	
Mileage	—				Mileage	14,100.33		
Passengers carried	69,658				Passengers carried	71,428		
(Excluding contract holders)					(Excluding contract holders)			

right) Car No. 2 is posed with its crew and intending passengers at Littleborough. The caption claims it is the first passenger car to leave Littleborough on 30 May 1905 but official records show that the first car ran the previous day.

Bystanders mingle with tracklayers as the new electric tracks near completion in Littleborough Square. The triangular junction allowed trams from Rochdale and from Summit to turn into the terminus in Station Road. Most of the buildings including The Wheatsheaf on the left can still be seen today. The first trams arrived on 4th July 1905.

A Tramways Manager at last

Although electric tramway operation was by now well established with nearly two years operating experience, the Committee had not found it necessary to appoint a Tramways Manager. The task of planning and implementing a whole new transport system had been left to the Borough Surveyor, Mr. Samuel Platt and the Borough Electrical Engineer, Mr. C.C. Atchison who had in effect been managing the tramway between them for the past two years. On 7th March 1904 the Committee finally agreed to advertise for a Tramways Manager at an annual salary of £300 *(£18,870)*. A total of 79 applications were received and five were selected for interview:

Mr A.A. Blackburn, AMIEE,
Car Sheds Superintendent, Manchester Corporation Tramways;

Mr J. Brindle,
Manager and Secretary, Bury, Rochdale and Oldham Tramways;

Mr Wm. Hutchings,
Traffic Manager, South Lancashire Tramways, Atherton;

Mr. J.D.S. Moffett, AMICE, AMIME,
Tramway Assistant, Borough Surveyor's Office, Rochdale;

Mr W. Smith,
Manager, Taunton and West Somerset Electric Railways and Tramways Co. Ltd, Taunton.

They were allowed second class rail fare and far travelled Mr Smith was allowed one guinea *(£66)* for hotel expenses. Mr Moffet, being the best qualified applicant, and the only internal candidate to be shortlisted, was duly appointed on 18th April 1904.

Crowds flock to witness Electric tram No.7 with its complement of dignitaries for the first inspection of the Littleborough route on 29th May 1905, only 18 days after the last steam tram. Passenger service began the same day. The location is the initial terminus at Eastwood Street on Church Street

The same month an invitation was received from the Chairmen of the Glasgow and Manchester Tramways Committees to attend a meeting at the Westminster Palace Hotel in London to discuss the ominous threat of Parliamentary sanction being granted to private companies over municipal tram routes. The Mayor and Chairman were deputed to attend. Two months later a specific request was received from the Conference of Local Authorities regarding the 'Tyneside Tramways and Tramroads Bill, 1904' enquiring if the Borough Member of Parliament could be asked to vote against the clauses giving the Tyneside Company compulsory running powers over Newcastle Corporation's tramways. Fearing a dangerous precedent, not least from the Middleton Tramways, the Committee agreed, and the M.P., Col. Royds C.B., was duly lobbied.

A posed photograph to record the end of steam as new electric trams take over. Car No.7 on the Thornham route is seen with a steam tram loco and trailer on the Littleborough route. (W.T.Carter)

New electric tram and last steam tram loco and trailer are seen outside the Wellington Inn at the foot of Drake Street. Most references give the date as 8 May 1905 but some sources quote the last steam tram as being on 11 May. (Eric Fielding)

Todmorden Corporation became one of the first municipalities to operate motorbuses when a route to Steanor Bottom opened in January 1907 with two double deck Critchley-Norris buses. It was to be nearly twenty years before Rochdale started its first bus route. (LHAS)

The post of Car Shed Superintendent was advertised at a salary of £3 *(£189)* per week. Candidates were interviewed from Birkenhead, Blackpool, Blackburn, Cardiff and Rochdale. Mr J. D. Galloway of Blackburn was selected. He took up his post on 18th July, the same day as Tramways Manager Mr Moffett.

Appointing a Traffic Manager and Chief Clerk was a more straightforward affair. Mr George Webster who held a similar post with the soon to disappear Bury, Rochdale and Oldham Tramways wrote to the Committee offering his services for the Corporation Tramways. They accepted and appointed him at a salary of £3 3s *(£198)* per week but his time and salary was apportioned between the Company and the Tramways Committee until his Company duties ceased.

In June heads of agreement with Heywood Corporation were tabled for the working of tram routes in Heywood by Rochdale Corporation. Predictably, a Sub-Committee was set up to consider them.

Rochdale could have become one of the first municipalities to operate motor buses if a suggestion from Mr W.W. Shaw of Rochdale had been accepted. He proposed running buses on the Healey route instead of converting it to electric trams. The Committee were sufficiently interested to ask the newly appointed Tramways Manager to visit Bolton Corporation who had already started a motor bus service. Presumably he returned unimpressed as the idea was not pursued and conversion of the Healey route to electric traction was confirmed.

Some ten miles distant across the forbidding Pennine hills, Todmorden Corporation had been one of the first to consider running buses when they informed Rochdale in January 1906 that they were seeking powers to run motorbuses from Todmorden to the tram terminus at Summit, Littleborough. Todmorden began to operate buses on 1st January 1907, only the second municipality (after Eastbourne) in Britain to do so.

For the first couple of years there were no specified tram stops and cars would pick up and set down as required, within reason. In July 1904 a sensible decisions was taken that fixed stopping places would be defined on all routes, the Routes Sub-Committee being given the task of deciding where their location.

When the new Mellor Street was opened on 23rd July 1904, connecting for the first time the two separate parts of the tramway, the Norden trams were re-routed to operate to the town centre via Mellor Street, Bridge Street, Dane Street and the Esplanade. The Spotland trams continued to use Spotland Road to terminate at Blackwater Street.

Open top 4-wheel cars 13 and 18 pass on the loop at Featherstall Road, Littleborough.   (LHAS)

A proposal by the Routes Sub-Committee to withdraw trams from Blackwater Street was rescinded by the Committee; instead Spotland cars were to run alternately to Blackwater Street and Cheetham Street. Only a week later Council referred the matter back and the Committee agreed to discontinue the use of Blackwater Street, making it one of the shortest lived route sections in the Borough. In November 1904 the terminus for the Spotland service was changed to Cheetham Street. According to one source, Blackwater Street was later re-constructed and the Spotland trams once again terminated at Lord Street from 29th September 1906. Cheetham Street fell into disuse and never saw trams again. Blackwater Street tracks were eventually extended to the Town Centre when Newgate opened in 1910.

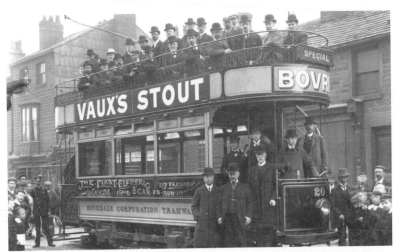

The caption handwritten on this photograph is 'The first electric car to run in Smallbridge May 24 1905'. The destination on Brush Car No. 20 shows 'Special' and the large number of dignitaries probably included members of the Tramways Committee. The official inspection and start of passenger service was on May 29 1905.

Steam tramways finally bow out

The long protracted negotiations to take over the steam tramways took another step when arbitration proceedings began between the Bury, Rochdale and Oldham Tramways Company and the various local authorities through whose districts their lines were working. Further delays resulted from the death of the first arbitrator, Sir Frederick Bramwell, following his inspection of the lines. His successor had to repeat the inspection and preliminaries. The proceedings were held at the Surveyor's Institution in Great George Street, Westminster on 31st May 1904. Rochdale and Bury Councils agreed to share the major costs as they had the most interest in the matter.

Finally in October 1904 the arbitrator set out the sums to be met by each local authority to make up the total sum of £162,675 8s 0d *(£10.23m)*. Rochdale's share was the largest at £70,790 6s 0d *(£.4.45m)*. With the completion of the purchase on 13th October, the Corporation became the not very proud owner of the steam tramways and redoubled their efforts to replace them as quickly as possible.

In May 1905 they gave notice to terminate the tenancy on the Entwisle Road Steam Depot on 31st May and to advertise the remaining engines and cars for sale. Tenders had to be in by 11th May, delivery after 15th May and all cars cleared by 31st May. Once again such timescales would be unachievable today. The last steam trams ran to Littleborough on 11th May. During their last month of working they ran 8,021 miles and carried 69,314 passengers, earning £360 14s 1d *(£22,600)* in revenue. One car body was retained for use as a waiting room at the end of Newbold Street on Milnrow Road. The 10 steam tram engines and 8 trailers were sold for £520 *(£32,570)*.

Another view of Car No. 20 on the same day, this time at Littleborough with the handwritten caption 'The first electric car to run in Littleborough May 24 1905'. The destination still shows 'Special' but this is the other side of the tram as the advertisements are different to those in the previous photograph. There are more people than at Smallbridge but some are noticeably the same people. Newcomers probably include members of Littleborough Council.

In the first month of electric operation the revenue was £1,021 12s 6d *(£64,000)*, proving the greater attraction of electric trams. The neighbouring borough of Heywood (absorbed into Rochdale in 1974) had also achieved short-lived status as a steam tram operator, but their Heywood to Hopwood route did not close until September 20th 1905.

The three steam tram depots were sold at auction and went for knock down prices. They had been valued at £26,887 by the company's valuer and even the authorities' valuer had estimated them at £15,861. This proved a little over-optimistic as they only fetched £580 between them, the Rochdale depot being sold to Mr. William Hailwood for only £400. The auctioneer commented that if ever a property was given away, this was the one.

Rochdale's steam trams had operated for only 22 years and only on four routes. Plans to extend them to Milnrow and Spotland were never realised. They were never a great success and the company had a somewhat chequered history. To their credit however, they laid the foundations for public transport in the Borough and made a significant contribution to the development of the town during the latter part of the nineteenth century.

Writing in 1906, after the last steam tram had gone, the Rochdale Observer commented:

"The presence of evil-smelling, lumbering steam tramcars in Rochdale streets is recalled almost with a shudder and it is difficult to realise that when they were introduced three-and-twenty years ago they were welcomed with enthusiasm as adding to the comfort and convenience of the townsfolk. Better steam cars than none, most people will say, though the true disciple of Ruskin would scorn to make terms with the ugly monsters".

But to be fair, would Ruskin have preferred to brave the rigours of a wild night at Facit on foot rather than in the relative comfort of a steam tram?

A more detailed history of the steam tramways can be found in Geoffrey Hyde's book 'The Manchester Bury Rochdale and Oldham Steam Tramway'.

For a short time in the summer of 1905, electric trams from Rochdale met steam trams operated by Heywood Corporation at the Rochdale boundary. A steam tram loco and double deck trailer wait to depart for Heywood while brand new Car 27 poses with smart crew and passengers before returning to Rochdale town centre via Sudden and Drake Street. *(Eric Fielding)*

EARLY ELECTRIC TRAM SCENES

Brush bogie car No.39 of 1905 leaves Broadway heading for Drake Street and Milnrow Road. The old tram shelter dates this picture to some time between 1905 and 1907.
(Edwards & Bryning Ltd., Rochdale)

A lady in a long skirt and large hat walks up the carriageway, followed by a horse and cart and a well loaded open top 4-wheel tram. The scene is Manchester Road, probably around 1910. (Eric Fielding)

Brush 4-wheel car No. 17 of 1903 heads along Oldham Road. A group of children, all wearing their hats, find the photographer more interesting.
(Eric Fielding)

10. Expansion in Rochdale and beyond.

Electric trams reach Littleborough

Work was progressing on the conversion of the Littleborough route. All outbound electric trams were to travel via Entwisle Road but inbound trams would alternate between Entwisle Road and Yorkshire Street and John Street, the reason probably being that John Street has a steep gradient and was only single track with no passing places. However in July 1905 it was decided that trams would operate alternately via John Street in both directions.

Two smartly dressed girls are more interested in the photographer than the approaching tram. Brush combination bogie car No.50 is on its way to Heywood on Bolton Road in Marland. (Eric Fielding)

The service from Cheetham Street/Yorkshire Street to Littleborough opened on 29th May 1905, initially terminating at Eastwood Street. On 4th July it was extended to Littleborough Square where a triangular junction was constructed to enable the proposed shuttle service to Summit to terminate at the station alongside the service from Rochdale. The final Summit section, which had never had steam trams, opened on 12th August. Only one tram was needed to operate the half hourly service.

A special dinner was held in the Littleborough Council Chamber at Hare Hill House in December to celebrate completion of the tramway, with well known local mill owners Gordon and Ernst Harvey amongst the guests. Recognising the significance of the occasion, the civic dignitaries feasted on eight courses including hare soup, turbot and lobster, oysters, pigeon, mutton, beef, turkey, pheasant, sweets and cheese. Eight toasts followed, with replies, including one by Councillor Rhodes to the 'Success of the Rochdale and

Littleborough Tramway Undertaking'. Tactfully, nobody reminded the councillor that there was in fact no such body!

Whitworth Urban District Council now enquired when they might expect trams to be extended along Whitworth Road. Rochdale replied that they were too busy building tramways to consider any other extensions at the moment. However, they did get round to considering it in September but decided that they could not secure the powers under a Provisional order and that Whitworth U.D.C. would be well advised to obtain the necessary powers under the Tramways Act 1870. Rochdale would then be prepared to operate the tramway in Whitworth on terms to be agreed.

Negotiations with Heywood Corporation

The success of the tramways encouraged other areas to demand trams to their locality. Trams were seen as clean, quick and comfortable and they contributed to the solution of the housing problem. As lines were laid to outer parts of the Borough, building land came onto the market. Although the new houses were not attractive for the poorer residents, they did relieve pressure in the town centre and rents therefore reduced. Council houses were not built until the twenties.

As explained above, Heywood Corporation decided to run a temporary steam tram service themselves after the takeover and they asked Rochdale if they could operate steam trams over the existing tracks inside the Rochdale boundary as far as Sudden. This was agreed in principle but then in January 1905 a draft agreement received from Heywood Corporation was deemed unacceptable.

An 8-wheel open balcony open top bogie double decker waits at the Littleborough terminus in Station Road. The shuttle trams from Summit terminated on the adjacent track. Crews had to be vigilant when turning the trolleys. (Eric Fielding)

LITTLEBOROUGH

Urban District Council.

Completion of ..
Tramways.

Children gather to witness the first tram to Littleborough while dignitaries look on from above. The date is shown as 24 May 1905 but records show that the official inspection took place on 29 May. As often the case, the children seem more interested in the photographer than the tram. (P. Lord)

COUNCIL CHAMBER,
HARE HILL,
LITTLEBOROUGH,
DECEMBER 6TH. 1905.

.. Menu ...

Sherry

PREMIER SERVICE.

SOUP
HARE.

———

FISH
TURBOT.   LOBSTER SAUCE.
SOLES AU GRATIN.

———

Claret

ENTRÉES
BOUCHÉES AUX HUITRÉES.
PIGEON SAUTIE AUX CHAMPIGNONS.

———

REMOVES
SADDLE OF MUTTON.
ROAST BEEF.   BOILED TURKEY.
OX TONGUE.

Champagne

SECOND SERVICE.

GAME
ROAST PHEASANTS.

———

SWEETS
MERINGUES AU CREAM.
CHAMPAGNE JELLY.

———

Liqueurs

SAVOURIES
FROMAGE CUIT.

———

DESSERT.

... Toasts ...

"THE KING" ... ... The Chairman

"THE QUEEN CONSORT, PRINCE AND PRINCESS
OF WALES, AND OTHER MEMBERS OF THE
ROYAL FAMILY" ... ... The Chairman

"SUCCESS TO THE ROCHDALE & LITTLEBOROUGH
TRAMWAY UNDERTAKING" ... Councillor J. Rhodes
REPLY { The Mayor of Rochdale, Counc. J. E. Jones
        { Councillor J. W. Lees

"THE OFFICIALS CONNECTED WITH THE UNDER-
TAKING" ... ... Councillor Holroyd
REPLY—S. S. Platt Esq.

"TOWN AND TRADE OF LITTLEBOROUGH"
Councillor J. C. Hudson
REPLY—E. Taylor Esq., C.C.

"OUR VISITORS" ... ... The Chairman
REPLY { Mr. W. H. Hickson
        { Mr. E. C. Harvey

"OUR COUNTY REPRESENTATIVES"
Councillor R. Brook
REPLY—A. G. C. Harvey Esq., C.A.

"THE PRESS" ... ... Councillor A. J. Law
REPLY—Mr. Clegg.

No expense was spared by Littleborough Urban District Council to celebrate the coming of electric trams. The eight course menu included hare soup, turbot with lobster sauce, pigeon, mutton, beef, turkey, pheasant washed down with claret and champagne.

The only traffic is a horse drawn wagon on Manchester Road near New Barn Lane as two intending passengers wait for the tram to Heywood via Drake Street.
(T. Pinder)

A meeting between Rochdale, Heywood and Bury Corporations was held in Rochdale on 28th May 1905 to draft a working agreement for the conversion to electric traction in Heywood with the following terms:

- Heywood to construct and maintain the track and electrical equipment and supply current;

- Bury and Rochdale to provide enough cars and staff to operate a 15 minute service, or as may be agreed;

- Receipts from the Heywood section to be handed to Heywood quarterly;

- Heywood to pay 4$\frac{1}{2}$d *(£1.04)* per car mile run on the section to Rochdale and Bury;

- Rochdale and Bury to repair and maintain the overhead equipment in good working condition;

- The equipment to be approved by the electrical engineers for Rochdale and Bury.

Six cars would be needed to work the Heywood system, four for the Heap Bridge to Heywood Parish Church section and two from the Rochdale boundary to the Parish Church. Heywood were to take over these six cars at the end of the tenancy, pay any remaining debt and meet the interest and sinking fund on the cars which would be maintained by Rochdale and Bury. The tenancy was for three years and then subject to three months notice on either side. The terms were finally agreed in September 1905.

New tram routes not pursued

Three new sections of tramway were proposed within Rochdale:

1. from the existing tramway at St Mary's Gate along Blackwater Street and Lord Street to the junction with Yorkshire Street;

2. from Lord Street junction with Yorkshire Street along Yorkshire Street to South Parade;

3. from the existing tramway at the Railway Station along Maclure Road to a junction with the existing tramway on Drake Street.

The Committee recommended an application to the Board of Trade for a Provisional order under the Tramways Act 1870. However the first two proposals were overtaken by plans for a new street, now known as Newgate, connecting Blackwater Street with The Esplanade. The Maclure Road plan was dropped in August 1906 and not revived for almost 20 years; no doubt objections to the application from frontagers on Blackwater Street, Lord Street and Maclure Road had an influence.

Another potentially forward thinking scheme also failed to reach fruition. Norden U.D.C. required a direct tram service to Rochdale Station. The British have never been very good at transport integration and true to form the Committee turned it down. There was no railway station in or near Norden and this would have given them direct access to the rail network. A century later and Norden is still waiting for its connection. There are five bus routes from Norden but none of them go to Rochdale Railway Station!

Car number 4 waits at the remote moorland terminus of the Littleborough-Summit shuttle service. The smartly dressed conductor and driver with point iron in hand pose for the photographer.
(MTMS)

However, the Committee did agree to increase the frequency on the Circular route, which served Rochdale Station, to every ten minutes in each direction for a trial period from 22nd December 1905 until 31st January 1906. This was later extended for another two months.

Through running achieved

One successful innovation was through running of trams between systems. South east Lancashire and north east Cheshire achieved one of the largest and most complex tramway networks in Britain with extensive joint operations between municipal operators, particularly into Manchester. Agreement on the basis for discussion was reached in January 1906 for through running with Oldham Corporation between specified points on their respective

Todmorden tramway would have been built to 3' 6" gauge, the same as Halifax. The steam trams then serving Littleborough were 3' 6" gauge but the replacing electric trams which ran on to Summit were of course standard gauge.

A second proposal for through running emerged on 6th July 1908 when a joint meeting of the Rochdale, Heywood and Bury Tramways Sub-Committees held in Heywood recommended:

1) that the Rochdale and Bury Corporations should work the Heywood Tramways at cost price;

2) that Heywood should receive the fares charged in respect of stages in Heywood and not in proportion to mileage as heretofore;

3) that through running should be instituted between Rochdale and Bury.

In this early view of the Tramway Centre, the steam tram tracks are still visible on the left on South Parade. Brush combination bogie car No. 38 waits to depart for Heywood (Touchstones Rochdale)

Rochdale agreed to a three month through running trial although it took another year to formalise arrangements. Rochdale had objected to the clauses in the Parliamentary Bills being promoted by Bury and Heywood for operation of their tramways, including powers over Rochdale tracks. The matter was settled during the Committee stage of the Bills allowing through working by Bury and Rochdale cars to extend from Rochdale town centre to Market Place, Bury. A draft agreement for the service was reached to allow the service to begin on 1st August 1909.

systems. The first Oldham tram to run on Rochdale tracks ran through the town centre and out to Norden in February 1906 with members of both Tramway Committees on board. It then returned through Oldham to Hathershaw with the members proceeding to Oldham Town Hall to debate the issues.

The joint working arrangements took a little while to resolve but on 16th April the Manager announced that through running from Hathershaw in Oldham to Rochdale and Norden would commence on 1st May. The service was later reported to be 'working satisfactorily'.

A more ambitious link would have taken trams across the Pennines almost into Yorkshire. The Municipal Journal for May 1902 reported that "Rochdale…will itself run cars through the urban district of Littleborough to within a mile or two of the Yorkshire border, to which it is anticipated the Halifax trams will go in a short time". This was prompted by Todmorden Corporation's tentative plan to lay a tramway from Todmorden to Summit, close to the Rochdale tram terminus, and lease it to Halifax. The line was never built and through running would not have been possible as the

The service duly began on that date but after a lengthy trial it was found that there was very little through traffic between Rochdale and Bury as the competing through train service took only about 20 minutes, much quicker than the tram, despite a much better tram frequency. Furthermore it was contended that the service to Sudden and Heywood had been adversely affected by the through trams with a consequent loss of passengers, in contrast to the through Oldham service whose receipts had risen and patronage was strong. Through working to Bury continued nevertheless.

Joint running to Bury via Heywood restored the link pioneered by the steam trams 25 years earlier, and Manchester was reached in 1925. At some point (it is not recorded when), the through service to Bury was discontinued. However by 1924 Heywood Corporation resurrected the idea of the through service between Rochdale and Bury and suggested a three way meeting to discuss the possibility. Agreement was reached and through operation recommenced on 13th July 1925 with cars running through after 12 noon each day.

CAR No 1 at SUMMIT

Car No. 1 at Summit with its blinds drawn in the front and rear sections. The smartly dressed crew pose for the photographer. The date is not known but the tram is looking decidedly shabby. It was withdrawn in 1919. (MTMS)

Car number 1 at Summit with the shutter blinds open, a more usual situation, again with posing crew and few passengers. (MTMS)

Single deck bogie car No. 1, Rochdale's first tramcar, poses at Summit with its crew and a policeman. Although not dated, this may well have been the official inspection on August 12th 1905. (LHAS)

Tramways in Rochdale completed

The electric tramways within the Borough were by now complete, apart from some relatively minor extensions. Twelve services operated as shown in Table 10.1. They all started from the Tramway Centre at the Butts/South Parade apart from the Spotland route which ran from Cheetham Street. The frequencies shown are those applicable to the weekday working day; services were augmented at peak periods and weekends. Additionally, the Hathershaw service was augmented between Rochdale and Kings Road and Thornham and some short workings operated on the Heywood service as far as Sudden in the mornings.

Table 10.1. Tram services and frequencies, 1906.		
	(minutes)	frequency (Trams per hour)
Littleborough via Entwisle Road	22	3
Littleborough via John Street	22	3
Littleborough-Summit	12	2
Firgrove via Milnrow Road	11	3
Town centre to Healey	17	3
Circular via High Level Road	12	4
Bamford via Bury Road	11	3
Spotland via Spotland Road	13	2
Norden via Mellor Street	18	3
Heywood via Drake Street	22	3
Heywood via Manchester Road	22	3
Sudden (short working, am only)	12	3
Hathershaw via Oldham	57	1 - 6

It is interesting to see that most routes enjoyed only a twenty minute service which would be considered rather sparse by today's tramway and light rail standards. Spotland and Summit only warranted half hourly services while only the Circular service and Oldham achieved a quarter hour headway or better. Perhaps this reflected the local nature of employment during the era 'when Cotton was King'. For many shorter journeys it was still quicker to walk. Average speeds were mainly between 8 mph and 9 mph, not a lot less than today's peak period bus speeds.

The build-up of the network is shown clearly in Table 10.2 below which gives the monthly mileage operated and passengers carried over the first four operating years. The initial excitement from the totally new experience for Rochdalians of travelling on a completely new mode of transport in the summer of 1902 died down rapidly in the winter of 1902/03 but recovered during 1903 to surpass the initial patronage figure, with only the initial three routes operating. The new routes and conversion of steam routes in the latter part of 1904 quadrupled the number of passengers and by mid 1905 it had almost reached three quarters of a million per month.

A marked seasonal difference was still evident, suggesting the trams were well used for leisure trips in the summer to the surrounding hills, dales and parks.

These impressive achievements would of course not have been possible if the groundwork had not been thoroughly prepared by the diligent officers of the Corporation. The Borough Surveyor had had the heavy responsibility of preparing all the engineering input to the Rochdale Corporation Act 1900 and the subsequent construction of the permanent way for the entire tramway including conversion and re-gauging of the former steam tramway. The old tracks were not reusable so had to be completely replaced.

On the 21st February 1906 the Committee recognised Samuel Platt's great achievement by awarding him a whole year's salary, £600 *(£36,613)*, as a bonus. It was well earned as he must have suffered many long hours and sleepless nights to install the entire tramway in only five years, about the same time it took to build Rochdale's renowned Town Hall. However the Council parsimoniously referred the matter back and the bonus was reduced from £600 to £500 *(£30,511)*, still a substantial sum.

The completion of the major part of the tramway enabled the meetings of the Tramways Committee to settle down to the more routine business of running a public transport department. The excitement of planning and building new lines and buying lots of new trams was replaced with more mundane matters such as passing monthly or weekly accounts, signing off the Requisition Book, making routine purchases of everything from uniforms and caps to notepaper, minor track repairs, dealing with complaints from the public and considering frequent applications for wage rises. Requests for shelters at termini or stops became another familiar item on agendas.

The Committee often adopted a fairly hard line on employees seeking to improve their remuneration but relented when two junior clerks asked for a rise in March 1906. Their salary was increased from 10/- *(£30.51)* per week to 13/- *(£39.66)* per week, a 30% rise. In contrast, the

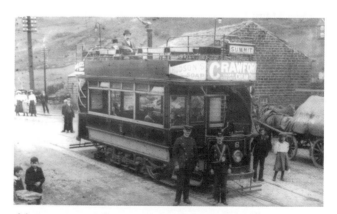

A busy scene at the remote Summit terminus with tram crew and assorted onlookers. Photographers were still quite a rare site. Car No. 8 is a 4-wheel single truck car to the same design as Car No.3 and built by the Electric Railway and Tramway Carriage Company in Preston. After this batch, future orders went to Brush for the next 18 years.

(Eric Fielding)

Table 10.2. Monthly mileage and passenger figures for first four years operation.

Year	Month	Mileage	Passengers*	Bury	Norden	Spotland	Circular	Thornham	Milnrow Rd	Sudden	Healey	Heybrook	Littleborough	Summit
1902	July	—	101,663	x	x	x								
	August	—	120,250	x	x	x								
	November	—	81,277	x	x	x								
	December	—	80,350	x	x	x								
1903	January	—	80,040	x	x	x								
	February	—	69,658	x	x	x								
	March	18,899	101,159	x	x	x								
	April	16,202	101,012	x	x	x								
	May	16,603	105,055	x	x	x								
	June	17,104	125,150	x	x	x								
	July	17,400	121,409	x	x	x								
	August	17,588	116,194	x	x	x								
	September	16,312	99,716	x	x	x								
	October	17,114	94,681	x	x	x								
	November	16,012	81,513	x	x	x								
	December	15,999	81,218	x	x	x								
1904	January	14,966	83,516	x	x	x								
	February	14,100	71,428	x	x	x								
	March	15,091	78,292	x	x	x								
	April	15,151	96,493	x	x	x								
	May	15,096	104,905	x	x	x								
	June	14,171	108,533	x	x	x								
	July	17,625	148,059	x	x	x								
	August +	22,310	172,310	x	x	x	x							
	September	26,926	226,010	x	x	x	x	x						
	October	40,625	323,471	x	x	x	x	x	x	x				
	November	40,882	291,778	x	x	x	x	x	x	x	x			
	December	58,019	430,523	x	x	x	x	x	x	x	x		s	
1905	January	58,568	415,906	x	x	x	x	x	x	x	x	x	s	
	February	55,679	389,644	x	x	x	x	x	x	x	x	x	s	
	March	62,549	469,312	x	x	x	x	x	x	x	x	x	s	
	April	65,489	526,344	x	x	x	x	x	x	x	x	x	s	
	May	63,860	482,972	x	x	x	x	x	x	x	x	x	s	
	June	78,013	658,902	x	x	x	x	x	x	x	x	x	x	
	July	82,465	735,250	x	x	x	x	x	x	x	x	x	x	
	August	89,418	748,090	x	x	x	x	x	x	x	x	x	x	x
	September	84,156	671,644	x	x	x	x	x	x	x	x	x	x	x
	October	83,999	652,887	x	x	x	x	x	x	x	x	x	x	x
	November	81,562	605,139	x	x	x	x	x	x	x	x	x	x	x
	December	87,030	675,164	x	x	x	x	x	x	x	x	x	x	x

* excluding contract holders.
x = section open or partly open.

+ including 15 days of circular route.
s = section operated by steam trams.

47

TRAMS BEYOND THE BOUNDARY

Crowds gather to witness the Board of Trade inspection car as it makes its way through Whitworth on 14 June 1910. It opened that day to Hall Street and was extended later in 1910 to Facit and Shawforth. Brush built Car 19 of 1903 was converted to an engineering car in 1927 and renumbered 1. *(Eric Fielding)*

A typical industrial area street scene as Brush bogie combination Car No. 40 heads for Whitworth. It is one 20 such cars delivered during 1905.
(Eric Fielding)

Steam trams last ran to Healey in September 1904. Two months later electric trams started. Brush 4-wheel car No. 12 built in 1903 stands at the terminus at Ending Rake. The cottages in the background can still be seen today. The line was extended to Whitworth in 1910 and right through to Bacup in 1911, one of the highest tram routes in Britain.

Tramway and Vehicle Worker's Association were refused six days holiday per year with pay and time and a quarter for overtime. They were told that their pay and conditions were already as good or better than the average for other neighbouring towns. A similar request from the Amalgamated Society of Engineers and Steam Engine Makers for an increase of 1/- *(£3.05)* per week for fitters and turners was granted. It was to apply to all skilled workmen.

A year later a further request from the Amalgamated Society of Vehicle and Tramway Workers achieved better success. Although their application for a week's holiday with pay for all inspectors, motormen, conductors and shedmen with a full year's service was turned down again, their request for a wage increase was partly accepted. An increase from $6^1/_4$d *(£1.56)* to $6^1/_2$d *(£1.63)* per hour for motormen and regular staff with two year's service was approved but nothing more for conductors or shedmen.

The value of good publicity was realised by the Committee on 14th May. A combined handbook and timetable in a handy pocket size was produced as the 'Official Guide and Illustrated Map of the Electric Tramway Routes, Walking Tours and Car Time Tables'. In addition to timetables and fare tables for each route, there were brief descriptions of walks from tram terminals, photographs of local beauty spots, trams and the car Shed (interior and exterior). A list of Tramway Committee members, extracts from the bye-laws and 'hints for passengers' completed this attractive and useful booklet. It was printed by Edwards and Bryning Ltd. of Rochdale and sold for 2d *(51p)*. The Guide Books could be purchased from the Timekeeper at The Butts, the commission being passed to the Corporation. Curiously it made no mention of the through route to Oldham although the Heywood route was included. An original copy of this guide with its colour cover and map can still be seen at the Local Studies Centre Touchstones Rochdale.

Brush open top 4-wheeler of 1903 squeezes past a horse drawn wagon on Market Street on its way to Whitworth, probably in 1910. A group of long skirted women stand on the pavement outside their stone terraced houses.

Rochdale's tramways quickly became an accepted and valued feature of the town. When the new Rochdale Golf Club 18-hole course was laid out at Bagslate in 1906, (which was 'expected to become one of the best in the district'), the site was acclaimed as very convenient because it was within one minute's walk of the Norden tram route.

Not surprisingly therefore, the prospect of competition from buses owned and operated by railway companies was a potential threat to the immense investment in their new tramways. The Municipal Tramways Conference resolved to secure the deletion of clauses deleted in Parliamentary Bills allowing railway companies to run buses. They would not agree to them running in any city, borough or urban district in which a local authority owned or worked tramways. The Rochdale M.P., Mr. Vivian, was asked to support a motion against the promoters of the Mersey Railway Bill and the Wirral Railway Bill. Happily, the offending clause was duly struck out and tramway operators could breath again. Competition from buses when high capital cost tram systems have been built largely with public funds is still a major issue for today's light rail proposals.

A Committee visit was made to the signals at the top of John Street. The approaches on each arm of the delta junction were single track so only one tram could pass through the junction at a time. It was recommended that the signal over the town side of John Street be removed to the other side of Yorkshire Street, the signals otherwise being satisfactory. As colour light traffic signals had not been invented it is assumed that it must have been some form of semaphore signal.

An industrial setting as Brush bogie combination car No.43 heads past the Liberal Club on its way to Whitworth. A horse and cart and a few pedestrians complete the activity.
(Eric Fielding)

WHITWORTH SCENES

A large crowd of children gather to watch Car No. 24 outside the Dog and Partridge public house on Market Street at Hall Street in Whitworth. Trams terminated here for a short time between June and July 1910 before being extended to Facit and Bacup.   (Eric Fielding)

The Whitworth Parish Church parade makes its way along Market Street in Whitworth in 1910. Brush combination Car No.57 eases past on its way to the terminus.   (Eric Fielding)

A Brush bogie combination car of 1905 heads along Whitworth Road on the Bacup Section, past typical stone terrace houses and women in full length skirts. The track was single with passing places but the overhead was double, to avoid having too many frogs.

Extensions into neighbouring Districts

In July 1906 the Committee decided to explore an extension of the tramway into Milnrow Urban District. A meeting was held with representatives of Milnrow U.D.C. two months later who were requested to apply for a Provisional Order authorising the construction of a tramway from the Rochdale boundary at Firgrove to Huddersfield Road in Milnrow. The tramway was to be worked by Rochdale on mutually agreeable terms. Detailed agreement was hard to reach but Milnrow did agree to make the application . Support for a tramway to Milnrow had never been totally unanimous. Two years earlier, the Rochdale Observer for 30 November 1904 had reported:

An open top tram is the only vehicle in sight as it trundles along a section of single track on Market Street in Facit. Trams reached Facit in 1910 and were extended to Bacup in 1911. (Eric Fielding)

"All who travel the Milnrow Road will be glad to hear negotiations for the widening of the canal bridge at Firgrove are being re-opened. It is a scandal that the present state of things has existed so long. Not only is the bridge very narrow but the gradients are bad and the place is a continual danger to vehicular traffic. It would be impossible, of course, to carry a tramway over the present bridge. It is said some influential folk in Milnrow are not anxious to have tramway communication with Rochdale. They are a little afraid of the borough and inclined to look upon any project for drawing the two communities closer together as a means of hastening annexation of their district".

In that latter respect their fears were justified! The line was duly included in the Rochdale Corporation Tramways Provisional Order, 1906 which received Royal Assent on 4th August 1906.

In December 1906 the Town Clerk reported the capital costs of the Corporation tramways:

Acquisition of the steam tramways	£80,205	(£4.894m)
Construction of electric tramways	£137,492	(£8.390m)
Other tramway purposes	£133,023	(£8.117m)
Total cost	£350,720	(£21.402m)

The acquisition of tramways allowed for £4,771 12s 4d (£291,173) in respect of loss on working steam tramways. It was subsequently agreed that this loss should be charged to the tramway revenue account, reducing the

A classic northern industrial scene as Brush 8-wheel bogie combination car No. 43 makes its way along Market Street past Facit Mill and terrace houses. Children gather in the road to watch.
(MTMS)

BACUP SCENES

A large crowd of children gather to welcome Car No. 26, a Brush built 4-wheeler of 1905. The location is Shawforth on Market Street on the Bacup route although the destination shows Whitworth .   (Eric Fielding)

Photographs of the Bacup route are scarce. This contemporary postcard shows an open top car standing on St James Street. The terminal tracks in the foreground are the double track layout favoured by Rochdale and lead a short distance into Bridge Street.
                    (Lillywhite Ltd, Halifax)

Brush bogie combination Car No.61stands at Bacup terminus at Town Head, Bridge Street. The Rawtenstall Tramways terminus was a few yards away but through running was not possible because of the different gauges. Power for Rochdale's tramway was fed from Rawtenstall's tramway and the feeder cables can be seen at the top of the photograph.
                    (Jackson & Son, Grimsby)

capital cost of tramway acquisition to £75,433 (£4.603m) and the total cost of the tramways to £345,948 (£21.110m). This seems to be the first time that capital costs appeared in the Tramways Committee minutes.

Increases in pay continued to be sought by individual employees or by the embryonic trade unions. In June 1907 the Amalgamated Association of Tramway and Vehicle Workers claim for an increase of 2s 6d per week for inspectors was rewarded with an increase of one farthing per hour (6p) taking their rate to 6¾d per hour (£1.69). This was equivalent to about half the claimed increase. The era of annual collective bargaining was still some way off.

present at the same rate as paid at Cheetham Street lavatory.

An offer from The National Telephone Company to install a telephone at the town centre office was received but declined.

An important milestone went apparently unnoticed in August 1907 when the monthly total of passengers carried, including those on the Heywood Section, passed the million mark for the first time. Summer traffic was higher than in winter, doubtless because in wet weather no one wanted to brave the tramcars' exposed open top decks unless there was no alternative. The total had been within

Single deck 8-wheel bogie combination car built by Brush in 1912 on the Milnrow route which was completed in 1912.
(Rochdale Observer)

In July 1907, approval was given for a building that was destined to become a Rochdale landmark for many years. The Corporation had recently provided a wide expanse of new paving between the Butts and South Parade by the expedient of covering the River Roch where it flowed through the town centre. Tramlines were laid in an anti-clockwise direction, thus allowing all boarding and alighting to take place on a central island. Upon the island stood the showpiece – a combined shelter, ladies' lavatory and parcels office – which soon became known as the "Tramways Centre". It was built by Messrs W A Peters & Sons, the contractor who had built the Car Shed and Tramway Offices.

The question of charges for the use of the new ladies lavatory was debated at length before the obvious figure was agreed. The Committee resolved:

1) That the Tramways Committee have charge of the ladies lavatory and the whole shelter.
2) That the waiting room be open from 8.00 a.m. to 11.00 p.m. daily.
3) That the charge for use of the closets be one penny (25p).
4) That the Manager engage a woman attendant for the

sight of a million since March but no doubt the August weather had brought out the crowds.

The importance of leisure traffic was highlighted in July 1907. At weekends if the weather was fine, all 60 trams could be pressed into service compared with only about 33 cars required on weekdays. On fine Saturdays no motormen or conductors were allowed to take time off and even on Sundays most had to work. The lightest traffic was Tuesdays which was early closing day.

The high standard expected from the platform staff was amply demonstrated when a conductor was prosecuted at the Borough Police Court for embezzling a penny fare (25p) from a passenger. He was fined 10/6d (£31.19) plus costs. No nonsense was tolerated from the public either. A farmer from Tottington received the same punishment for obstructing a tramcar on Manchester Road. Passengers were also sometimes prosecuted for bad behaviour such as a Castleton man who was fined 21/- (£62.38) and costs for offensive conduct while on a tramcar.

However, the Committee was equally capable of magnanimity. Motorman Newsome managed to stop Car.

No.11 "in exceptional circumstances" and was called before the Committee so that the Chairman could commend him for his prompt action. His loss in wages was made up by the Committee.

A new road and more extensions

In October 1907 the Committee resolved that its next application to Parliament should include powers to build a tramway in the new street to be built between Blackwater Street and the Esplanade, now known as Newgate. It was subsequently agreed that the street should be widened from 14 yards *(12.8m)* to 16 yards *(14.6m)* to permit double tracks to be laid in the centre.

The next extension to the system came a step closer in July 1908 when the Routes Sub-Committee recommended negotiations with Whitworth Urban District Council for a northward extension from the existing terminus at Ending to a point on the main road below Shawforth Station. Agreement was reached that Whitworth Council would make an application under the 1896 Light Railway Act to construct the line as a light railway and to bear the cost of construction, electrical equipment and renewals although Rochdale would be responsible for maintenance and would work the line for an agreed period. On investigation Whitworth Council realised that a Light Railway Order might be difficult to obtain and agreed to seek a conventional Tramway Order instead.

Terms were agreed with Whitworth U.D.C. on 21st October 1908 for the extension of the tramway to the Red Lion at Shawforth, 'Tramway No.1'. Not surprisingly the Lancashire and Yorkshire Railway lodged an objection to the Bill as the proposed line closely paralleled their branch line from Rochdale to Bacup opened in 1870. The

Tramway Order was confirmed in July 1909 but with a protective clause for a drawback to the Lancashire and Yorkshire Railway in respect of any loss on the tramways in Whitworth. Preparations were then made to begin construction of the extension in spring 1910.

These developments aroused the interest of the Borough of Bacup at the head of the valley whose Town Clerk raised the possibility of extending the tramway from Facit to Bacup. The Committee inspected the route on Monday 13th September 1909 and by October had agreed to open negotiations with Bacup Corporation and Whitworth Urban District Council on an extension northwards from Shawforth to the centre of Bacup, to be worked by Rochdale Corporation. Terms were agreed in November on a similar basis to those for Whitworth, except that Bacup sought a Light Railway Order rather than a Tramway Order.

The 13th October 1909 saw agreement reached with Whitworth UDC to construct 'Tramway No.2' from Shawforth to the Bacup boundary at Britannia, where it would connect with the Bacup Light Railway. On 10th November agreement was reached with Bacup Corporation for the construction and operation of tramways in Bacup and the Light Railway Commissioners held an enquiry at Bacup on 1st February 1910 and expressed their approval. Royal Assent was obtained on 5th August 1910.

Whitworth Tramway No.1 was opened in 1910 in three sections: Healey terminus to Hall Street on 14th June; Hall Street to Station Road, Facit on 20th July; Station Road Facit to Red Lion Shawforth on 6th September.

In December 1908 the Committee had approved an increase in the General Manager's salary from 1st January 1909. Mr Moffet was awarded an extra £50 *(£2,930)* per annum taking his salary to £350 *(£20,509)*. It was to be

Trams reached New Hey in 1912, the last extension until Maclure Road was built in 1924. Bogie car No.69 of 1912 waits at the terminus at the junction of New Hey Road and Huddersfield Road. This view is much the same today apart from a lot more traffic .

(Eric Fielding)

increased by a further £25 *(£1,465)* per annum for the next two years.

On 15th September 1909 terms were finally agreed with Milnrow UDC. to construct the tramway extension for 1.78 miles *(2.85 km)* through Milnrow to terminate at Huddersfield Road in Newhey. The UDC applied for a Provisional Order in the current session of parliament, Royal Assent being obtained in 3rd August 1910.

The Routes Sub-Committee visited Oldham on 12th October 1909 to inspect Oldham's route from Thornham to Hathershaw, the new repair depot and the main car shed at Mumps. They took the opportunity to complain to members of the Oldham Tramways Committee about the dirty condition of Oldham trams working through to Rochdale. Their hosts promised no expense to be spared in remedying the situation.

The winter of 1909/10 was severe with several heavy snowstorms. The Department spent over £160 *(£9,375)* on salting and keeping the track and roads open. Car maintenance costs also increased. The Annual Report comments that if this expenditure had not been incurred some roads would have been closed to vehicular traffic for days. The trams had their uses!

A deputation from the residents and shopkeepers on Cheetham Street was heard by the Committee on 20th July 1910. They were protesting about the loss of their tram service, with a 1600 name petition, the Spotland route having been diverted to terminate in Blackwater Street in 1906. The Chairman intimated that they "could not at present see their way to sanction the reopening of this section". The Cheetham Street section had opened as recently as 1904 so had enjoyed a tram service for only two years. The rails were certainly not worn as when they were taken up in 1916 they were used to replace worn track on John Street.

In August 1910 it was reported that the description 'Bury Road' on the Bury Road cars was misleading and it was agreed to change it to 'Cemetery' in future. There was a good reason: there were then two Bury Roads, the one that leads to the Cemetery and one between Sudden and the Heywood boundary which is now Bolton Road. The following May they decided to change it again, this time to 'Bamford' which is far more misleading as they stopped at least a mile short!

An Agreement was signed between Rochdale and Bacup Corporations on 6th March 1911 whereby Rochdale would construct the extension into Bacup 'with all due speed'.

When trams finally reached Bacup on 25th July 1911 it became one of the highest tram routes in the country, reaching a height of 965 ft. *(294m)* above sea level at Britannia. During severe winters the line could be snowed up for days and on bad winter nights, some residents of Shawforth and Whitworth would appear in the roadway with a jug of tea and something to eat for the frozen tram crews. The same happened at Summit but sadly today's bus drivers are unlikely to experience such generosity. A small four car depot was provided on the descent into Bacup to save mileage on the long haul into Rochdale, and crews would stay overnight in Bacup before bringing the first trams out in the morning.

Although Bacup Corporation never owned any trams itself, it had the unusual distinction of owning two sections of tramway: the standard gauge route along Rochdale Road, St James Street and Bridge Street operated by Rochdale Corporation and the four foot gauge line in Newchurch Road and Market Street leased to Rawtenstall Corporation. The two termini were only a few yards apart but of course through running was not feasible.

Illuminated trams and Bundy Clocks

One of the many advantages of electric trams was that they had plenty of electric power on tap to light up lots of bulbs and illuminated trams became very popular for celebrations all kinds. The first recorded visit of an illuminated tram to Rochdale was made by an Oldham car in June 1911. It was probably one of Oldham's open top 4-wheel double deckers decorated with bunting, shields, evergreens, coloured lights and large illuminated letters 'LONG LIVE THE KING'. The occasion was the Coronation of King George V and Queen Mary on 22nd June 1911.

On 3rd August it was Bolton's turn to send an illuminated tram, to the great pleasure of the Corporation and townsfolk. An illuminated Bolton tram returned to Rochdale two years later on 23rd July 1913, a further visit being recorded in February 1917 .

During 1911 a Bundy time recording clock was installed at Healey at a cost of £18. It was equipped with a paper tape transport with recording printer and a transfer drive spindle to synchronise the two units. The driver placed a key, coded to his duty, in a slot in the centre box and turn it; the print mechanism then printed his key number and the arrival time on the paper tape. The results were pronounced 'satisfactory', enabling actual arrival times to be accurately recorded for the first time.

One reason given for installing the clocks was that previously the trams had been fitted with conventional clocks which unfortunately proved unreliable. Drivers observed the tram clock even if it was fast or slow, to the annoyance of passengers. The tram clocks were removed and seven more Bundy clocks were purchased and installed at the Railway Station, Bamford terminus, Spotland Bridge, King's Road, Kiln Lane, Smallbridge and Facit. Similar clocks were still in use for buses in several areas until the nineteen sixties.

In November 1911 Councillor Dunning, who had been a member of the Tramways Committee since it started and had chaired it since November 1903, was made an Alderman of the Borough, continuing as Chairman for another year but then resigning. Placing on record their deep appreciation of his nine years service and his dedication to the interests of the undertaking, the Committee expressed regret to Alderman Dunning that he had not seen his way to continue to serve on the Committee. Councillor Joseph Fielden was elected Chairman in succession.

11. Tram routes to everywhere.

In the reign of King George II, Daniel Defoe, in his wanderings through England, has described a fearsome snowbound walk over the moors from Rochdale to Halifax in which he had almost given himself up for lost. Twentieth century Rochdale folk disdained any such fears.

A remarkable booklet first published in 1908 under the title 'Where to go by Car' (tramcar, not motor car) showed the extent of tramways in the early years of the twentieth century, and the radical social and economic changes that they brought. John Lingard, a Manchester printer, had researched a mine of information about routes, timetables and fares across innumerable tram systems in the north west and beyond. In the days when trains were the main mode for longer distance travel, and before cars, buses and coaches had become commonplace, travelling by tram and walking where trams didn't reach, offered a real alternative.

In his introduction Lingard comments:

"It is now possible to travel long distances, splendid opportunities are opened up to those who desire to see both town and country in a way which is quite impracticable when travelling by train. Many people have already discovered the attractions of long distance tram travelling. It has this advantage over the ordinary means of travel, that the passenger can alight where his fancy suits him. He can ramble in the woods or the fields, explore some picturesque farmstead, and when he is tired of this he can make his way back to the highway and join the next tram in whichever direction he desires to go"

Lingard highlights the egalitarian qualities of the tram, which no previous form of transport could claim:

"A long tram ride is an excellent way of getting an insight into the character of the people in the various towns and country places. Everybody on a tramcar is on an equality, there is no distinction of classes, the artisan who pays his penny is on a par with the rich man and this rubbing of shoulders is destined to have a beneficial effect all round, it tends to eliminate the aloofness which is fostered by railway travelling, and leads to an exchange of ideas which to anyone of an observing turn of mind is most interesting, especially the different shades of dialect spoken on a journey".

Lingard's routes were based on Manchester and listed the destinations that could be reached, the distance, fares, tram frequencies and estimated journey times. While most were electric tram routes, a few bus routes were listed where they provided a link between tram routes such as the Todmorden Corporation bus service between Steanor Bottom, 300 yards from the Summit tram terminus, and Todmorden, plus another from Todmorden to Sandbed from where it was a 1$^1/_2$ mile walk to the Halifax tram at Hebden Bridge. At that period, Rochdale trams on Whitworth Road only ran as far as Healey leaving a five mile walk through Whitworth, Facit and Britannia to Bacup where steam trams still ran down the valley to Rawtenstall.

Long walks across the hills between tram termini were no deterrent to the new generation of tramway explorers. Two routes from Manchester to Bradford were offered, both travelling via Middleton, Sudden, Rochdale and Littleborough. The first then continued via Todmorden, Hebden Bridge and Halifax, a distance of 39$^1/_2$ miles including the 1$^1/_2$ mile walk between Sandbed and Hebden Bridge. It took four hours and cost 2s 6d *(12$^1/_2$p) (£7.43)*. The second continued with a 7$^1/_2$ mile walk up Blackstone Edge and past the White House to Triangle and then via Sowerby Bridge and Halifax, a distance of 34$^1/_2$ miles. It took four hours including the walk (although for some the walk alone would probably take four hours!) and cost 1s 7$^1/_2$d *(8$^1/_2$p) (£4.83)*. It is described in more detail in the later edition.

The 11 mile journey from Rochdale to Manchester took 1 hour 10 minutes (about the same time it now takes by car in the morning rush hour!) and required changing trams at Sudden and Middleton. The cost was 7$^1/_2$d *(3p) (£1.86)*. Sixteen years later the fare had risen to 10$^1/_2$d *(4p) (£2.60)*.

Car No. 3 approaches Littleborough town centre on Todmorden Road, alongside Holy Trinity parish church, on the shuttle service from Summit. Note the complete absence of other traffic.

More long distance trips by tram

An expanded and updated version of Lingard's guide was published in 1924 with the slightly changed title of 'Where to go by Tram'. More tram routes and extensions had opened since his 1908 guide, there were more bus routes but all the steam trams had gone. Rochdale was near the heart of his 'tram and walking' network which stretched from Morecambe to Leicester and from Shrewsbury to York. Some links where there were no trams could be made by motorbus but many others were shown as walking routes including some quite long stretches, like the Blackstone Edge route. Either people must have been much fitter than today or time was not of the essence; maybe both. On the other hand, how many people actually availed themselves of these alluring possibilities?

The places that could be reached by tram in Rochdale are set out in Table 11.1 below.

This example of integration across a vast network is rarely matched in today's deregulated bus networks. Most journeys could be made entirely by tram, changing at the boundaries between systems, or in some cases riding through on cars of joint operators. Sometimes bus links were needed to bridge gaps in the rails. The longest possible tram ride was from Littleborough Summit to Liverpool, about 52 miles.

Routes to or through Rochdale included Manchester to Bradford (in Yorkshire, not the Manchester suburb), Burnley, Castleton, Halifax, Hebden Bridge, Leeds, Littleborough, Middleton, Mytholmroyd, Rochdale, Sowerby Bridge, Todmorden, Wakefield and Whitworth. Many of these were based on the 48¹/₂ mile *(77¹/₂ km)* Manchester to Leeds route shown in Table 11.2 below. The average time for the journey was 5 hours giving an average speed of 9.7mph *(15.5 km/hr)*.

Table 11.1.	Tram routes in Rochdale, from Lingard's 'Where to go by Tram' (1924 edition).				
Rochdale to:	Frequency (minutes)	First tram AM	Last tram PM	Fare (old pence)	Fare (current equivalent)
Bacup	20	7.30	11.10	8d	£1.19
Bamford	10 & 20	7.35	11.20	1¹/₂d	22p
Britannia	20	7.30	11.10	6¹/₂d	96p
Bury via Heywood	10 & 20	7.35	10.55	9d	£1.34
Facit	20	7.30	11.10	5d	74p
Healey	20	7.30	11.10	2¹/₂d	37p
Heywood	10 & 20	7.35	10.55	4¹/₂d	67p
Littleborough	10	7.40	11.10	4d	59p
Milnrow	20	7.45	11.15	3d	45p
New Hey	10 & 20	7.55	11.15	4d	59p
Norden	10 & 20	7.40	11.00	3¹/₂d	52p
Shawforth	20	7.30	11.10	6¹/₂d	96p
Spotland Bridge	10 & 20	7.40	11.05	2d	30p
Sudden	10	7.25	11.15	2d	30p
Thornham	10 & 20	5.00	11.10	2¹/₂d	37p
Whitworth	20	7.30	11.10	4d	59p
Littleborough to:					
Summit	30	7.35	11.05	2d	30p
Middleton to:					
Castleton (F)	15 & 30		10.35	4d	59p
Chadderton (S)	12		11.25	3d	45p
Oldham (S)	12		11.25	4d	59p
Rhodes (S)	12		11.00	3d	45p
Slattocks (F)	15 & 30		10.35	3d	45p
Stanycliffe (F)	15 & 30		10.35	1¹/₂d	22p
Sudden (F)	15 & 30		10.35	5d	74p
Thornham Lane (F)	15 & 30		10.35	3d	45p

(F) – from Middleton Fountain. (S) - from Middleton Station

Special early workmen's cars ran in addition to the times in the table at lower fares up to about 7.30 a.m.. The first cars on Sundays were 9.35 a.m.

Direct car routes from Manchester were listed and "all cars, (except where stated) meet at the different termini."

For those who fancied a day out by tram, Lingard listed some circular car rides from Manchester, two of which passed through Rochdale. Being circular tours, one could of course start and end at Rochdale. A 63¹/₂ mile *(101¹/₂ km)* tour ran from Manchester to Blackburn via Pendlebury, Bolton and Darwen and via Accrington, Burnley Todmorden, Summit and Littleborough to Rochdale. Return to Manchester was via Sudden and Middleton. All sections were by tram except for Dunscar (Bolton) to Higher Darwen, Accrington to Burnley, and Towneley to Summit which were by motorbus. The total cost was 6s 3d *(£11.13)*

A shorter round trip from Rochdale lay via Thornham to Oldham and then to Manchester Piccadilly, returning from Manchester High Street via Middleton and Sudden. This was all by tram and cost 1s 10d *(£3.27)* for the 23¹/₂ miles *(37¹/₂ km)*.

Lingard's combined 'Car and Walking Tours' reached much further into the countryside. Destinations listed extended to Sheffield, Northwich, Huddersfield, Holmfirth and even Birmingham although most of these involved long walks and some bus rides. The breathtaking example from Manchester to Bradford via Blackstone Edge, a distance of 34¹/₂ miles *(55 km)* is described in more detail. Three trams were needed from Manchester to Rochdale, changing at Middleton and Sudden. The next tram would take you to Littleborough tram terminus, opposite Holy Trinity Church.

The directions then were:

" take the Halifax Road to the right. It is a splendid walk of 7 miles over the moor to Ripponden village. On reaching the historic White House, 1350 ft. above the sea level, a splendid view of Hollingworth Lake and the surrounding countryside is obtained. You then descend to Ripponden".

The next part of the journey to Triangle was by bus but then 3ft. 6ins. gauge Halifax trams took you to Sowerby Bridge, Halifax and Shelf and then 4ft 0ins gauge Bradford trams into Bradford. The total cost was 2s 9½d (£4.97) plus no doubt a fair amount of shoe leather and plenty of fresh Pennine air to create a healthy appetite.

Preparation of a new guide book to the tramways was offered by Mr James Ormerod of Milnrow Road. He would include the interesting features along the routes. For some reason the Committee decided not to progress it although the 1906 guide must have been out of print by then and was in any case out of date.

Table 11.2.	Tram journey from Manchester to Leeds via Rochdale. *(based on Lingard's 'Where to go by Tram'.)*			
From	**To**	**Frequency (minutes)**	**Fare (old pence)**	**Fare (Current)**
Manchester (High Street)	Middleton	10	3½d	*52p*
Middleton	Sudden	15	5d	*74p*
Sudden	Rochdale	10	2d	*30p*
Rochdale	Littleborough	10	4½d	*67p*
Littleborough	Summit	30	2d	*30p*
Summit	Todmorden	30 (bus)	5d	*74p*
Todmorden	Hebden Bridge	30 (bus)	6d	*89p*
Hebden Bridge	Halifax	30	1s	*£1.78*
Halifax	Shelf	30	6d	*89p*
Shelf	Bradford	15 & 30	4½d	*67p*
Bradford	Stanningley	10	4½d	*67p*
Stanningley	Leeds	10	5d	*74p*
Total			5s 0d	*£8.91*

For 10 years from 1906 to 1916, a long through tram service was operated jointly with Oldham Corporation Tramways between Norden and Hathershaw. An open top 4-wheeler stands at Norden terminus on Edenfield Road at Industry Street.

(Eric Fielding)

A classic Rochdale bogie single decker sets off for Bamford past Rochdale's splendid Town Hall. A Bury open balcony car is just visible in the background.
(Lilywhite, Halifax)

A tinted postcard of the Tramway Centre before the waiting shelter was built.

Two open top double deckers are seen on an early postcard of 'Broadway', the name sometimes given to the area between The Butts and South Parade. The Wellington Hotel and some of the buildings on the right still exist.

A tinted postcard shows an open top bogie car leaving the loop at Passmonds en route to Norden. The building behind the trees on the left is Passmonds House, now a residential care home. The three story building on the left was demolished to widen the road but the two storey cottage is still there.

A busy colour tinted view of the Tramway Centre in 1906, looking towards Yorkshire Street from Drake Street, probably taken from the Wellington Inn. Four single deck bogie cars, two double deck open top four wheelers and a double deck open top bogie car are waiting to depart for all corners of Rochdale on the newly completed electric tramway. Pedestrians cross roads undisturbed by any other traffic.

An early tinted photograph of Broadway showing the Tramway Centre and single and double deck cars. The livery should not be assumed to be very accurate!

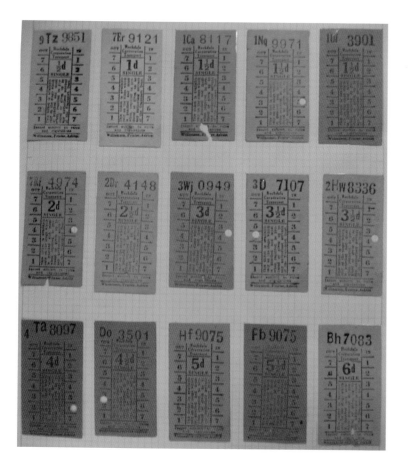

Example tickets from the TMS archives at Crich. (NB These are all marked 'Rochdale Corporation Transport' and could be tram or bus tickets.

The Rochdale coat of arms was applied to each side of every tram. Probably the only surviving example is this wooden section, cut out from the side of one of the last trams.
The motto 'Crede Signo' means 'Believe in the sign', quite appropriate for a tramway!

Note: detail clearer on this version but colour more accurate on version above left.

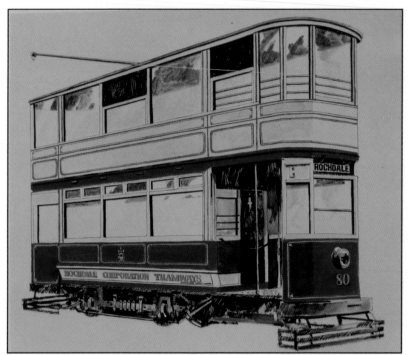

Colour photographs of Rochdale trams are probably non-existant but tinted photographs do exist. This relatively modern example shows car No. 80. (The maroon colour is probably too red and should be more chocolate brown).
(MTMS)

The Tramway Workshops on Mellor Street had an even shorter working life with trams, barely ten years. The building is not architecturally noteworthy, unlike the office opposite, but it does still exist. (A.P. Young)

The Mellor Street Tramway Offices were only used for their original purpose for 28 years but still stand proudly after more than a century.
(A. P. Young)

The ornate terra-cotta doorway main entrance to the Tramway Offices on Mellor Street can still be seen. No longer required for transport purposes but the building is still in use. (A. P. Young)

The legend 'Tramway Offices' stands out over the doorway.
(A. P. Young)

64

MAP TO ACCOMPANY THE PROSPECTUS OF

THE MIDDLETON ELECTRIC TRACTION COMPANY, LIMITED.

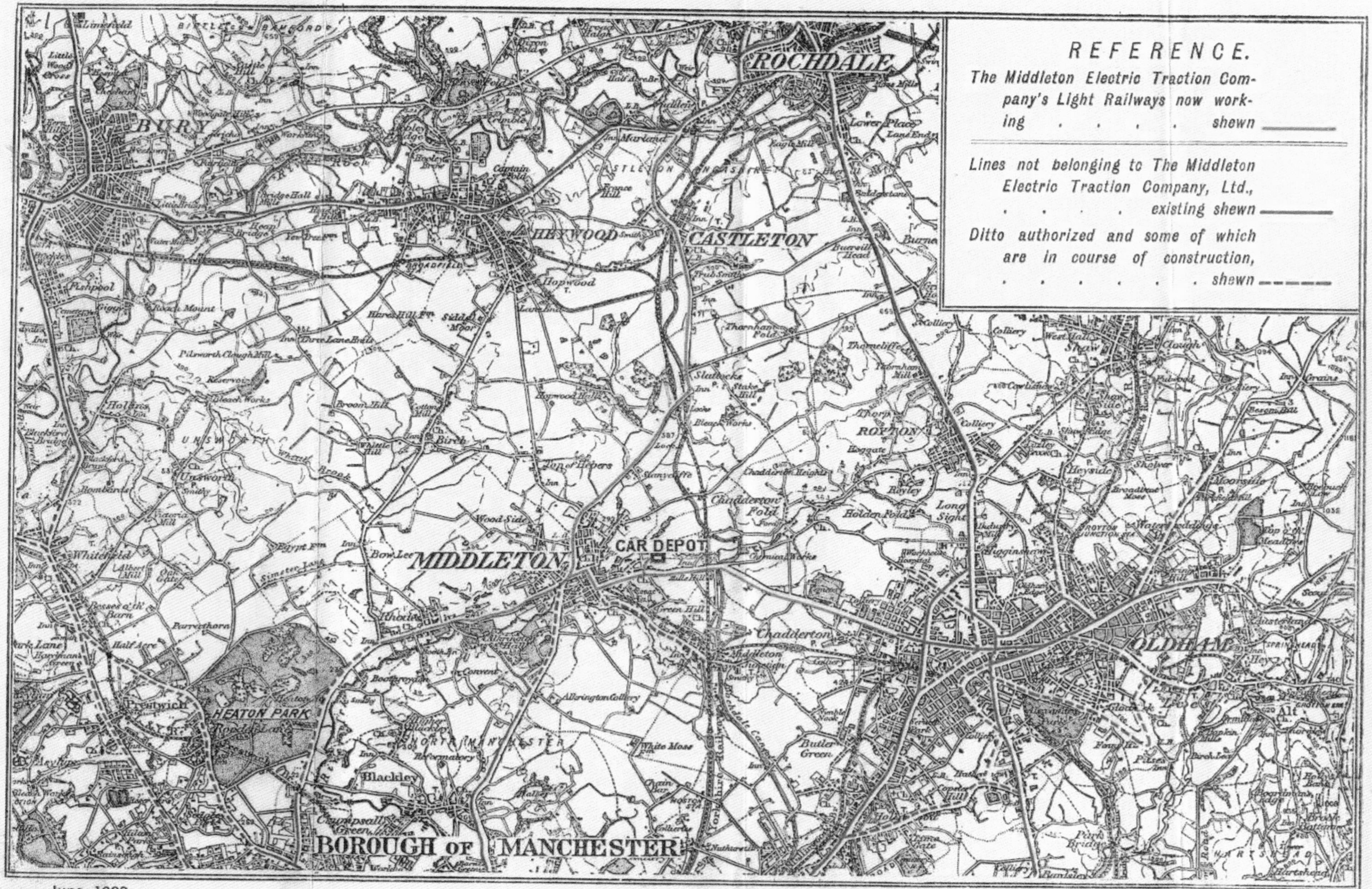
REFERENCE.
The Middleton Electric Traction Company's Light Railways now working . . . . . shewn
Lines not belonging to The Middleton Electric Traction Company, Ltd., ... existing shewn
Ditto authorized and some of which are in course of construction, ... shewn
ROCHDALE
BURY
HEYWOOD
CASTLETON
ROYTON
MIDDLETON
CAR DEPOT
OLDHAM
HEATON PARK
BOROUGH OF MANCHESTER
Chadderton
Blackley
Prestwich
Whitefield
Unsworth
Hopwood
Shaw
Thornham Fold
Lower Place
Chadderton Fold

June, 1902.

Scale 1 inch to the statute mile.

Spottiswoode & Co. Ltd. Lith. London

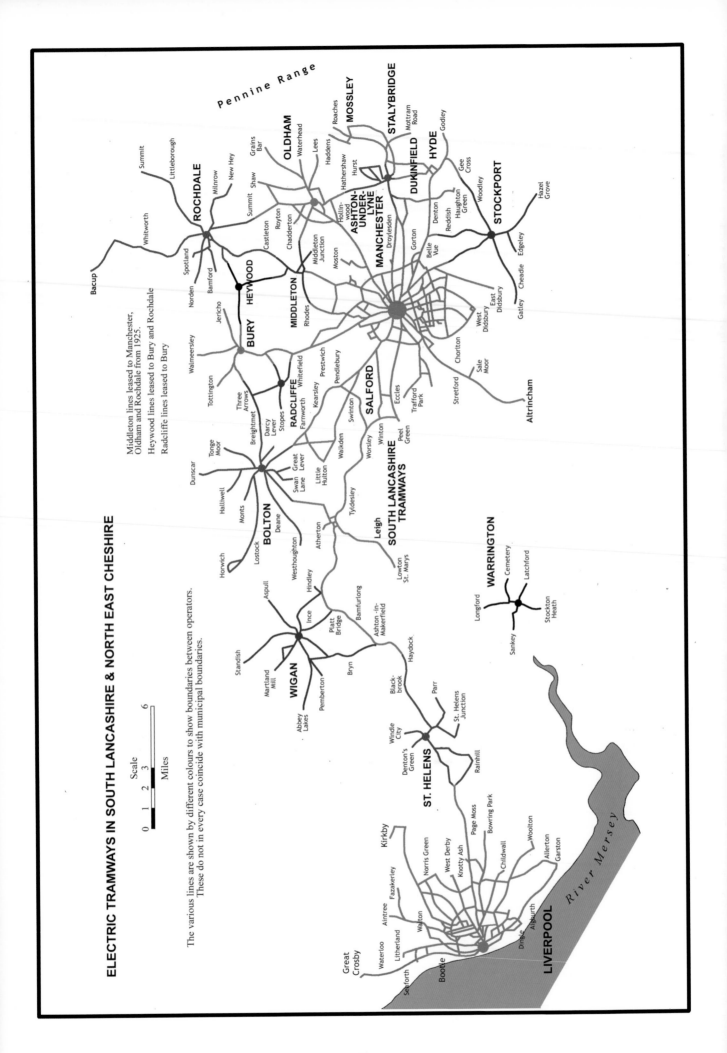

ELECTRIC TRAMWAYS IN SOUTH LANCASHIRE & NORTH EAST CHESHIRE

Middleton lines leased to Manchester, Oldham and Rochdale from 1925.

Heywood lines leased to Bury and Rochdale

Radcliffe lines leased to Bury

The various lines are shown by different colours to show boundaries between operators. These do not in every case coincide with municipal boundaries.

Scale

Miles

0 1 2 3 6

Pennine Range

ROCHDALE

Summit
Littleborough
Milnrow
New Hey
Whitworth
Spotland
Bamford
Norden
Heywood
Bacup

OLDHAM
Waterhead
Grains Bar
Lees
Shaw
Royton
Haddens
Roaches
MOSSLEY
Summit
Castleton
Chadderton

STALYBRIDGE
Mottram Road
Hathershaw
Hurst
ASHTON-UNDER-LYNE
Hollinwood
DUKINFIELD
HYDE
Godley
Gee Cross

Middleton Junction
Moston
MIDDLETON
Rhodes
MANCHESTER
Droylesden
Gorton
Denton
Reddish
Haughton Green
Woodley
STOCKPORT
Hazel Grove
Edgeley
Cheadle
Gatley
East Didsbury
West Didsbury

BURY
Jericho
Walmeersley
Tottington
Three Arrows
Breightmet
Darcy Lever
Stopes
RADCLIFFE
Farnworth
Whitefield
Kearsley
Prestwich
Pendlebury
Swinton
Belle Vue
Chorlton
Sale Moor
Stretford
Altrincham

SALFORD
Eccles
Trafford Park
Winton
Worsley
Peel Green
Walkden

BOLTON
Dunscar
Halliwell
Monts
Deane
Lostock
Horwich
Tonge Moor
Swan Lane
Great Lever
Little Hulton
Tyldesley

SOUTH LANCASHIRE TRAMWAYS
Leigh
Atherton
Lowton St. Marys

WIGAN
Standish
Marttand Mill
Aspull
Ince
Platt Bridge
Bamfurlong
Ashton-in-Makerfield
Haydock
Pemberton
Abbey Lakes
Bryn
Blackbrook

Hindley

ST. HELENS
Windle City
Denton's Green
Parr
St. Helens Junction
Rainhill
Bowring Park
Page Moss

WARRINGTON
Longford
Cemetery
Latchford
Stockton Heath
Sankey

Great Crosby
Waterloo
Litherland
Seaforth
Kirkby
Fazakerley
Aintree
Walton
Bootle
Norris Green
West Derby
Knotty Ash
Childwall
Wootton
Allerton
Garston
Dingle
Aigburth
LIVERPOOL

River Mersey

12. Service cuts and wartime.

Coal strike, more extensions and a new manager

A coal strike in March 1912 caused the Committee to consider a temporary curtailment of the tramway services but it was left to the Chairman and the Manager to decide. By the end of March the situation was sufficiently serious for tram services to be withdrawn completely from the Spotland, Bury Road, Circular route and Summit Sections and a 20 minute service operated on the remaining routes. All Sunday services were withdrawn.

In March it was the turn of the General Manager, Mr. J.S.D.Moffet, to ask for an increase in Salary. He was granted an immediate increase from £400 (£24,826) to £425 (£26,378) per annum straight away and to £450 (£27,930) in April 1913. By contrast a new office boy was appointed at 8/- (£24.28) per week, equivalent to £20 8s 0d (£1,238) per annum.

steam tramway through Wardle towards Littleborough to electric traction, which had been completed, but did not make provision for any other routes within the Urban District.

Another extension which never happened would have run from Bacup to the village of Weir on the road to Burnley. Bacup's Town Clerk wrote to the Committee asking if they would be prepared to work this extension to the Bacup Light Railway on the same basis as the existing line, but nothing came of the request.

Mr Moffet, General Manager of the Tramways since April 1904, tendered his resignation in June 1913 following his appointment as General Manager of West Ham Tramways in London. The Committee placed on record their high appreciation of his services as General Manager

'Kitchener wants more men, your pals are calling for you' – an open balcony 4-wheeler is pressed into service to persuade volunteers to sign up for the war against Germany. (MTMS)

An extension which did not materialise was suggested in September 1912 when Wardle Urban District Council requested a meeting to discuss terms for Rochdale to lay and run electric trams along Wardle Road. A deputation attended the meeting but were told that the Committee could not "see their way to recommend the Council to construct and work a tramway along Wardle Road except as provided for in Section 29 of the Rochdale Corporation Act, 1900". This Section covered the conversion of the

and "the zeal and efficiency which he has displayed throughout his tenure of that office". They offered their congratulations and best wishes for his future.

The Chief Clerk and Traffic Manager, Mr. George Webster, lost no time in applying for the vacant post and the Committee appointed him on 16th July 1913 without any further discussion or interview. His salary was £350 (£21,248) per annum, rising to £400 (£24,283) by two annual increments of £25 (£1,518) each.

A number of consequential appointments followed:

Mr. E. Sedgwick Rolling Stock Superintendent at a salary of £4 *(£243)* per week;

Mr. G. Phillipson Overhead Equipment Superintendent at a salary of £2 15s 0d *(£167)* per week;

Mr. F. Ogden Chief Clerk at a salary of £2 2s 0d *(£127)* per week;

Mr. R. Bentley Chief Traffic Assistant at a salary of £2 2s 0d *(£127)* per week.

Other increases approved were:

Motormen: 6³/4d *(£1.71)* per hour after three years satisfactory service; 7d *(£1.77)* per hour after five years satisfactory service;

Conductors: 6d *(£1.52)* per hour after three years satisfactory service; 6¹/4d *(£1.58)* per hour after five years satisfactory service;

Cleaners: 5¹/4d *(£1.33)* per hour; 5¹/2d *(£1.39)* per hour after six months satisfactory service;

Inspectors: 7d *(£1.77)* per hour; 7¹/4d *(£1.83)* per hour after two years satisfactory service;

A number of clerks were also awarded wage increases.

Timekeeping for public transport has always been a problem and in January 1914 it was reported that the clocks in the cars were not keeping time satisfactorily. Presumably they had not been removed in 1911 as previously reported but this time they were taken out and replaced by recording clocks at points along the routes:

Littleborough Section:	Wardle Lane;
Bacup Section:	Facit;
Milnrow Section;	Kiln Lane;
Thornham Section:	King's Road;
Norden and Spotland Sections:	Spotland Bridge;
Bamford Section:	Bamford Terminus;
Circular Route:	Railway Station.

It is not clear whether these were the Bundy clocks previously installed in 1911 at these locations or a new type.

First World War brings cut-backs

The outbreak of the First World War demanded restrictions. The Manager was left to amend tramway services as necessary and expenditure was curtailed for the duration of the war. Requests for free travel were treated rather more leniently than in the past for various workers involved in wartime activities. The validity of workmen's cheap fares was widened.

By October 1915 a new problem arose. Recruitment of large numbers of men into the armed forces left a dearth of tram conductors. Nearly 30% of employees had joined up. The Committee decided to allow the Manager to recruit female conductors if he had difficulty in recruiting 'suitable applicants for the post of conductors'. Until then, tramway operations had been an all male affair with women being considered 'unsuitable'. The war changed all that. In fact the service could not have been kept going without women, a situation which was to be repeated in the second world war.

The shortage of labour and spare parts took their toll on the state of the tramway and a backlog of maintenance built up. Track, overhead and rolling stock were all affected and this contributed to the ultimate demise of the trams fifteen years later. Wartime brought rapid improvements in technology, notably the internal combustion engine which eventually made the motorbus an irresistible competitor.

Trams did not depend on imported fuel and did not use rubber tyres so there was no need to restrict services to conserve scarce imports. Moreover they could easily carry extra crowds. When the second world war started, the trams had all been replaced with buses and severe restrictions had to be imposed, illustrating another advantage of tramways. The blackout caused added problems for buses which had to be steered; the trams would still have had their rails to follow.

Another impact of war soon began to be felt. Reports trickled through from the War Office of Rochdale tramwaymen killed in active service. Conductor Lance Corporal Arthur Swaine, motorman Lance Corporal H Hardiker and motorman Sergeant Walter Boothman all died from wounds received in Gallipoli. The following year, four conductors and two motormen, all Privates, were killed in action in France. Committee resolutions expressing their regret and stopping the half wages they were being paid while serving became almost routine. Any moneys retained were paid to widows or mothers.

The war lasted much longer than anyone had expected and in 1917 the Board of Trade appointed a 'Special Tramways (Board of trade) Committee' to give every possible assistance to tramways and light railways which were considered essential to the war effort and to deal with questions of new or increased services, or closing tramway services.

Before the war the number of passengers had been fairly steady, between 1.1 million and 1.2 million per month. It rose slightly in the summer months and dropped back during the winter. This pattern continued into 1915 and 1916 but then gradually rose, probably as other means of transport became more scarce and as workers to munitions factories increased. In June 1917 the total topped 1¹/2 million per month for the first time. Traffic on the Heywood route had doubled in about six months.

Another casualty was the through route to Oldham which ceased on 26th December, 1916, cars terminating at Thornham. However this was not due to the war but to a disagreement between Oldham and Rochdale. Oldham were fitting their trams with top covers but they would not fit under Rochdale's low bridges. Through running had lasted only ten years, but still longer than the through route to Manchester which only ran for seven years. Some trams reportedly still worked through including football specials and a Bury Corporation tram carrying sacks of flour from Oldham to Bury during the war!

Car 24 was decorated to celebrate victory at the end of the First World War in 1918. A number of Rochdale tramway crewmen died in the hostilities but most returned to resume their duties.
(Eric Fielding)

There were now a large number of tramway operators in the north west and networks were still expanding. In December 1917 the tramway authorities in Lancashire and Cheshire decided to form a Federation to be known as "The Lancashire and Cheshire Tramway Federation" with each authority nominating two representatives together with their tramway manager. Rochdale were also members of the Municipal Tramways Association which included all the municipal tramway operators in Great Britain and Ireland. Topics of common interest often revolved around wage rates and conditions, fares and new statutory measures affecting tramways.

Claims for increased wages including wartime bonuses continued at not infrequent intervals with the Committee endeavouring to resist as long as possible. Eventually in March 1917 it became a national issue with an application for an increase for tramway employees being made by the National Transport Workers' Federation. Arbitration before the Committee on Production resulted in substantial increases which prompted the Tramways Committee to seek urgent approval from the Board of Trade to obtain Parliamentary sanction to increase fares by up to 50%. Materials and power costs were also rising.

Great War ends

The end of the war in November 1918 was an enormous relief to everyone. Car No. 24, which by then

had been vestibuled, was decorated for the celebrations. Notification was received when any tramway employees were discharged from the Army. A total of 163 tramway employees had joined the armed forces of whom 18 were killed, two died from disease and one died since discharge. All except two of those surviving returned to the tramway. However it did not mean an immediate end to shortages and restricted coal supplies for electricity generation meant that the reduced levels of tram service had to continue. Sunday morning services were resumed in April 1919.

The years-long gloom and drabness were finally dispelled by the signing of the Peace Treaty and a welcome visit by Liverpool's spectacular illuminated tram on a marathon tour of Lancashire by way of St. Helens, Bolton, Bury, Rochdale, Oldham, Manchester and Stockport.

Mr Ernest Sedgwick resigned as Rolling Stock Superintendent in March 1919. The post was advertised as Rolling Stock and Works Superintendent, reflecting the addition of the new tramway workshops. The short list included applicants from Atherton, Wakefield, Belfast, Dover and Bexley Heath, a much wider geographic spread than in earlier years. The successful candidate was Mr. A. R. Williams of Bexley Heath in Kent at a salary of £300 per annum *(£8,250)*. The following month the Manager's salary was increased from £500 *(£13,750)* to £600 *(£16,500)* per annum.

13. Roaring twenties and soaring costs.

Increased costs and tramway losses

Economic conditions in the early twenties were difficult. Some employees actually had their wages reduced and unemployment was rising. The first recorded move towards strike action came on 3rd April 1920 when the Amalgamated Society of Tramway and Vehicle Workers gave notice of withdrawal of labour because of the failure of the Corporation to pay the 44/- *(£2.20, £52.62)* increase on pre-war rates that had been awarded. Wage claims were also received from office staff who were granted a 15% increase. Mr Webster, the Tramway Manager received a 33% increase taking his salary to £800 per annum *(£19,140).*

That month the Tramways department finances showed a net loss of £2,682 11s 10d *(£64,170)* for the financial year 1919/20 so another application to the Minister of Transport to increase fares by 50% was urgently lodged.

Five trams from the Middleton Electric Tramways were acquired by Rochdale Tramways in 1925. Car No. 12 in the M.E.T. fleet, built by Brush in 1905, became No.12 in the Rochdale fleet and is seen at Sudden in 1925 still with MET logo and livery. *(MTMS)*

The 1921 coal strike lasted for three months and the labour unrest culminated in the ten day general strike in 1926. The Under Secretary for Mines issued an order to reduce electricity consumption by 25% to conserve available stocks of coal. A special meeting on 25th April 1921 decreed that all Sunday tram services would be withdrawn and ordinary weekday services reduced. Sunday services were restored six weeks later and weekday services were back to normal after another couple of weeks on 4th July.

Throughout the pre-war years and right through the war the Tramways had turned in a comfortable profit. Galloping inflation turned this into a significant loss in 1920 and the deficit rocketed to £19,130 *(£709,400)* in 1922. With a return to stability, the account returned to profit in 1923 and remained so until the end of the decade.

The last tramway extension

The first postwar extension to be built was proposed in April 1922. The line was to run from Drake Street along Maclure Road to join the High Level Road route at the railway station. All trams to and from Tweedale Street would use the new double track link, allowing the High Level Road tracks to be abandoned. Double track junctions were provided at Drake Street and Tweedale Street.

Following a Special Meeting of the Council on 9th November 1922, an application was made to the Ministry of Transport for a Provisional Order. The Draft Provisional Order authorising construction of the tramway was approved by the Ministry in April 1923 and received Royal Assent in August. The estimated cost was £8,500 *(£305,130)* and loan sanction was sought from the Ministry of Transport. Loan sanction and approval to the track layout and construction was received in March 1924.

The new Maclure Road section was inspected by Major Hall from the Ministry of Transport on 9th August 1924 and services began operating the same day although the official start of operation was two days later on 11th August. Although the High Level Road route was no longer needed, a siding was kept at the Station end until the end of tramway days and it could still be seen for some time afterwards. Some Heywood and Sudden cars were diverted to operate via Maclure Road and Tweedale Street to improve links to the railway station.

An official opening ceremony was held on 25th September, 1924 for the Esplanade improvement. It was performed by the Minister of Transport, who also opened a new road in Castleton, accompanied by Sir Henry Maybury, Director General of Roads.

Tramway costs and revenues

A breakdown of the total capital costs of the tramway as in 1927 is given in Table 13.1 below.

A 4-wheel open top Rochdale tram waits behind a double deck Manchester bogie car on the jointly operated 17 route at the Tramway centre. Joint operation began in 1925 and only lasted 7 years.(MTMS)

Table 13.1.   Capital cost of Rochdale electric tramways.

Item	Capital cost	Capital cost at current prices
	£	£
Permanent way	148,800	6.16m
Electrical equipment of lines	66,458	2.75m
Power stations and sub-stations	1,990	0.08m
Other land and buildings	53,065	2.20m
Cars and equipment of cars	85,506	3.54m
Other purposes	3,660	0.15m
Total (lines and works open for traffic)	359,479	14.89m
Old lines and works now superseded	85,450	3.54m
Preliminary expenses including legal and parliamentary	858	0.04m
Total capital cost of tramway	**445,787**	**18.46m**

Table 13.2.   Income and Expenditure for Rochdale tramways, 1927-28.

Income	Revenue/Cost	Revenue/Cost at current prices
	£	£
Passengers	173,448	7.18m
Parcels and mails	3,150	0.13m
Through running	(7,775)	0.32m
Total revenue	168,823	6.99m
Advertising and miscellaneous	887	0.04m
Total Income	**169,710**	**7.03m**
Expenditure		
Permanent way maintenance	11,896	0.49m
Electrical equipment maintenance	3,779	0.16m
Car maintenance	16,704	0.69m
Miscellaneous repairs and renewals	786	0.03m
Total maintenance and renewals	33,165	1.37m
Traffic expenses	70,168	2.91m
Electrical power	20,850	0.86m
Rates and taxes	3,846	0.16m
Compensation and insurance	2,245	0.09m
General expenses	6,512	0.27m
Through running expenses	(4,487)	0.19m
Total working expenses	**132,299**	**5.48m**
Balance to net revenue account	37,411	1.55m

The revenue income and expenditure for 1927-28, the peak year for tramway operations, are shown in Table 13.2 below. This was a considerable improvement over the previous year when the combined effects of rising costs of materials and electricity as a result of the coal strike, and nine days stoppage due to the general strike, had reduced the surplus to almost zero.

Middleton tramways acquired at last

In October 1920 the Town Clerk had reported that he had received a visit from a representative of the British Electric Traction Company to discuss the sale of the Middleton tramways. As with all important issues, the matter was referred to a Sub-Committee but Middleton

Borough declined to discuss the matter for the time being. Nevertheless, it was raised again in August 1921 when the Chairman and Managing Director of the Company called on the Town Clerk to enquire whether there was any intention on the part of the Corporation of purchasing their respective part of the Middleton Light Railway. The Committee still declined to act.

It was not until November 1923 that a special joint committee was set up in with Middleton Corporation and Chadderton Urban District Council to negotiate the purchase of the undertaking. It was finally reported on 20th May 1925 that agreement had been reached for the joint purchase of the undertaking by the Councils of the three authorities. Rochdale's share of the total purchase price of £79,000 was £10,861 which included all the company's double deck cars and the route between Sudden and the expanded Borough Boundary at Castleton. Manchester Corporation took over the routes in Middleton while Oldham Corporation took over those in Chadderton.

The Middleton tramways were operated temporarily from 16th June to 9th August as a joint undertaking with revised fares, until the various track connections were made. Then each authority took control of its own section. In the past, disagreements over the years had meant that through running over Middleton's tracks had never materialised but now things could begin to change.

The takeover date was set at 25th June 1925 although it was brought forward to the 16th. Alderman Clark, Chairman of Rochdale's Tramway Committee, was thanked for the able way in which he had conducted the negotiations. Tenders were immediately sought for the points and crossings to make the track connections between the two systems at Sudden, and to set the fares for the through service to Slattocks. A trial through run was made on 7th August and a service to Castleton and through to Manchester began on 9th August. This was the last new tram service to be introduced in Rochdale.

Although the Middleton tramways had been taken over in June, the Minister of Transport did not approve loan sanction for their purchase until November. The loan included the cost or the Sudden trackworks which had also been completed months earlier. Sanction for loans of £10,681 (£387,560) for the purchase of the Middleton tramways and £2,519 (£91,260) for the trackworks at Sudden was received in December 1925, repayable over 20 years.

Bus competition threatens

The Roads Act 1920 had included a clause inserted allowing a right of appeal against decisions of licensing authorities in regard to omnibus services. The General Purposes Committee protested on the grounds that they had not been afforded reasonable opportunity to consider the provision before it was inserted. The Ministry of Transport remained unmoved.

Decorated trams appeared from time to time to advertise events or celebrations. No. 21 was advertising the Rochdale Health Homes and Fashion Exhibition held in the Drill Hall, Baron Street from 14th to 24th September 1927 (?). The tram is turning from Maclure Road at the junction with High Level Road approaching Rochdale Railway Station. The notice on the dash panel states 'Passengers entering or leaving the car whilst in motion do so at their own risk and danger'. Another panel announces 'Do not miss the daily gas cooker lectures'. (MTMS)

The first trial of strength came with an application to the Watch Committee in April 1921 by Holt Bros. (Rochdale) Ltd., (destined to become the renowned Yelloway Motor Services), for a bus service from the Town Hall Square to Wardle and Hollingworth Lake. The Tramways Sub-Committee recommended that the application be refused on the grounds that the route was one of the busiest tramway routes in the Borough. In their opinion the frequent stopping of both tramcars and omnibuses in Entwisle Road and Halifax Road, which were only sufficiently wide for the existing traffic requirements, would be dangerous. Probably no one realised that this was a portent of things to come that would eventually see the end of the trams.

Another application to run buses was granted, but only on a temporary basis for one month during the coal strike. The applicants were the Middleton Electric Traction Company who wanted a temporary license to run buses from Sudden along Manchester Road to the boundary at Slattocks but only if they needed to withdraw their trams.

A much more ominous threat arose from a Parliamentary Bill promoted by various railway companies including the Lancashire and Yorkshire Railway who were seeking powers to use road vehicles in any district for the conveyance of merchandise or passengers and their luggage, and to apply their funds for that purpose. A conference of authorities was called in London to oppose the Bill and Rochdale joined the opposition. Happily, the threat evaporated when the promoters removed the offending clauses from their Bill.

The Committee raised no objection when Messrs. Holt Bros. proposed a bus service from Bamford to Heywood as it linked two localities without competing with the trams. Another application to run a bus from Rochdale to Wardle was made by Mr. F. Biggin in September 1923. He undertook not to pick up or set down passengers along the tram route and only to serve the Town Hall Square for which he would pay the usual fee. The Watch Committee approved the application, also subject to these conditions.

A more familiar name appeared on the scene in October 1923 when Ribble Motor Services applied to run a bus service from Rochdale to Blackburn via Norden, Edenfield and Haslingden. The Watch Committee gave permission subject to the terminus being in the Town Hall

Joint operation in action – Rochdale all enclosed car 86 of 1926 passes Bury open balcony car 34 outside Rochdale's impressive Town Hall. The newly completed Post Office is opposite.
(J.S. King)

TOWN CENTRE SCENES

Men are much in evidence in this turn of the decade view of the Tramway Centre. All enclosed Car 85 of 1925 leaves for Drake Street while open balcony Car 75 loads on the central island. The policeman does not seem to have much traffic to direct.

(J.S.King)

A busy town centre scene in the late twenties at the junction of Drake Street and South Parade. 1920 built Car 78 has just been waved through by the policeman on point duty while a classic Brush 4-wheeler waits at the tramway centre, still in original open top condition. *(Eric Fielding)*

Open balcony car No. 76 arrives at the Tramway Centre from Drake Street before departing to Marland. A bogie single deck car in original condition approaches from Smith Street, probably in the late twenties. *(Premier Photo).*

Square, at the usual fee, and to minimum fares at least 50% higher than the ordinary tram fare from Rochdale to Norden. The service began operation in July 1924 to become the first regular stage carriage bus service in Rochdale. It ran every two hours with additional short workings at weekends to 'Owd Betts', a popular moorland pub near Knowl Hill. A protective fare of 6d was applied to avoid abstraction from the Norden tram service. This bus service continued in various forms until final withdrawal in 2005. Owd Betts can now only be reached by car or on foot or cycle.

An invitation was received in November 1923 from Messrs. C. F. Rymer to a demonstration of a trackless trolleybus. The Committee decided to take no action although trolleybuses had been operating in nearby Ramsbottom since 1913.

The last tram to be built by a manufacturer for Rochdale was English Electric Car 92 of 1926. It had a Brill 21E truck and Brush motors and controllers. It is standing at the Thornham Summit terminus where passengers for Oldham had to change to an Oldham tram or bus, like the one emerging from Thornham Lane.   (Eric Fielding)

Rochdale decide to run buses

Competition was growing between company operators keen to exploit their new buses and municipal operators wanting to protect their heavy investment in tramways. In Rochdale this prompted a decision in August 1924, (ironically the same month that the last tramway extension opened), when the Committee unanimously agreed to promote a Bill in the next session of Parliament for powers to operate buses in Rochdale and district. It was specified that they would be 'linking up from the tramway termini'; there was no suggestion at that stage that they would replace the trams. A Special Meeting of the Council on 10th November 1924 confirmed the decision to promote a Bill in Parliament to authorise running buses within and outside the Borough and to seek further powers in respect of the tramways.

In nearby Rawtenstall, an inquiry was held in September 1924 to consider an application from Rawtenstall Corporation to run buses between Burnley and Bury and an appeal by Ribble Motor Services against their refusal to grant them a licence to run in Rawtenstall. The same month an inquiry in Manchester heard the North Western Road

Car appealing against Manchester's refusal to grant them a licence. Ribble had also applied for licences to operate from Rochdale to Halifax and Huddersfield but as no approvals had been obtained, they signalled their intention to appeal to the Ministry of Transport.

The Rochdale Corporation Bill, 1925, had its first reading in the House of Lords on 11th February 1925. Ribble Motor Services and Heywood Corporation had deposited petitions against the Bill. The Middleton Electric Tramways also made representations regarding the proposed acquisition of their company and a clause was inserted to protect their interests in the event of the purchase not being completed. Negotiations for the acquisition were still ongoing at that time. A month later, a Special Meeting considered and approved a proposal for a scheme linking up the border towns of Lancashire and Yorkshire by a motor omnibus service. It would be controlled by a Joint Control Committee with representatives from Rochdale, Oldham, Halifax, Huddersfield, Ashton and Stalybridge.

The Rochdale Corporation Act, 1925 which received Royal Assent on 31st July 1925 (some reports give 24th June), gave the Corporation powers to operate buses up to five miles from the Town Hall or along any tram route operated by their cars. The way was now open to replace the trams although it was not even considered at that time.

North Western's long awaited reply to their application to run buses in Rochdale eventually came over a year later in June 1925. North Western wanted to licence a total of 79 buses, their entire fleet, for use within the Borough. The Committee refused the application and instead approved an application from the Joint Committee to run services including the following bus routes:

Route No. 1   Rochdale and Halifax, via Littleborough, Blackstone Edge, Ripponden and Sowerby Bridge;

Route No. 1A   Oldham and Ripponden for Halifax, or alternatively to Blackstone Edge, Littleborough and Rochdale;

Route No. 2   Oldham and Huddersfield, via Austerlands, New Delph, Standedge, Marsden, Slaithwaite and Linthwaite;

Route No. 2A   Rochdale and Delph, via Milnrow, New Hey, and Denshaw, linking up with the Oldham bus for Huddersfield and Delph.

In the summer additional services were proposed including:

Rochdale and Oldham to Huddersfield via Denshaw, Nont Sarahs, Outlane and Lindley.

An aerial view of the Tramway Centre with the Town Hall and Post Office in the background. Even in the late twenties trams were almost the only vehicles to be seen. (Eric Fielding)

The Watch Committee resolved that "the North Western Road Car Co. Ltd. be informed that in view of the consent of the Council to the running of omnibuses in the Borough by the Joint Control Committee of Halifax, Rochdale, Oldham and Ashton-under-Lyne Corporations and the Stalybridge, Hyde, Mossley and Dukinfield Joint Tramways and Electricity Board, this Sub-Committee cannot see their way to recommend the granting of licences to the North Western Road Car Co. Ltd."

Ribble had a more favourable response to their request to licence all their vehicles for use in Rochdale. The Watch Committee agreed, subject to only one vehicle being on the Town Hall Square at any one time. It was also agreed that all char-a-bancs plying for hire within the Borough must be licensed.

In August, The Corporation made applications to its neighbours to run buses in Milnrow, Norden, Littleborough, and Wardle. Wardle U.D.C. were one of the first to respond positively.

The Chairman dies in service

The Tramways Committee Chairman, Alderman Taylor, died in service in July 1925. He had been chairman for over 11 years including the difficult years through the First World War. The Committee sent their respectful sympathy to Mrs Taylor and their family. Alderman Clark was appointed Chairman for the remainder of the year.

The Committee set up a further Sub-Committee to consider the equipment which would be required for motor bus operation. The question of a depot site also had to be investigated and the Borough Surveyor was asked to submit a scheme and costs for the erection of a bus garage at Mellor Street, adjoining the existing tramway shed.

A Special Meeting of the Tramways Committee was held on 6th August 1925 to consider a proposal by Henry Mattinson, General Manager of Manchester Corporation Tramways, that Rochdale and Manchester should commence the operation of their respective portions of the Middleton Light Railways on Sunday 9th August. The route was to run via Slattocks, Middleton, Blackley and Harpurhey to a terminus in High Street, Manchester. Proposed joint running arrangements between Rochdale town centre and Manchester High Street were for a 15 minute service commencing at 8.30 a.m. until 11.15 p.m. on Mondays to Saturdays and a 15 minute service on Sundays commencing at 9.45 a.m. until 10 p.m. This proposal was agreed and a test run across the new track connection took place on 7th August 1925. Through services on this 12 mile interurban route to Manchester began on 9th August. Additional short workings to Castleton operated after 12 noon with some journeys via Tweedale Street.

A tramway office and public conveniences was proposed in August 1925 to be sited at the junction of Faulkner Street and Samuel Street, close to the present Smith Street. A two storey building accommodated six W.C.s and twenty urinals for men and 13 W.C.s for women, together with the tramway parcel office and mess room. The existing ladies' accommodation in the tramway waiting room in the town centre was still retained but the remaining accommodation at the shelter was adapted for use as a tramway cash office and enquiry office.

The devastating General Strike hit Rochdale on 3rd May 1926 when tramway employees unilaterally stopped work at midnight under instruction from the Transport and General Workers' Union. They were acting on a decision by the Trades Union Congress in relation to the national stoppage in the coal industry.

The Chairman offered to address all the tramwaymen at Mellor Street depot at 9.30 a.m. on Monday morning. He

offered to re-instate them on the old terms if they all returned to work. The Chairman attended at 9.30 a.m. but nobody else did. Rochdale remained tram-less for the ten days of the strike.

Not surprisingly, in the financial year ending 31st March 1927, the profit on tramway operations was just £304 8s 8d (*£12,610*) compared with £2,231 9s 4d (*£92,410*) on the buses which had been operating for barely a year. The following year the tramway profit was £3,796 19s 2d (*£158,500*) with the buses making a healthy £6,955 9s 2d (*£290,340*). Although buses were taking some passengers from the trams, the trams remained reasonably profitable.

The first Manchester Corporation tram to reach Rochdale was No. 674, seen at the Tramway Centre displaying its No 17 route number and destination boards indicating 'Manchester, Middleton & Rochdale'. Rochdale tram 73 has pulled up behind. The date was 9th August 1925. (A.M.Gunn)

Manchester's first 'Pilcher' domed roof tram was No.266 which entered service in 1930. It ran on the long joint route 17 from Manchester High Street to Rochdale but only for less than two years. The 17, the only Rochdale route to have a number, was the last to be withdrawn in 1932. It is seen on its way from Rochdale to Manchester on Rochdale Road in Blackley. (Whitcombe Collection, Science Museum)

14. Fares and ticketing.

Fares on the first tram routes

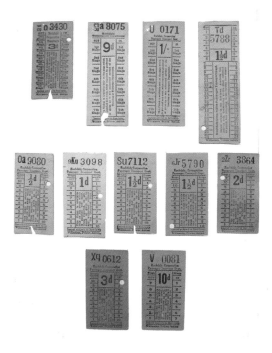

Example tickets from the TMS archives at Crich. (NB These are all marked 'Rochdale Corporation Transport' and could be tram or bus tickets.)

The Committee resolved at their April 28th 1902 meeting to adopt the Ticket Registering Bell Punch system for fare collection. It was used throughout the tramway era and Bell Punch machines were used for the next 53 years, well into the bus era, although T.I.M. machines were introduced in 1946. The Borough Surveyor was asked to obtain a supply of tickets, punches and collection bags, there being no Tramways Manager appointed.

The fare for the Bury Road route was to be a single penny stage from the Presbyterian Church, Manchester Road, (on the corner of Manchester Road and Dane Street and now occupied by an undertaker) to the Borough Boundary on Bury Road. No free passes were to be issued but season tickets would be considered by the Committee.

Fares for the Norden route were approved at the meeting on 9th June 1902:

Lord Street to Spotland Bridge:	1d *(27p)*
Lord Street to Bagslate Moor:	2d *(54p)*
Lord Street to Norden terminus:	3d *(80p)*
Lord Street to Spotland Fold:	1¹/2d *(40p)*
Workmen's Cars to Spotland Fold:	1d *(27p)*

There were no ¹/2d fares. A one penny fare was later introduced on the Spotland section between Clarke's Lane

and the White Lion terminus. As the trams were to carry parcels, rates were approved for their carriage:

Any distance for 14 lbs. and under:	2d *(54p)*
Any distance above 14 lbs. and not more than 28 lbs.:	3d *(80p)*
Any distance above 28 lbs. and not more than 56 lbs.:	4d *(1.07p)*

Parcels carried by passengers were free up to 28lbs but cost 2d *(54p)* over that weight.

Norden Urban District Council objected to the 3d *(80p)* fare to Norden which they considered too high and asked for a review. Their request was politely refused. A fare of a different kind was approved in August 1902 when the Committee agreed to allow the Norden cars to carry the Post Office mails from Norden to Rochdale once daily for the sum of 1/- *(£3.22)* per week. This may have been too generous as it was soon revised to a charge of 1¹/2d *(40p)* per bag. An early morning workmen's car to Norden was introduced in August with a fare of 1d (27p) for two stages and 1¹/2d *(40p)* for the whole journey .

A Sub-Committee was set up in September 1902 to consider the issue of contract tickets. They reported back on 13th October with suggested scales for ordinary passengers and scholars as shown in Table 14.1 below. These were approved.

Table 14.1 Contract tickets.

Ordinary Passengers	3 months	6 months	12 months
1d stage	£ 15s. 0d	£ 1 5s 0d	£ 2 7s. 6d
1¹/2d stage	£ 18s. 0d	£ 1 11s. 3d	£ 2 18s. 9d
2d stage	£ 1 1s. 0d	£ 1 17s. 6d	£ 3 10s. 0d
3d stage	£ 1 8s. 0d	£ 2 7s. 6d	£ 4 10s. 0d
Scholars			
1d stage	£ 9s. 0d	£ 15s. 0d	
2d stage	£ 15s. 0d	£ 1 5s. 0d	
3d stage	£ 1 0s. 0d	£ 1 15s. 0d	

Tramway employees were allowed to travel free but only to and from work and only if in uniform. Initially children under five were allowed to travel free provided they sat on a lap. This was later changed to children under three being allowed to travel free and those between three years and twelve years at half fare.

In August 1904 the fares for the Circular route were approved as:

From The Butts via Drake Street, Oldham Road, High Level Road to end of Tweedale Street (Manchester Road end):   1d *(27p)*.

From the end of Tweedale Street
via High Level Road, Oldham Road
and Drake Street to The Butts: 1d (27p).

From The Butts via Drake Street,
Manchester Road, Tweedale Street
to the Station: 1d (27p).

From the Station via Tweedale
Street, Manchester Road and
Drake Street to The Butts: 1d (27p).

The last two did not make sense as Drake Street would not be traversed if travelling from the Station to The Butts via Manchester Road. Perhaps the last 'and' should have been 'or'. It would have been much easier to specify a flat fare of 1d (27p) as that was the actual fare for any journey on this service .

A fare of 1d (27p) was agreed for Oldham Road from The Butts as far as Kings Road. The fare from The Butts to the Milnrow Road terminus was also 1d (27p).

In October 1904 these fares were rescinded and revised fares were approved.

Oldham Road section:
Centre to King's Road	1d	(27p)
Centre to Broad Lane	1¹/2d	(40p)
Centre to Borough boundary	2d	(54p)
High Level Road to Broad Lane	1d	(27p)
Kings Road to Yew Tree Inn		
(Thornham New Road)	1d	(27p)
Broad Lane to Borough boundary	1d	(27p)
Kings Road to Borough boundary	1¹/2d	(40p)

Manchester Road section:
Centre to New Barn Lane	1d	(27p)
Centre to Sudden (Windmill Lane)	1¹/2d	(40p)
Pinfold to Sudden	1d	(27p)

The fare from King's Road to the Borough boundary was subsequently rescinded by full Council. A further fare of 1¹/2d (40p) between High level Road and Yew Tree Inn was added.

Fares for the Healey Section were approved in November 1904:

Cheetham Street loop to Gale Street	1d	(27p)
One Ash Gates to Wesleyan Chapel	1d	(27p)
Gale Street to Ending	1d	(27p)
Cheetham Street loop to Ending	2d	(54p).

In January 1905 the fares to be charged on the electric trams on the Littleborough section were agreed although steam trams were then still operating . Fares were:

Cheetham Street to Albert Royds Street		
(with transfer ticket)	1d	(27p)
Heybrook to Wardle Road	1d	(27p)
Spotland Fold to Sherriff Street	1d	(27p)
Spotland Bridge to Cheetham Street	1d	(27p)
Sherriff Street to Heybrook	1d	(27p)
Spotland Fold to Cheetham Street	1¹/2d	(40p)
Spotland Bridge to Heybrook	1¹/2d	(40p)
Spotland Fold to Heybrook	2d	(54p)

Some additional fares were also agreed for the Norden route:
Town centre to Ings Lane	1¹/2d	(40p)
Ings Lane to Norden	1¹/2d	(40p)
Junction of Dane Street and		
Bridge Street to Ings Lane	1d	(27p)

Additional fares on the Sudden route were agreed in April 1905:

New Barn Lane to Borough boundary	1d	(27p)
Castle Inn to Borough boundary	1¹/2d	(40p)
Town Centre to Borough boundary	2d	(54p)

Fares on the Littleborough Section were revised in May 1905 as follows:

Rochdale and Albert Royds Street	1d	(27p)
Wardleworth Station and Wardle Lane	1d	(27p)
Cloverdale and Wardle Lane	1d	(27p)
Albert Royds Street and Halliday Lane	1d	(27p)
Halliday Lane and Littleborough	1d	(27p)
Rochdale and Wardle Lane	1¹/2d	(40p)
Wardle Lane and Littleborough	1¹/2d	(40p)
Rochdale and Halliday Lane	2d	(54p)
Albert Royds Street and Littleborough	2d	(54p)
Rochdale and Littleborough	3d	(80p)

The Healey Section fares were revised in June 1905:

Town Centre to Gale Inn	1d	(27p)
Mizzy Road to Methodist Chapel	1d	(27p)
Gale Inn to Ending	1d	(27p)
St James's Church to Methodist Chapel	1¹/2d	(40p)
Mizzy Road to Ending	1¹/2d	(40p)
Town Centre to Ending	2d	(54p)

Cheap travel for some

A request for blind persons to be allowed to travel free was refused by the Committee. They had received requests from a number of bodies including nurses, policemen and other public sector workers for free travel but all were turned down. It was agreed that the senior managers of the tramway, and those of some neighbouring authorities, would be allowed free travel in their areas.

Workmen's cheap fares were available on early morning and evening trams. Originally special workmen's cars ran and if they missed them they had to pay full fare. For example workmen's cars ran from Norden at 5.30 a.m. and 6.10 a.m. with just one returning from Rochdale at 5.30 p.m. Healey had two in the morning at 5.25 a.m. and 6.00 a.m. with two returning at 5.10 p.m. and 5.40 p.m. There were no return fares.

Contract tickets had been available but by 1907 they were falling out of favour. It was considered that if people could afford the £3 or £4 outlay which a contract cost then they could afford to pay the normal fare. There was a growing feeling of equality but contracts were seen as unfair because the holders could make as many journeys as they liked without any extra payment. Fraud was another good reason for stopping them. Some holders gave their contract tickets to others to use who then effectively travelled free.

A change in the system started on 16th March 1909 when 1½d fares were issued for the first stage from the Town Centre on all sections up to 7.30 a.m. and all returning cars up to 6.30 p.m. On 29th June 1911 it was resolved that on the first stage only from the Town Centre on the early morning cars the fare would be one halfpenny with penny return tickets for the first stage valid until 6.30 p.m. The following year on October 23rd a 2d return was issued to and from the Town Centre where the workmen's fare was 1d. On 16th September 1914 the time limit for workmen's tickets was extended to 8.30 a.m. and special workmen's fares were abolished. This was to accommodate workers being on short time due to the war. After the war, on 14th July 1920, workmen's tickets could be used at any time up to 9.00 a.m. Rochdale was therefore generous in offering a return journey for a single journey fare up to 9.00 a.m. when other towns only allowed them up to 7.00 a.m.

Fare revisions were made not infrequently, often in response to specific requests from other councils or groups. Many requests were refused. In September 1911 a number of overlapping stages were introduced on the Bacup route with fares up to 5d (£1.31) for the section from Mizzy Road (Cronkeyshaw Common) to Bacup.

Example tickets for ordinary 1d, 1½d, 2½d, 3½d, and 4d and Workman 3d.

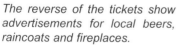

The reverse of the tickets show advertisements for local beers, raincoats and fireplaces.

From 2nd December 1912 workpeople's 2d (54p) return tickets were issued for all stages where the workpeople's fare to and from Rochdale was 1d (27p). The return journey could be made at any time on the day of issue up to 6.30 pm on weekdays or 1.00 pm on Saturdays. On 5th October 1914 the times were extended to allow workpeople to buy tickets up to 8 30 am instead of 7.30 am and to return any time until the last car on weekdays and up to 3 pm on Saturdays.

An application for ex-servicemen's passes was refused in September 1919 but was eventually granted in 1925.

Free passes for blind people had also been refused but they were introduced in June 1920 in Rochdale and later extended to include Heywood and Manchester.

Another 'Williamson' operator

Bett and Atkinson (Ref. 15) comment on the tickets used on Rochdale Tramways:

"This was yet another operator who has been faithful to Williamson for very many years though some very early tickets were printed by J. R. Williams of Liverpool. 'Geographical' tickets seem to have abandoned remarkably soon; certainly some at least were of numerical stage type as early as 1911. Ordinary tickets of the 1911-1919 period were very stubby with a small number of stages (only 6 on the 1d and less on some higher values). The stages were always set out in the form '1st Stage, 2nd Stage…etc.' with the addition of a space 'W', possibly for a workman's single. The heading was 'Rochdale Corporation Tramways' with the fare as a red overprint.

The number of stages was later increased and still later fare overprints were abandoned in favour of figures in the text. The title was altered to 'Rochdale Corporation Passenger Transport Dept.' about 1931. Not long afterwards there appeared a more compact ticket with 10 stages indicated by numbers only, without repetition of the word 'Stage'."

Tickets were issued for adult single, child single, adult and child returns and workmen's returns. Colours were ½d pale green, 1d white, 1½d buff (various shades), 2d blue/grey, 2½d yellow, 3d pink, 3½d lilac, 4d brown, 4½d red, 5d dark pink, 5½d dark red, 6d pale turquoise.

A conductor going out on duty was issued with a tin box containing tickets made up in packs of fifty and his waybill with the starting serial numbers. On return he had to fill in the finishing numbers and if his cash did not match the waybill he had to make up the difference. The ticket punch registered every ticket issued providing an additional check. It was claimed that conductors could often pay in over £100 from a shift but were rarely more than a few pence out. Conductors were considered careful, trustworthy and honest. Anything otherwise would result in dismissal.

A new agreement for the carriage of Mail bags was made in September 1911 but on the same terms and conditions as before. It was also agreed that Postmen and other officials in the employ of the General Post Office would be carried at ordinary rates.

Fares for the Milnrow Section were approved in December 1911 as set out in Table 14.2 below.

The first major increase in fares was proposed in September 1918 when an application was made to the Board of Trade for an Order authorising revised fares:

• an additional ½d on all 1d , 1½d and 2d stages;
• an additional 1d on all 2½d, 3d and 3½d stages;
• new 1d stages up to about ¾ mile from the town centre.

Table 14.2	Fares and stages for the Milnrow Section, December 1911.						
	Town Centre	Molesworth Street	Kenworthy Street	West Street	Kiln Lane	Council Offices	Huddersfield Road
Town Centre	-	1d	1d	1¹/2d	2d	2¹/2d	3d
Molesworth Street	1d	-	1d	1d	1¹/2d	2d	2¹/2d
Kenworthy Street	1d	1d	-	1d	1d	1¹/2d	2d
West Street	1¹/2d	1d	1d	-	1d	1d	1¹/2d
Kiln Lane	2d	1¹/2d	1d	1d	-	1d	1d
Council Offices	2¹/2d	2d	1¹/2d	1d	1d	-	1d
Huddersfield Road	3d	2¹/2d	2d	1¹/2d	1d	1d	-

[1d (26p) 1¹/2d (39p) 2d (52p)   2¹/2d (66p) 3d (79p)]

Norden U.D.C. objected to the proposed increases but withdrew when the Committee agreed to reduce the fare from Rochdale town centre to Norden from 3d to 2¹/2d. Objections from other surrounding Districts were also resolved but Littleborough would not withdraw their objection. A proposal in February 1919 for a new penny stage from Littleborough Centre to the Gale Inn and limits on other increases was not enough to persuade them. The fares increase was finally approved by the Board of Trade on 24th March 1919 and was implemented three days later.

Charges for parcels were also increased:

all parcels up to 7 lb.   2d (23p) any distance;
7 lbs. to 14 lbs.   3d (34p) any distance;
14 lbs. to 21 lbs.   4d (46p) any distance;
21 lbs. to 28 lbs. (maximum)   5d (57p) any distance.
(7lbs = 3.18 kg.)

The charge for leaving a parcel at the town centre Parcels Office was increased to 1¹/2d (17p) with an additional charge of 1d (11p) per day if left over 24 hours.

When the Middleton Electric Traction Company wanted to apply for a fares increase Rochdale objected, as did the authorities in Middleton and Chadderton. Their objection was later withdrawn on condition that the increases were limited to specified amounts, were only to be valid until 1st June 1924 and that they should not increase the purchase price of the undertaking. The Light Railway Commissioners issued an Order confirming the increases in March 1920.

Free passes and more increases

The Committee seemed to be relaxing their previously strict opposition to free passes. Over the years many different groups, including blind persons, had asked for free travel on the trams but been given a stiff rebuttal. In June 1920 Rochdale and District Society for the Blind were granted their request for free passes, subject to conditions prepared by the Manager and Town Clerk. Conditions for workmen's tickets were also relaxed with validity extended to any tram arriving in the town centre up to 9 a.m.

Fares were increased again on 26 June 1920 as soon as the Tramways (Temporary increase in charges) Act 1920 was passed. Adjustments to fares with additional penny stages or other minor changes continued to be made over the next few years.

In December 1923 the age under which children could be carried at half fare was raised to 15 years. In December 1925 free travel was extended to ex-servicemen with 60 per cent or more disablement. How this was defined is not recorded.

A revision to return fares was made in April 1928 for the longer distance journeys, as shown in Table 14.3.

Cheap long distance tram fares were introduced in October 1929, possibly in response to bus competition. The fare between Rochdale and Manchester, Rochdale and Bury, and Rochdale and Bacup was 6d (£1.03) each way with a fare of 5d (85p) from Castleton (Albion Street) to Manchester.

As buses began to replace trams, separate fare scales were devised which in many cases meant higher fares. The reasons may include the cost of new buses, and the lower seating capacity of buses compared to some trams. However it was agreed in October 1930 that tram replacement buses on Sunday mornings would charge the lower tram fares.

Table 14.3	Return fares for long distance riders, April 1928.		
Section	**Journey between**	**Single fare**	**Return fare**
Bacup	Rochdale and Whitworth	4d and 4¹/2d	7d
	Rochdale and Tong Lane	5d	8d
	Rochdale and Bacup	9d	1s 2d
Littleborough	Rochdale and Littleborough	4d and 4¹/2d	7d
	Rochdale and Littleborough and Summit	6¹/2d	10d
Norden	Rochdale and Norden	4d	7d
Newhey	Rochdale and Newhey	4d and 4¹/2d	7d
Castleton	Rochdale and Castleton boundary	4d	7d

[4d (70p), 4¹/2d (78p), 5d (87p), 6¹/2d (£1.13) 7d (£1.22), 8d (£1.39p), 9d (£1.57)
10d (£1.74) 1s 2d (£2.44)]

15. Tramway rolling stock.

What type of tram for Rochdale?

The most important feature of any tramway, and the most visible, is the rolling stock.

The Committee considered the question of what types of tram would be right for Rochdale. Although some standard tram designs were available, notably the Preston 4-wheel open top double decker, most towns wanted to develop their own designs which would not only meet their operational needs but also present a distinctive image for the town.

At the dawn of the electric era, on 4th February 1901, Mr Lacey, the Electrical Engineer, submitted designs of electric cars to the Tramways Committee but he was asked to prepare further designs and estimates for cars of various types, suggesting that the Committee wanted a wider choice. Furthermore they resolved to inspect various trams in operation in different parts of the country.

Accordingly, a week later on 11th February the Committee and the Borough Surveyor visited Preston to inspect different types of tram, firstly at the Electric Railway

Despite all these visits, the Committee could not decide which type of rolling stock to purchase and deferred their decision until the next meeting, to be held on 18th March when they asked Mr Lacey to prepare specifications for six trams of different types:

One single deck combination car, bogie trucks with two motor equipment (Southport);

One maximum traction car, two motors (Blackburn);

One double-truck car, four motors (Blackburn);

One double-truck car with reversible staircase;

One double-truck car, two motors (Bournemouth);

One small single-truck car, single deck (Manchester).

(Systems in brackets operated the types of car to be specified.)

The Committee's tactics were not unusual, indeed other municipalities acted likewise twenty or thirty years later when choosing their initial fleets of motorbuses or trolleybuses. The 'combination' car was so called because it combined a central enclosed saloon with end compartments for smokers. It was destined to become a popular style for Rochdale, partly because of low railway bridges on the Oldham Road and Milnrow Road.

Rochdale's first tram was a single deck 8-wheel combination car built by ER&TCW in Preston. It had Brill 22E maximum traction trucks and Dick Kerr electrical equipment.

The tenders were considered by the Committee on 17th June 1901. According to the Committee minutes, British Thomson-Houston won the tenders for 'types A, B and C' and Dick Kerr won the tenders for 'types D, E and F'. In fact Dick Kerr won the tender for the combination car, the maximum traction car and the single truck car with BTH (Brush) winning the other three types. At some stage the specification for the single truck car was changed from single deck to double deck. A month later, on 18th July, the tenders were accepted with some revisions to tender prices and the inclusion of spares and steel tyres. The cars as listed above became Nos. 1, 2, 6, 4, 5 and 3 respectively.

and Tramway Carriage Works and then at the Electric Engineering Company's works. (The ERTCW became The United Electric Car Company in 1905 and later English Electric). They then went on to Birkenhead, home to Britain's very first tramway in 1860, to inspect the various types of tramcar at the works of George Milnes & Company. They also visited Loughborough on 4th March to see the tramcars built by the Brush Electrical Engineering Company.

Rochdale's second tram, open top eight wheel maximum traction Car No.2 is resplendent with curtains and full lining out. It was built by the Electric Railway and Tramway Carriage Works Limited in Preston in 1902 and fitted with Brill 22E trucks. (Eric Fielding)

The first two Rochdale trams were 8-wheel bogie cars but No. 3 was a shorter 4-wheel Brill 21E single truck car. Like Nos 1 and 2 it was built by the Electric Railway and Tramway Carriage Works Limited in 1902. It was eventually fitted with a top cover but not for another 28 years, only 2 years before it was scrapped!

(Eric Fielding)

left) Car No. 4 is the only one known to have been fitted with a snow plough. No photographs have yet come to light of it ploughing snow, but harsh winters were common in those days.

right) Car No. 5 was another open top 8-wheel double deck bogie car with enclosed platform Milnes body but with Brush B reversed maximum traction bogies. They were later replaced with Brush D equal wheel bogies.

(Eric Fielding)

Excitement must have been building up when the Borough Surveyor presented samples to the Committee on 23rd December 1901 of window curtains and seat covers for the trams. Samples of lettering and decorations for the trams and notices to be displayed for passengers, prepared by Mr Lacey, were considered on 17th February 1902.

The first trams arrive

At the end of April 1902, Car No. 2 was reported as having arrived at Rochdale Station. With the minimum of delay, it was delivered to the temporary Bury Road Depot at Coptrod, the Borough Engineer having been authorised to extend the shed to accommodate it. However all was not quite well as at his inspection of the Bury Road route, Major Druitt raised some concerns about the steps on the 'Combination' car, referred to as "the Southport Improved car" in his report. This was Car Number 1, an eight wheel single deck bogie combination car. Major Druitt's report stated:

"The steps, even when folded up, project too far from the sides of the car, and there is always a danger of their not being folded up when not in use. The hanging gate of the lifeguard needs deepening so as to hang nearer the ground, and also to be placed further in front of the lifeguard proper. Wire netting should be added on both sides of the car between the bogies, as the car body is very high from the ground."

Car No.10 was the first of a long line of orders to go to Brush in Loughborough. It had a Brush AA single truck with 25 h.p.Brush motors and Brush 3A controllers. It is seen in as new condition in the depot yard. *(Ian Yearsley)*

Car No.10 spent most of its working life as a 4-wheel open top balcony car but was fitted with enclosed platforms and hexagonal dashes in 1928 and fitted with an English Electric top cover in 1930. It was sent to the breakers yard only two years later. *(Eric Fielding)*

The other car inspected, referred to as the "Liverpool Type Car", was a four wheel double decker, No.3. (referred to as the 'Manchester type' car on the tender list). The Report commented:

"...the car... is suitable if fitted with the Tidswell lifeguard. In view of the heavy gradients on some of the Rochdale Corporation lines, I strongly advise the adoption of Type (b) as slipper brakes will be essential on the steep gradients and these are more easily applied to four wheeled cars. Also four-wheeled cars are more economical on steep gradients than bogie cars."

Type (b) was the four wheel double decker so it was clear that the Major favoured these rather than the bogie cars. He would be proved right some years later after several accidents with bogie cars on gradients although four wheelers were not immune. The report included a reminder that if there were any low bridges on the Rochdale tramway routes, there must be 6ft 6ins (1.98m) clearance at least between the top decks of double decked cars and the underside of any overbridge.

The extent of gradients on tram routes in Rochdale is shown in Table 15.1 below.

To satisfy the concerns of the Major, modifications were made to the four wheel double decker at Coptrod and also to three double deck bogie cars at the temporary Bridgefold Depot. Ordinary slipper brakes were fitted to the four wheeler and pneumatic slipper brakes to the three cars at Bridgefold.

It should be explained that slipper brakes were used where the hand brakes on early electric trams were not adequate to hold a car on steep gradients, which were plentiful in Rochdale. They consisted of an iron or sometimes hardwood block which was suspended in a shoe between the wheels over each rail. The handwheel operated by the driver pressed the blocks down onto the rails to apply the braking forces. They were separate from the normal handbrake. The slipper brake was a mechanical pre-cursor to the more familiar electro-magnetic track brake.

In June it was reported that Cars Nos. 2 and 3 on the Bury Road Section were to be fitted with slipper brakes and transferred to the Norden Section while Cars Nos. 5 and 6 would be transferred to the Bury Road Section. Slipper brakes were ordered from Dick Kerr for Nos. 2 and 3 and from British Thomson-Houston for Car No. 4, replacing the previous resolution regarding slipper brakes. The exchange of cars between the

Table 15.1	Examples of gradients on tram routes in Rochdale.		
Road	**Section**	**Gradient**	
		Ratio	Percent
John Street	Robert Street to Pagan Street	1 in 11.5	8.7 %
	Baillie Street to Yorkshire St. (average)	1 in 14.7	6.8 %
Blackwater Street	Brickcroft to St Mary's Gate	1 in 13.1	7.6 %
	Lord Street to St Mary's Gate (average)	1 in 15.3	6.5 %
Rooley Moor Road	Spotland Bridge to Blair Street	1 in 10.6	9.4 %
Edenfield Road	Spotland Bridge to Willbutts Lane	1 in 13.4	7.5 %
Milnrow Road	Brocklebank Road towards canal bridge	1 in 13	7.7 %
Drake Street	Opposite Drake Hotel	1 in 19.4	5.2 %

Source: Borough Surveyor's Office, Rochdale.

two temporary depots was entrusted to Dick Kerr and BTH for their respective cars. There was at that stage no track connection between the depots and the moves were probably made with the aid of a traction engine. The single truck Car No. 3 was selected to be fitted with Jerrard's track cleaner as an experiment.

Tenders for three additional cars, Nos. 7, 8 and 9, were considered at a special meeting 28th July. Dick Kerr were the successful bidder for the double deck open top standard width cars with Brill 21E trucks and DK35A motors. The livery including lettering and decoration was to be identical with Car No.3. The order was placed in August 1902 and delivery had to be within four weeks of receipt of the order! In today's modern efficient world it would take about two years.

The numbers of standing passengers allowed was one third the number of seated passengers on the lower deck. Conductors were instructed to permit standing only on Saturdays, Sundays and special occasions or when the weather was inclement.

The first service vehicle in the fleet was a tower wagon for the repair and maintenance of the overhead line which the Borough Engineer procured in August 1902 together with the necessary tools from Messrs. McElroy. An arrangement was made with the Watch Committee to use their Weights and Measures horse drawn wagon during the daytime in the event of overhead emergencies.

The question of advertising on the trams was raised in May 1902 when a request was considered from Messrs. Grifiths & Millington Ltd. They were prepared to make an offer for the advertising rights but the Committee said they were not yet in a position to entertain the matter. Two months later Mr Thomas Kershaw of 9, Corporation Street, Manchester was asked to fit Car No.3 with sample advertisements for Committee approval. It was soon agreed to advertise on the decency boards and ventilator windows on all tram cars but then Mr Kershaw offered to pay £18 per annum for each running car for the sole right to advertise for 5 years from 4th November 1902. Adverts would be placed on the two top sideboards (the 'decency boards'), two circular top end spaces and all ventilating window panels inside. The outside adverts would be enamelled or painted while the interior ones would be embossed glass. The Committee accepted his offer.

The tram fleet expands

A major expansion of the tram fleet was heralded in May 1903 when the Committee asked Mr Lacey to prepare specifications and drawings for forty one more cars of similar types to those already in operation. Three types were specified:

Rochdale purchased 24 open top 4 wheel cars from Brush between 1902 and 1905. The last 10 had Brush Conaty radial trucks like No. 23 with Brush 25 h.p. motors and Brush 3A controllers. (Eric Fielding)

Originally the same as Car 23, Car 24 was fitted with platform vestibules. It was decorated in 1918 and is seen at the Tramway Centre, passing Williams Deacons Bank, now the HSBC Bank. (Eric Fielding)

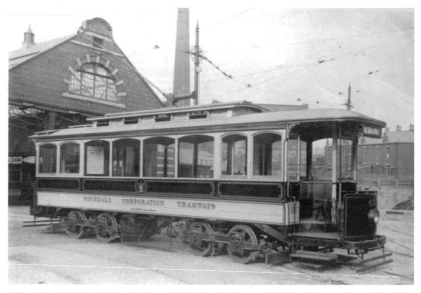

The classic Rochdale design of single deck car with Brush maximum traction equal wheel bogies. No.42 is seen in original condition with open platforms and clerestory roof at the Mellor Street depot. (Eric Fielding)

Another view of the classic Rochdale design of single deck combination car. No.36 is seen in original condition with open platforms and clerestory roof at the depot. (J.S. King)

- 20 single truck double deck cars with 'Bellamy' reversed staircase (as No.3);
- 5 combination bogie cars with two motors (as No. 1);
- 16 double deck bogie cars with two motors and 'Bellamy' reversed staircase (as No. 4).

Tenders were opened on 10th August but visits to three tram factories were organised before they were considered. Decisions were reached on 21st September with the whole contract being awarded to the Brush Electrical Company of Loughborough. All the bogie cars were specified as having "equal wheel maximum traction" bogies, an apparent contradiction in terms since maximum traction bogies normally have unequal diameter wheels. The difference was that these bogies had off-set bolsters to bring the weight as close as possible to the driven wheels. Confusingly, Brush used the same designation, type 'D', for both bogie variants: the centre bolster type for four motor cars and the offset bolster type for two motor cars. All Rochdale's bogie cars were thus 'equal wheel maximum traction' except Cars Nos. 1 and 2 which had conventional maximum traction bogies.

The choice of equal wheel maximum traction bogies created a potential problem. The floor would have to be high enough to allow the wheels to pass under it on sharp curves, making boarding even more difficult. The solution adopted was to have the floor supports underslung from the steel car body underframe which allowed a floor height

similar to conventional bogie cars. This unusual design was attributed to Mr Moffet who became the Tramways Manager in April 1904. It is thought that the bogie design was unique to Rochdale while the only other example of this type of underframe was on the Potteries Electric Traction system. Also probably unique to Rochdale was the Brecknell, Munro and Rogers Ltd trolley base, supporting a

Brush built double deck bogie car 49 of 1905 was fitted with an English Electric top cover in 1930 but retained its open balconies and open platforms. Two years later it had gone. It is seen on The Esplanade passing the building that is now the Touchstones Gallery and Local History centre.

BOGIE CAR SCENES

A batch of six double deck bogie cars were purchased in 1905 before orders reverted to single deck bogie cars for the next 7 years. Car No. 45 has Brush D equal wheel bogies, Brush 35 h.p. motors and Brush Type 3A controllers. They were fitted with top covers in 1930, only to be scrapped two years later. (Eric Fielding)

Brush built double deck bogie car 45 of 1905 was fitted with an English Electric top cover in 1930 but retained its open balconies and open platforms. Two years later it had gone. (Eric Fielding)

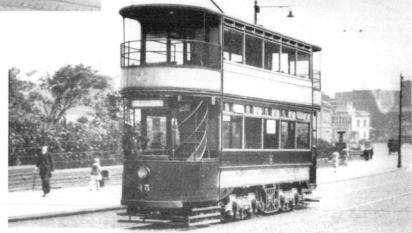

Another batch of 10 Brush combination cars were delivered in 1906 with Brush equal wheel maximum traction bogies. No 54 was one of a few to have their platforms enclosed in the 1920's. (J.S.King)

SINGLE DECK BOGIE CARS

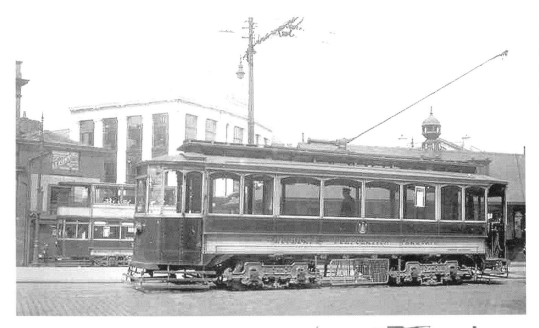

Brush bogie car No. 52 appears to be heading in the wrong direction as it stands at the Tramway Centre. An open balcony car stands on the Butts.

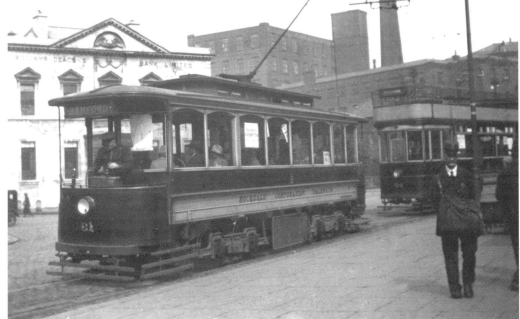

Bogie car No.61 waits at the Tramway Centre before climbing the long gradient up Bury Road. It is followed by open top double decker No.24. The date is probably the late twenties.
(Eric Fielding)

Bogie single decker No.63 of the 1912 batch tucks in behind double decker No.27 at the Tramway Centre. It was built to the same design as the 1905 deliveries, still with open platforms and clerestory roof.
(Eric Fielding)

FOUR WHEEL DOUBLE DECKERS

In 1920 the first enclosed cars were purchased although still with open balconies. Car 74 was one of 10 built by English Electric with Brill 21E trucks after years of buying everything from Brush. It is travelling along Mellor Street past the tramway workshops building. (Eric Fielding)

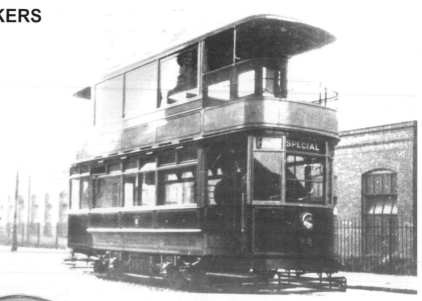

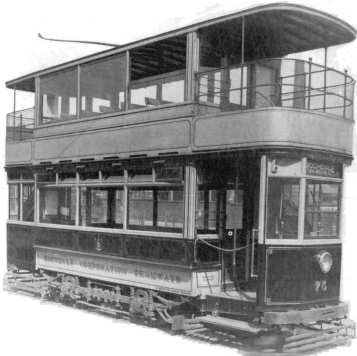

After nearly twenty years of buying Brush cars, 10 enclosed double deckers with open balconies were delivered from English Electric in Preston in 1920. They were the first new double deckers for 15 years and were mounted on Brill 21E four wheel trucks. No. 75 is one of the batch numbered 70 to 79. (MTMS)

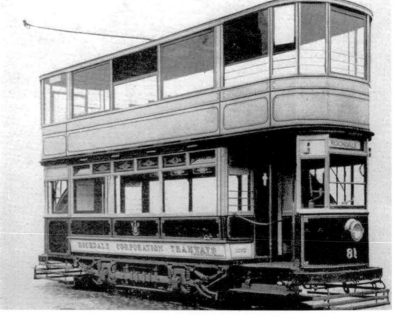

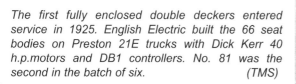

The first fully enclosed double deckers entered service in 1925. English Electric built the 66 seat bodies on Preston 21E trucks with Dick Kerr 40 h.p.motors and DB1 controllers. No. 81 was the second in the batch of six. (TMS)

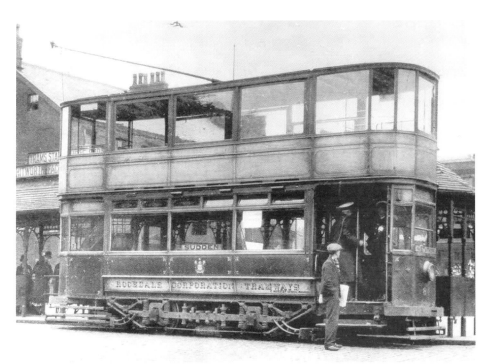

All enclosed tram 84 was built by English Electric on a Preston 21E truck in 1925. It was looking rather old and shabby when photographed at the Tramway Centre ready to depart for Sudden via the Railway Station, probably towards the end of the system. (MTMS)

supplied with garden type seats in the open portions at each end of the car.

The names of Sub-Committees seem to be used rather illogically because it was the Traffic, Staffing and Car Shed Sub-Committee which responded in May with their recommendation for the numbers of cars to be to be purchased. The original order for 20 single truck double deck cars, 16 bogie double deck and 5 combination car single deck was changed to 25 single truck double deck cars, 6 bogie double deck and 10 combination car single deck, keeping the total at 41 cars. Of these, 10 single truck double deck cars and the 10 combination cars were to be constructed forthwith and as previously resolved four single truck double deck cars and two combination cars were to be delivered as early as possible. The Committee changed the order yet again to 20 single truck double deck cars, 6 bogie double deck and 14 combination car single deck, reducing the total to 40 cars. Of these, ten four wheel double deck cars, Nos. 10 to 19, had already been delivered in 1903.

No.4 trolley mounted on the car roof. Brush 35 h.p. motors and Brush 3A controllers were fitted.

Ashley Best writes of these cars: "The design of the tram makes use of angled platforms to maximise the size of the smoking saloons at the expense of the platform staff. The driver had a very cramped space in which to stand. The seats in the smoking compartment were even more basic than the usual wooden seats of the period and did not appear to be any more than simple benches lacking backs. The livery has been described as deep hide brown and primrose yellow, the dark panels being lined in gold and the primrose panels in hide brown. The lettering on the car sides was gold shaded blue as were the numerals on the dash. At the time the trams were built, with their elaborately painted and lined out exteriors, they must have been regarded as handsome vehicles. They had well proportioned, almost architectural appearance of so many trams of their time and were indeed more attractive than most."

In March 1904 the Committee asked Brush Electrical Engineering to deliver four of the single truck double deck cars and two double bogie combination cars as early as possible, but records indicate that no cars were delivered in 1904. There was some debate about the numbers of cars to be ordered from Brush, and the Brakes Sub-Committee were asked to settle the question. It was agreed that whatever cars were ordered would be fitted with the 'Hudson Bowring' type of life guard and edge-wise lath type seats. The combination cars were to be

Yet another Sub-Committee was set up, this time to look into brakes. They considered the desirability of adopting the Westinghouse magnetic brake, the British Thomson Houston brake or "any other brake which may be brought to their notice".

A further four all enclosed double deckers bought in 1926 were similar to the previous batch but had narrow opening windows below roof level. No. 87 was the second of the batch. They were destined to have very short working lives.

(Eric Fielding)

Westinghouse 'Newell' track brakes were specified for three single truck cars and one combination car and B.T.H. magnetic track brakes with mechanical hand operated gear on one double deck single truck car and one combination car. All the cars were fitted with 'run backs' to prevent running backwards on gradients. It was later decided to fit one new combination car with a Spencer track brake in place of the B.T.H. brake.

All the double deck cars were ordered as open top but as early as May 1904 consideration was being given to providing top deck covers, no doubt influenced by the unpredictable Pennine weather. The Traffic Sub-Committee was asked to consider the options but in the event it was to be another fifteen years before any trams had top deck roofs.

The ten double deckers for early delivery had the Brush standard type of staircase. In September 1904 it was decided to order radial

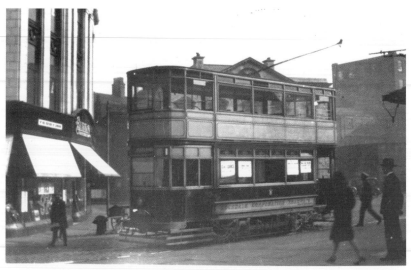
All enclosed Car No. 93 was built in the Corporation tramway workshops on a Brill 21E truck with Metro Vick 65 h.p. high speed motors and Metro Vick controllers. It was fitted with an English Electric top cover. (Eric Fielding)

The last Rochdale tram was No.94, built in the Corporation's tramway workshops on Mellor Street on a Brill 21E truck with Metro Vick 50 h.p. motors and Metro Vick controllers. It entered service in 1928, just 4 years before the last tram ran. (Ian Yearsley)

trucks for one of the new four-wheel double deck cars as an experiment. On October 17th the Borough Electrical Engineer was asked to put in hand 10 single truck cars from Brush but to withhold delivery of nine until the one with the radial truck had been tried. The following year, Car

No. 20 was delivered with a Brush Conaty radial truck and was quickly followed by Car Nos. 21 to 29. The combination cars Nos. 30 to 43 and the double deck bogie cars Nos. 44 to 49 were also delivered in 1905, all with Brush 'D' equal wheel bogies.

A little explanation is needed about the terms used to describe this bogie. The 44 to 49 batch had Brush D bogies to the McGuire pattern, often referred to as 'Mountain and Gibson'. This type of bogie was first built by the McGuire Company in Bury to an American design. One of McGuire's senior engineers moved to work for Brush who then started to produce the same bogie as their type 'D'. Meanwhile McGuire went into liquidation and the Mountain and Gibson firm established itself at Bury and produced the same truck. After they ceased production the same bogie was produced by Brush, UEC, Hurst Nelson and others.

Rochdale buys steam trams!

Rochdale Corporation's brief spell as a steam tramway operator was enabled by a decision in October 1904 to purchase nine steam tram engines and seven trailers from the company so that they could continue to operate the Littleborough route until the following year. It was agreed that the depots be sold by auction as quickly as possible but that the Rochdale depot would be occupied by the Corporation until 31st May 1905.

More works vehicles were sought with an order in November 1904 for three salt wagons from Messrs. Milnes Voss & Company.

In December 1904, the Car Shed Sub-Committee recommended purchase of six double deck bogie cars and four single deck combination cars from the Brush Company. This was a continuation of the 1903 order.

An offer was received in April 1905 to purchase some of the steam tram engines and trailers that had been retained for the Littleborough route. The Committee replied to Mr Thomas Rawstron of River Street that they would be advertised for sale shortly. He subsequently submitted his tender which was accepted.

A request from the Brush Company to exhibit one of Rochdale's bogie double deck cars at the Tramways Exhibition in London was granted. The Exhibition was held in London in July.

Slipper brakes were again on the agenda in May when it was resolved that 20 cars comprising eight double deck bogie cars, six combination cars and six radial truck cars would be fitted with Westinghouse brakes. In December eight Westinghouse magnetic brakes were ordered for three combination cars, four radial truck cars and Car No.3. Six additional brakes of the same type would be acquired when needed for cars Nos. 2, 4, 7, 8, 9, and 31.

Problems at Brush

An early failure was reported to the Committee in November 1905. Two Brush truck side frames had broken. The matter was considered sufficiently serious for the Manager and one Councillor to attend tests of the broken frames in Sheffield. This was followed by a Works Sub-Committee visit to Brush works in Loughborough to seek an explanation for the defective frames. The Brush proposals were referred to consulting engineers for their observations.

Further problems with Brush products emerged in March 1906 with an exchange of correspondence regarding the cars supplied by them, particularly the motor suspension bearings and commutators. Further cars with broken frames included four of the 30 to 43 batch of single deckers and all of the 44 to 49 batch of double deckers except 48. In total 17 side frames were broken. The Manager was empowered to arrange terms of settlement. It must have been somewhat embarrassing for Brush who had featured Rochdale in their advertisement in The Tramway and Railway World in December 1905, alongside London and Auckland, New Zealand.

Evidence of modifications to truck frames emerged many years later when Philip Groves was examining some of his photographs of cars with Brush D bogies. He noticed

that there were variations as if some truck sides had been strengthened. This applied to single and double deckers including some of the later 60 to 69 series. This problem may not have been unique to Rochdale.

Amazingly, despite all the problems with defective trucks, Mr Moffet managed to turn out 48 of his 49 cars on busy Saturdays. The allocation of cars to routes was:

Bury and Milnrow Road	6
Norden and Thornham	12
Spotland	2
Circular route	2
Heywood	10
Healey	4
Littleborough	10
Summit	2
Total cars	48

The Manager estimated that he needed one spare car for every fifteen to twenty cars to allow for repairs, general overhauling and accidents, equating to a spares ratio of only 5% to 7% which not many operators could achieve today. Another common occurrence was heavy loading on radial truck cars resulting in hot bearings which could result in the car being returned to the depot for the rest of the day. He was so short of cars that on two occasions he had to take Car No. 3 out of the paint shop when only partly painted and put it into service. Traffic was growing and the coming summer period would put further strains on his limited resources.

More cars needed

Mr Moffet therefore calculated that he needed a minimum of six more cars:

Heywood Section to Sudden	2 cars
Littleborough Section to Wardle Lane	2 cars
Milnrow Section	1 car
Norden Section	1 car
Total	6 cars

Manchester City Tramways bogie car No 1040 is seen on route 17, the only one in Rochdale to carry a route number, at the Tramway Centre. Most Manchester trams were built in Hyde Road Works but this one was built by English Electric in 1928.   (MTMS)

Each new car would cost £700 making a total of £4,800 plus interest and sinking fund at 6% adding another £252. To strengthen his case, he also calculated that for all other tramway systems in the UK the average number of trams per route mile was between 3 and 11 with an average of about 5 cars per mile. Rochdale's figure was only $2^1/_3$ cars per route mile, less than the lowest average figure.

When specifying the type of car most suited to Rochdale's needs, the Manager had no hesitation in recommending the single deck combination car. It was the most popular with the travelling public and would ease the storage problems as, being single deck, they could easily be covered with tarpaulins if needed. Another six cars could be housed in the car shed by removing the salt wagons and making better use of the workshops. There were no traffic or engineering reasons given for this choice.

Acceding to the General Manager's pleas, in March 1906 the Committee asked for separate quotations for an additional six and ten combination cars. A quotation from the Brush Company, seemingly the only one obtained, was accepted just nine days later comprising ten single deck combination cars, to be fitted with runback preventers, side guards between trucks and Brush 1202 B pattern motors and Brush controllers. The contract was subject to delivery within ten weeks from the date of order. Once again the timescales were unbelievably short. Today you would be lucky to get 10 new trams from anybody in much under two years! In April it was decided to fit magnetic track brakes to these 10 combination cars which became 50 to 59 in the fleet and also to cars 35, 39 and 43.

A notice was placed on the top deck of double deck cars requesting smokers not to smoke in front of the trolley standard. Presumably this was to avoid their smoke blowing back into other passengers faces, all double deckers then being open top. Following complaints, a notice was fixed: 'Persons spitting in or on the car will be dealt with according to Bye-Law No. 5. Penalty 40/-' (£122).

The Committee inspected a double-deck single truck car and a single deck combination car which had been fitted with sample route indicators for alternative routes on the Littleborough and Heywood sections. Approval was given to fitting them to the necessary number of cars.

In March 1907 it was resolved to purchase a horse drawn tower wagon. The following month the tender of Messrs Rawlinson and Sons of Blackburn was accepted. A separate tender was sought for hire of the necessary horse for ordinary purposes and for emergencies.

The horse drawn tower wagon must have proved to be too slow, taking well over an hour to reach some parts of the network. It was deemed essential to be able to deal with overhead line breakdowns properly. In September 1909 it was

The water tram's main function, as its name implies, was to spray water across the carriageway, seen here in Mellor Street near the depot. As this photo demonstrates, it had quite a good range.
(Arthur Hodgson)

The water tram shows off its power outside the Town Hall on the Esplanade.
(Eric Fielding)

decided to make enquiries about the cost of a motor wagon complete with tower and a motor chassis without tower. The Routes Sub-Committee inspected suitable chassis from Halley, Leyland, Daimler and Commer. On receipt of the prices, they decided to purchase a chassis and fit one of the existing towers to it. Messrs. Halley and Company of Yoker, Glasgow won the tender for supply of a motor tower chassis at a cost of £597. *(£37,250)*

When the new tower wagon had been delivered, the Routes Sub-Committee decided to put it through its paces. On April 1st 1910 it negotiated Sparrow Hill and College Street with ease in second gear. Spurred on by this success they took it through to Littleborough and up Blackstone Edge in top gear! Crossing into Yorkshire at Ripponden, they returned over Saddleworth Moor to Huddersfield Road, Newhey. The wagon tackled many curves and steep hills, all but one in top gear. The trial was deemed satisfactory, and presumably a good day out was had by the Committee!

A combined rail grinder, drilling and sawing machine was obtained from Messrs Robson & Co. of Sheffield and proved very satisfactory.

It was not until December 1910 that it was decided to provide all trams with used ticket boxes. A total of 116 Baywood boxes were supplied, enough to fit all the trams then in service at each platform.

The Cleansing Committee wanted to use a watering car to help keep the streets clean. In December it was agreed that a watering car be provided at a charge of 6¹/2d *(£1.69)* per car mile plus a yearly contribution of £70 *(£4,368)* to cover interest and sinking fund on the cost of the car.

Yet more combination cars

Tenders were invited for ten more combination cars in May 1911 and for the Watering Car. Brush were again the favoured supplier for the bodies with Brush D bogies, Westinghouse controllers and British Westinghouse brakes. On 6th June 1911 the Routes Sub-Committee visited the Brush factory in Loughborough to inspect improvements made to the trucks and equipment. Brush agreed to modify trucks, motors and car bodies to meet their requirements and also offered to exchange 12 old 35 hp motors for 12 new 42 hp motors. On 14th June the Sub-Committee agreed to recommend award of the contract to Brush.

The cars were delivered in 1912 as Nos. 60 to 69 and were the last combination cars to be purchased. Brush also won the tender for the Watering Car which cost £800 13s 0d *(£49,690)*. It was equipped with oxy-acetylene plant and a rail grinding appliance and was also fitted with a snowplough which proved very useful in clearing snow from the tracks in the winter months. Its main function was to clean the tracks and water the roads to keep the dust down.

The Borough Surveyor recommended in June 1913 that the principal streets should be swept at night time using brushes hauled by the tramway watering car. Two new sweeping machines would be purchased.

A number of changes were made following Lieut.Col.

Driutt's report into the accident on John Street on 14th February. The Tramways Sub-Committee met on 19th May to consider his report and recommended:

1) to convert the sanders on all cars to the improved continuous sander type;

2) to fit a car with, and make a test of, the Westinghouse Patent Skid-Proof attachment to the magnetic track brake;

3) to fix water jets at the tops of the following gradients for the intermittent watering of the rails during greasy weather:

Drake Street, John Street, Blackwater Street, Meanwood Brow and Coldwall Brow. *(Meanwood Brow is on Rooley Moor Road north of Spotland Bridge and Coldwall Brow is on Spotland Road east of Spotland Bridge).*

The test under item 2 was successful and it was recommended that cars using John Street and Blackwater Street should be fitted with new magnets and the skid-proof attachment. The Committee rode to Norden on Car No. 63 which was fitted with this equipment to witness tests of its efficiency. They agreed to scrap the Type 23 magnets on all cars using John Street and Blackwater Street and fit No. 25 magnets of a more powerful type together with the skid-proof attachments. British Westinghouse Electric and Manufacturing were awarded the tender for supply 82 brake magnets and 32 skid-proof attachments.

The Manager reported on 1st September 1915 that Cars Nos.1, 8, 19 and 20 were in poor condition. It was agreed that they should be rebuilt.

In October 1914 it was agreed to purchase one set of Aberdeen type adjustable wind screens for trial on one of the cars, at a cost of £7 3s. 6d per car set. In July 1916 the Committee agreed to consider providing windscreens on all the cars. Driving trams without protection from the weather was fine in the summer but must have been excruciating in a howling winter gale, especially on the hills beyond Littleborough or up to Bacup. However in that more Spartan era, there were some who considered it healthy to drive unprotected from the wind or rain and that any form of windshield would be unhealthy and reduce visibility.

The Manager wrote to 71 other municipal tramway operators seeking their experience with either windscreens or vestibules for the protection of motormen. The Committee decided to consult their motormen who predictably supported the idea, the Leeds type being considered the best. The Sub-Committee went on a day trip to find out. On return they decided not to recommend them at present, perhaps because of the cost, but might experiment with one or two cars on the Bacup route. Meanwhile the Manager was authorised to purchase special winter caps for motormen, hardly a substitute for a windscreen.

The Cleansing Committee decided in August 1916 to purchase a sand spreader to be attached to the tramway watering car. In September the tender from Rochdale wheelwright Mr A. Holden of Upper George Street was accepted for a four wheeled wagon to be towed behind the watering car or a motor vehicle. It would carry sand or salt for spreading on the streets.

Another service vehicle was needed in July 1919 in the form of an additional motor tower wagon. Also the existing tower wagon was in need of repair. The tender from Halley's Industrial Motors was accepted in October.

Double deckers back in favour

Also in October the manager submitted a report recommending purchase of ten new cars, the type of car and funding method being left to the Routes Sub-Committee to consider. The following month the lowest total tender from English Electric of Preston was accepted for supply and delivery of ten single truck double deck top covered tramcars, the first in the fleet to be fitted with top covers from new. The tenders received are shown in Table 15.2 below. Metro-Vick tendered for electrical equipment only.

The lowest complete tender was accepted and by November 1920 half the batch of new double deck cars had been delivered, the rest being delivered in December, taking the numbers 70 to 79. They were the first to come from English Electric after a long run of Brush built cars. They were reported to be giving great satisfaction and were much appreciated by passengers. Loan sanction for £24,200 (£732,210) was sought in April 1921 by which time most of the cars were already in service. Their arrival enabled the Norden service to operate alternately via Spotland Road and Mellor Street and an accelerated service to be operated on some other routes.

The loan was approved, repayable over 20 years. The Committee could not have foreseen that they would still have eight years to pay on the loan when the trams were scrapped. The Ministry specified that:

1) where necessary the interval between the centres of double track would be increased to 8ft. 6ins. (2.59m) with the necessary additional clearances on curves when the tramways were reconstructed;

2) the folding step at the leading end be raised when the car was in motion; and

3) sideguards should be provided on each side at both ends.

Rochdale's first all-enclosed trams were ordered on 26th August 1924, English Electric being the successful tenderer for the single truck top covered cars with entirely enclosed upper decks and vestibules. They became cars 80 to 85 and had Preston 21E trucks, English Electric bodies, Dick Kerr 40 h.p. motors and DB1 controllers. Wooden seats were fitted throughout with close slat longitudinal seating in the lower deck and 'lath and space' garden type seats on the top deck. Loan sanction for £11,000 (£391,900) for their purchase, repayable over 20 years, was obtained. The six cars entered service at the end of 1924.

About this time some of the pre-war single deck cars were modernised, Car 54 being converted from three to two compartments and given a full length monitor roof. No. 50 retained its three compartments but was vestibuled and given a full length monitor roof; Cars 38, 52, 53 and 57 enjoyed similar improvements.

Table 15.2   Tenders for ten single truck double deck top covered tramcars, 7' 6" wheelbase.

Name of Tendering Firm	Bodies	Trucks	Electrical Equipment and Brakes	Total Cost	Delivery	Remarks
British Thomson-Houston Co. Ltd.	Not builders; agree to sub-let to English Electric Co. at prices quoted by that firm £12,675 £2,360		7,900	£22,935	Motors 4 months. Brakes, cannot give definite promise	40 h.p. ventilated motors built in the United States. B.T.H. Magnetic Brakes.
Brush Electrical Engineering Co. Ltd.	£12,000	£2,650	£7,725	£22,375	8 months for first 3 or 4.	1218 H type of motor; not ventilated. 40 h.p. rating. Westinghouse magnetic brakes.
English Electric Co. Ltd.	£12,675	£2,360	£7,000	£22,035	7-8 months	40 h.p. ventilated type. Westinghouse magnetic brakes.
Metropolitan-Vickers Electric Co. Ltd.	—	—	£7,116 10s	£7,116 10s	7-8 months	33 h.p. ventilated type motors & brakes only. Westinghouse magnetic brakes.

On completion of the takeover of the Middleton Electric Tramways Company, several cars were transferred to Rochdale plus a single truck double deck tram which had been allocated to Manchester in the distribution of Middleton cars but which they did not want. Double deck four wheel open top cars 12 to 15, built in 1905, retained their Middleton fleet numbers while similar car number 11 was renumbered 2 in the Rochdale fleet, replacing a car that had been scrapped in 1919.

The next order for trams in August 1925 called for four new cars, three new car bodies with top covers and three pairs of sideframes. Tenders were not advertised but English Electric were awarded the contract on 27th October with delivery to begin in three months. Application for loan sanction was made for the total cost of £10,250, *(£371,920)*. They became Nos 86 to 89 and were similar to the previous batch, 4-wheel double deck enclosed cars on Preston 21E trucks. A distinguishing feature was the 'top lights' (small windows) above the upper saloon windows. Approval was given by the Ministry of Transport in December, the loan to be repaid over 15 years.

Brakes in the news again

The second runaway tram on John Street in 1922, Car No. 57, revived the question of brake efficiency. A remarkably detailed explanation was given in the Rochdale Observer on 15th February 1922:

"It may be said at the outset that the appliances are wonderfully effective and provided that (1) they are in working order and (2) are properly applied, it is quite impossible for a car to run away, even down the steepest gradient.
The braking appliances on Rochdale cars are twofold:-

(1) The hand brake. This works by pressing a brake block against the rim of the wheel. There is a brake block for every wheel and they are all operated exclusively by the hand brake which is the brass handle on the driver's right hand side.

(2) The magnetic brake. This applies braking power first by a rheostatic action which will be explained later and secondly by magnetising the 'slipper' which is situated between the bogey trucks on either side of the car. When magnetised, the slipper grips the rails.

The magnetic brake is applied by means of the larger handle on the controller, which the driver operates with his left hand. On the top of the controller are a series of notches, those on one side being to regulate the amount of driving power passing through the motors, and those on the other side controlling the retarding power of the magnetic brake. It is only a momentary operation to convert the full driving power into the greatest braking force by turning the handle from one side to the other. When the driver turns the controller handle to one of the braking notches, all current ceases to pass through the motors, and by reversing the order of the field leads in the controller the motors are converted into dynamos and, driven by the wheels, generate power for themselves. This power is passed through a series of resistances into the slipper; and according to the greater or less number of resistances brought into operation the slipper is magnetised to a greater or less extent and grips the rails with a greater or less keenness. In addition to this slipper action the magnetic brake has also a rheostatic braking action for this reason: when the motors are being driven by the current from the overhead wire in the ordinary way, the revolution of the motors is in the same forward direction as the force of gravitation. But when the motors are converted into dynamos by the reversing of the field leads, their energy is developed in the opposite direction. Hence if the car is descending a hill the force of gravitation is pulling one way and the motors are exercising power in the opposite direction, with the result that a considerable braking effect is developed.

Having explained the theory of the magnetic brake let us examine its practical operation. As has been stated the brake depends on the generation of electricity by the revolution of the car wheels acting on the motors. Hence it follows that immediately the car stops dead, or the wheels cease to revolve, the slipper becomes demagnetised and leaves the rail. From this we reach a further conclusion, that the magnetic brake can only stop a car dead for a moment, since the very stoppage causes the brake to lose its effect, and the car - if proceeding down a hill – will move forward under its own weight. The corollary of these facts is that though a car may be momentarily stopped dead on a hill by the magnetic brake, it can only be held there by the hand brake.

We will now imagine a car proceeding down John Street. If the regulations are obeyed the car will be stopped dead at Pagan Street and held on the hand brake. The motorman should then apply his magnetic track brake by turning the handle to the top of the braking notch, and should release the hand brake. Since the controller is in the braking section no power is passing through the motors, but the car begins to move down the hill under its own weight. Before it had gone more than few yards the wheels would be generating sufficient electricity to magnetise the slipper and the car would stop dead with a violent jerk. As previously explained, this stoppage would automatically put the magnetic brake out of action and again the car would start off under its own weight, only to be pulled up with another jerk after a few yards progress when the wheels had begun to generate again. Consequently if the controller handle was kept on the top braking notch the journey down John Street would be a series of starts and stops every few yards as the magnetic brake automatically came into operation and then

momentarily ceased with the stoppage of the car. Such a journey would obviously be very uncomfortable for the passengers and consequently the experienced motorman, as soon as he finds that the car is generating properly, turns the controller handle to the next braking notch. This brings in more resistances and slightly decreases the braking power, allowing the car the car to travel downhill a little more quickly and without the jerks mentioned above. From this notch the motorman may go to the next or 'coasting' notch which allows a speed of six to seven miles (per hour). At any moment he can put the handle to a higher braking notch to reduce speed or stop dead.

If the brakes are applied in this way the risk of accident is infinitesimal. Supposing for instance that when the car starts off from Pagan Street, the driver finds that his car is not generating as it ought to do. If he has stopped dead at Pagan Street the speed of the car by the time he makes this discovery will only be such that the hand brake would stop and hold the car."

This explanation would have done justice to a school physics book! It carefully considered all eventualities, except the one which occurred three years later when a collision took out the controller and left the driver unable to control the tram. The reporter was fortunate enough to have the benefit of a demonstration of the magnetic track brake from the Tramways Manager, Mr. George Webster, and the Chief Engineer Mr. A.R.Williams.

The last new trams

In October 1926 the Manager reported that Cars Nos. 42, 51 and 55 were completely worn out and that three new cars were needed as replacements. The order was then extended to include another three cars, again of the same type except that they had Brush 1202 motors and Brush 3A controllers. As these types were no longer in production they must have been salvaged from scrapped cars. They

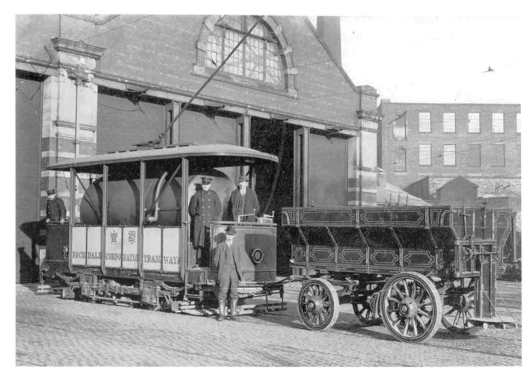

The water tram could also tow a sand trailer. The crew, including former steam tram driver Charles Hodgson, are justly proud of their charge. It was new in 1912 and even the trailer and its wheels are ornately lined out.
(Arthur Hodgson)

became Nos. 90 to 92. Philip Groves notes that as cars 42, 51 and 55 had Brush 1202 motors and were withdrawn in 1926, Cars 90 to 92 probably inherited their equipment.

The replacement of worn-out trams by new Corporation-built rolling stock continued with Car No. 93 in 1927 and No.94 in 1928. They were 4-wheel double deck cars fitted with transverse seats and English Electric top covers and like 86 to 92 they had top lights above the upper saloon windows. They became the last two trams in the fleet.

Car No.23 was undergoing reconstruction in early 1928 but progress must have been slow. The Manager recommended purchasing one top cover, two truck side frames and two motors to accelerate the work. Tenders were not invited. It was decided to fit the car with transverse upholstered seats. It is possible that in its modified form it became car 94.

As a means of modernising cars at low cost, the Manager reported in December 1929 that after carefully examining the open top cars he found that eleven of them were sufficiently strong to take a light type cover. He recommended that these cars be fitted with light canopy tops and that the quotation of English Electric to provide and fit the covers be accepted. The order was placed in February 1930. Cars fitted comprised Nos. 3, 10, 11, 20, 29 and 44 to 49. They were destined to spend less than two years in service in this form.

Also in 1929 English Electric car 89 was fitted with high speed 50 h.p. motors and upholstered seats, with barely 18 months left in service. At the time the decision to abandon the tramways had not been taken. The Tramways Committee members sampled the re-equipped tram as well as a new single Dennis deck bus on 20th March 1929. The bus took them to Castleton where they boarded No. 89 to experience the quality of ride on the new tracks laid by Manchester Corporation on the route to Middleton. At Hollin Lane, Middleton, they re-joined the bus to return to the Town Hall for afternoon tea and speeches. Alderman Clark, the Chairman, stated that trams were still best for busy town centre sections but buses were better for long distances. In an unwitting prediction of future changes, he noted the very high cost of track renewals and that new trams cost more than buses although they lasted much longer. The fact that trams stopped far more often than buses was one of the things that told against them. The Tramways Committee would have to consider cutting the number of stops to speed up the service.

The press reported the event (although they thought it was car 91!):

"Car 91 embodied several new features. The seating on the lower deck is transverse (i.e. similar to buses) and the seats are most comfortably upholstered. This arrangement reduces the seating capacity only by two, 20 as against 22 in the other cars. The new car is fitted with two 50 h.p. motors, as compared to the maximum 42 h.p. on any previous vehicle, and it is decidedly the speediest tram car in the service."
Referring to the ride on the new track they commented:

"Under such conditions all the customary objections to tramcars fall to the ground. Except when entering or leaving loops the running was wonderfully smooth, fast and free from noise."

Despite this glowing endorsement for new trams, their future in Rochdale was sadly very limited.

Abandonments reduce the fleet

Until 1930 only eight trams had been withdrawn. Over 90% of the fleet was still in service. At its maximum there were 88 cars in the fleet. Towards the end of 1930 the scene was about to change radically and irrevocably. Abandonment of the Littleborough and Summit routes in October 1930 was followed by the closures of the Norden and Bamford routes in January 1931. These reduced the tram fleet by 16 cars. Offers were invited for one or more car bodies, with or without the plate glass windows.

By the end of 1931 about 45 trams had been withdrawn leaving another 45 to be withdrawn during 1932. Route closures continued in quick succession with the Bacup route going in May, the Circular, Bury and Thornham routes going in July, and Milnrow in August. The final closure was to Castleton and Manchester on 12th November 1932.

The last tram in service on the last day was No. 80, a fully enclosed double decker only eight years old. A few trams survived into 1933 - Cars Nos. 46, 90 and others from these batches were seen in Mellor Street yard as late as 23rd March 1933.

The end of the trams, almost!

Despite some of Rochdale's trams being less than six years old, all went to the scrap heap, except for some trucks. Research by Philip Groves, who was born in Rochdale and spent his early childhood days there, shows that 15 sets of Brill 21E trucks were purchased by Hull Corporation Tramways from Rochdale Corporation in 1933, after the system had closed. The trucks included box frame 40 horse power DK30B motors, the type fitted to cars 70 to 89.

Hull's tramway closed in 1945 but 42 trams were sold to Leeds City Tramways including 15 with Brill 21E trucks. It is quite likely that these included some from Rochdale. One of the ex-Hull trams, No.96 of 1901, became Leeds works tram No.6 and was used as a stores car, rail grinder and snow sweeper until the end of Leeds trams in 1959. It has now been restored to carry passengers and operates regularly at the Heaton Park Tramway Museum in Manchester. It is just possible that its truck was originally from Rochdale. Unfortunately tramcar trucks did not have chassis numbers!

16. Tramway trackwork.

Borough Surveyor specifies the track

The Committee approved the type of track to be used on the new tramway at their meeting on 18th March 1901 and asked for advertisements to be issued for:

'1,400 tons of steel rail (girder section) according to the design submitted by the Borough Surveyor of both 45ft and 60ft lengths, with the necessary fishplates, bolts, nuts and washers, tie bars, 'anchor' joint and sole plates, points and crossings and drain rails.'

Old narrow gauge steam tram tracks are torn out of the roadway to make way for the new standard gauge electric tram tracks in May 1905.

No time was lost and at the meeting on 1st April 1901 tenders were accepted from Leonard Cooper of Leeds for anchor soleplates, Askham Bros. and Wilson of Sheffield for tie bars and Ibbotson Bros & Co. of Sheffield for nuts and bolts. Tenders for rails, fish plates and cement were invited. The Borough Surveyor was instructed to lay the tramways numbered 15 and 6 and parts of Nos. 18,7,8,9,11,12,13 and 14 without delay using direct labour. Wood paving was to be used in front of places of worship to reduce the noise levels.

The next meeting on 15th April agreed the supply of steel girder rails for straight and curved track and fishplates from P & W McLellan & Co.of Glasgow, to be supplied from Angleur Works near Liège, Belgium. Up to 1,200 tons of cement were to be supplied by Skelsey's Adamant Cement Co. of Hull and were to be delivered either by rail to Rochdale Station or by barge to the Canal Wharf.

Plans showing the mode of construction (see Fig 16.1) were drawn by Mr S S Platt, the Borough Engineer in May 1901. Grooved rails were laid on a 6in concrete base, bolted to upturned rails of the same section at anchor soleplates to provide additional strength (see Fig 16.2). Granite setts 6in wide were then laid on a one inch sand bed to form the carriageway level with the top of the rails. The

setts were laid between the standard gauge rails and for 1ft. 6in. from the outer edge of the rail, as required by the Tramways Act 1870. An alternative paving using 5 in. beechwood blocks was shown with the concrete increased in depth.

Employing direct works to construct such an innovative form of transport demanded experience and skill. Mr William Marshall, having been Permanent Way Foreman to the Bury, Rochdale and Oldham Tramway Company, knew the area and was familiar with tram track, albeit for steam trams. He offered his services and the Committee agreed to appoint him as Permanent Way Foreman, reporting directly to the Borough Surveyor, at a wage of £4 10s per week *(£283)*, including expenses but not night or special work for which he would receive extra. The Committee also appointed Mr Joseph Thorley of Nuneaton to the post of Concreting Foreman at a wage of three guineas per week, £3 3s *(£198)*. All the construction works were carried out by Corporation workmen under the supervision of the Borough Surveyor and his staff with up to 600 men being employed.

The first track is laid

Notice was given to the Road Authority under the Tramways Act 1870 that track laying was to start from the Borough Boundary at Cutgate on Edenfield Road to Norden (Tramway No.18). Under the Rochdale Corporation Act 1900 a plan showing the proposed method of construction and materials to be used was forwarded to the Board of Trade for approval and to the Local and Road Authorities.

A technical description was given by the Borough Surveyor. Rails were 7 inch by 7 inch girder type, 102½ lbs per yard, with a 1⅛ in. by 1⅛in. groove on straight track and 60 ft length rails. On curves of 50 ft. radius or less, rails were about 105 lbs. per yard and mostly 45 ft. lengths. The

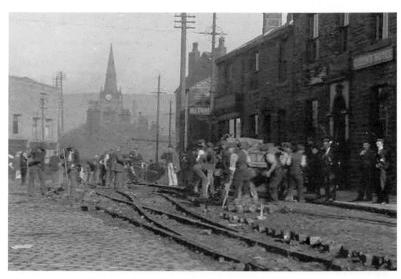

The last steam tram has run and the narrow gauge tracks have to come out to make way for the new standard gauge electric tracks. The poles and span wire for the overhead line have already been erected. Amazingly the conversion was achieved in less than three weeks.

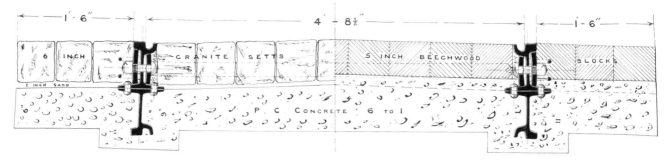

Fig 16.1 A cross section of typical tramway street track in 1901 showing the options for granite sett paving or beechwood blocks.(MTMS)

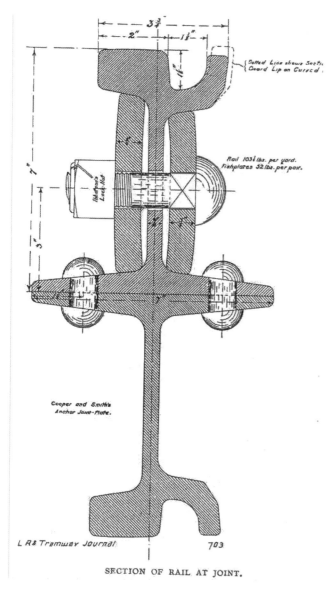

SECTION OF RAIL AT JOINT.

Fig 16.2 Cross section of tram rail joint. A short section of tram rail was bolted to the running rail upside down to strengthen the joint. (MTMS)

fishplates 27 ins. long, weight 53 lbs. per pair, were supplied mainly by Walter Scott of Leeds Steel Works with some from P & W McLennan Ltd. of Glasgow and Angleur Steel Works Ltd, Liege, Belgium. Fishplates were secured to the

rails by six 1 in. diameter bolts with lock nuts. (See Fig 16.3). Each joint was strengthened by a Cooper & Smith's anchor soleplate, 27 ins. long, of similar section to the rails but 'upside down' which was secured to the bottom flange of the rails by six 3/4 in. rivets on each side.

Points and crossings were supplied by Hadfield's Steel Foundry Co. Ltd of Sheffield, the crossings and tongues of the points being of manganese steel. Some of the special trackwork at junctions was supplied by the Lorain Steel Co. Ltd. of Philadelphia, Pennsylvania, U.S.A. and some by Hadfield's. The track was bonded by two 'Neptune' bonds at each joint with cross bonds every 50 yards, double track being bonded together every 100 yards.

All the track was laid on 5 in. to 6 in. of six to one Portland cement concrete with 1 in. of packing composed of three parts of hard granite chippings to pass through a 1/2 in. mesh to one part of Portland cement, with deeper recesses at joints for concreting round the anchor soleplates. Concrete between the rails was finished off with about 11/2 in. of four to one concrete. The sides of the rails were plastered with mortar composed of three parts of sand to one part of Portland cement and the whole was paved with granite setts 6 ins. deep. Joints between the setts were run with an asphalt mixture and finished off with cement grouting. Opposite places of worship, 3 in. by 5 in. creosoted beechwood or Australian hardwood blocks were used in place of granite setts to ensure quieter running during times of divine service.

There must have been some concerns about the tenders for steel girder rails and fishplates. The approval was referred back to the Tramways Committee by the Council meeting on 2nd May and a special meeting of the Committee on 6th May proceeded to rescind the order. Instead 1,000 tons of rail to the 'Salford Section' and 35 tons of fishplates were authorised, from the same sources. In addition 400 tons of the same section rail and 15 tons of fishplates were to be purchased from Walter Scott Limited of Leeds. It was noted that the tie bars would be spaced 7ft 6ins apart.

Yet another special Council meeting was called for 11th May to ratify the changes but it was reported that Walter Scott's tender was based on supplying 1400 tons of rail and that the price would increase by 5/- per ton *(£15.71 p)* if they only supplied 400 tons. The Committee resolved to accept the increased costs. Perhaps they wanted to ensure that at least part of the order went to home producers, or

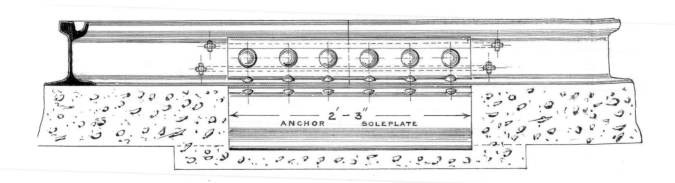

2' - 3"

ANCHOR SOLEPLATE

Fig 16.3 Elevation of fishplate joint. (MTMS)

ELEVATION OF POINT

Track construction on the Norden route at Spotland Bridge in 1901. The tracks from the right are from Spotland Road (formerly Clarke's Lane) and those leading to the left are for the link to the depot on Mellor Street which had not then been built. In the background, the route to the left was the Norden route up Edenfield Road and that to the right was the Spotland route up Rooley Moor Road. All the buildings are still existing, the one centre background being the After Eight Restaurant until 2006. The warehouse on the left was increased to four storeys, as seen in the view of Spotland Bridge on Page 27. (Touchstones Rochdale)

perhaps other operators' experience indicated that better materials were available.

In some of the later work, cross anchors were placed under the rails every 30 ft. or in some cases every 20 ft. and the length of the points was increased from 8 ft. 6 ins. to 12 ft. or 14 ft. Drain rails and boxes were freely placed on the track to intercept rainfall above points and at low lying places.

Where the road width would permit, and the density of the tramcar traffic would justify it, the lines were laid as double track with crossover roads every half mile. Elsewhere track was single with passing places at frequent intervals located so as to enable drivers to see the next passing place in either direction. The steepest gradient was 1 in 11.7 *(8.5%)* on John Street and the sharpest curve was 35 ft. central radius (10.7m). Later measurements showed that Rooley Moor Road near Spotland Bridge was slightly steeper at 1 in 10.6 *(9.4%)*.

Crowds marvel at the new tram tracks at the junction of Drake Street and Oldham Road in the summer of 1904. The conversion from steam to electric traction was completed in four months. (MTMS)

Meetings were being held at ever increasing frequency to cope with the rapid development of the tramway. Another tender, this time for points and crossings, was approved at the Committee on 13th May from the Hadfield Steel Foundry Company of Sheffield. The rail saga continued with an offer from Walter Scott's of Leeds to supply an extra 300 tons of rail and the necessary fishplates. The offer was accepted but the cost is not recorded. One of Borough Surveyor's staff, Mr H. C. Richards, was given the task of inspecting the rails and fishplates before they left the suppliers. The trip to Leeds was not far but the trip to Liège must have been rather more of an adventure.

The first section of rail was ceremoniously laid in Norden on 13th June 1901 by the Chairman of the Norden Urban District Council Tramways Committee, Councillor R. A. L. Hutchinson. A similar ceremony was performed the same day by the Rochdale Tramways Committee Chairman, Councillor W. H. Duncan, at Cutgate, just inside the Rochdale boundary. The whole Tramways Committee of Rochdale was invited to lunch in Norden to celebrate.

More track needed

Almost before the concrete had set, the need for more track was realised. The Borough Surveyor sought approval from the Committee on 8th July for an additional passing loop on Edenfield Road at Bagslate Moor Road and for double track in Bridge Street, (now part of Mellor Street). Approval was given, subject to the normal third party consents. The Board of Trade later agreed, subject to the space between the nearest rail and the kerb being not less than 9' 6" *(2.9m)*. Ten days later another change on the Norden route was approved, this time to replace single track with double track between Spotland Bridge and a point 210 yards *(192m)* west of Willbutts Lane. This required the widening of Edenfield Road and the acquisition of part of St Clement's churchyard although this is not recorded in the minutes.

Round the corner on Meanwood Brow, objections were raised to construction of tram lines but the Committee did not see sufficient reason to alter their plans. Objections also emerged in Blackwater Street from frontagers, pointing out "the inconvenience anticipated in consequence of the unloading of lurries *(sic)* in front of their premises". The Paving Committee was asked to alter the pavement opposite the premises and replace the flagged footpath with a paved crossing. Such concerns are still commonplace today with new light rail systems where they run on street. *[Blackwater Street no longer exists. It ran parallel to, and to the west of, Toad Lane from St Mary's Gate and disappeared with construction of the Exchange Shopping Precinct.]*

There was very little road traffic at the turn of the century and virtually all of it was horse drawn. Nevertheless some control was needed to combat the inevitable disruption caused by construction of street tramways. The Committee requested the Watch Committee to provide the necessary police for the regulation of traffic in streets where tramways were being or would be laid, "as occasion may require". Traffic control was still a problem a few weeks later when the Town Clerk wrote to the Middleton Electric Traction Company stating that unless better arrangements were made for the regulation of traffic, and for shorter lengths of road being taken up at the same time, proceedings would be instituted against them. After many complaints about inconvenience to traffic along Manchester Road, Castleton, the matter was referred to the Chief Constable.

Another track change was approved on 5th August when the Borough Surveyor considered it advisable to shorten the length of the passing place at the top of Blackwater Street on account of the "quick curve" and the type of car adopted. It is not stated whether this refers to the short 4-wheel cars or the longer bogies cars; the precise reasoning seems a little obscure. The Board of Trade disagreed because of the steep gradient and stipulated that the length of double track should be maintained.

Meanwhile, a request from Rochdale Unitarian Church to provide wooden setts outside its chapels on Blackwater Street and Spotland Road to reduce traffic noise was turned down because of the gradients and other factors. However when a similar request was received from St Martin's Church School in Castleton, it was accepted provided that the School Managers paid the extra cost. Traffic noise is not merely a present day problem.

Noise continued to dominate the agenda when a joint meeting of the Tramways and the Paving, Sewering and Scavenging Committees 9th October agreed to recommend wood paving opposite St Edward's School in Castleton Moor but not opposite St. Martin's School, thus reversing their previous decision. The general principle was established with a further recommendation for wood block paving, outside the tramway track, in front of places of worship provided that the managers or trustees paid the extra cost over and above the cost of granite paving, and to pay any extra maintenance costs. This was further clarified by the Tramways Committee on 31st October when a revised resolution specified that "in any case where wood paving shall be laid (except between the rails and for 18 ins. outside thereof opposite places of worship) the extra cost incurred thereby shall be defrayed by the owners of the properties opposite which such wood paving is laid."

Progress on the Norden route was apparently held up by delays in supply of points and crossings from Hadfield's in Sheffield.

On 4th October the Borough Surveyor was asked to defer laying some tramways previously agreed on April 1st. They were:

Tramway No.6 along Hudson Street, Hope Street and Duke Street;

Tramway No.11 along Station Road and Richard Street;

Tramway No. 14 along Molesworth Street and Wood Street.

No reasons were given but none of these sections were ever built, perhaps a realisation that they would not be profitable. The reason for Tramway No.11 was probably the new road proposed to link Drake Street directly with the Station which was eventually constructed in 1906 as Maclure Road. It did not become a tram route until much later in 1924 when tracks were laid providing a similar link to Station Road and Richard Street. Maclure Road will once again be a tram route if Metrolink comes to Rochdale town centre.

An inspection by Major Druitt and Mr A.P.Trotter of the Board of Trade of the works authorised by The Middleton Light Railway Order 1898 was made on 21st March 1902. Mr Sellon, Engineer to the British Electric Traction Company was joined by the Chairman and the Mayor to represent the Tramways Committee, presumably only for the sections in the Rochdale area as the inspection covered the whole system, mostly in the Borough of Middleton.

When Major Druitt and Mr A.P.Trotter inspected the first section of tramway in Rochdale, the Bury Road route, on 15th May 1902 they noted that "the lines are laid in the usual manner, rails 103½lbs per yard, with a 1⅛ in. groove."

Next, a formal application was made to the Board of Trade for a deviation from the deposited plans along the Esplanade. The tracks would be close to the northerly footway instead of in the middle of the carriageway. This may have been to allow construction of the electric tramway while the steam tramway was still in use. Mr Brindle, Secretary of the Bury, Rochdale and Oldham Tramway Company, wrote to the Committee in response to an invitation to comment from the Board of Trade. He referred to the proposal being to "construct and work a tramway on the Esplanade parallel to the Company's lines". They had pointed out to the Board the public danger and impeding of road traffic which would result. Two adjacent double track tramways would indeed have been a major safety hazard. They also considered the proposal to construct the line without their consent "a departure from an honourable undertaking come to during the progress of the Corporation's Tramway Bill". Honour was presumably upheld as the two systems never ran side by side; the last steam tram along the Esplanade ran in June 1904 and the first electric trams began in August.

Track changes in the town centre

Early in 1903 the Borough Surveyor reported on a proposal to change the routing in the town centre and divert the trams from Blackwater Street to continue along St Mary's Gate into Cheetham Street. Some problems had been experienced with the sharp curve from St Mary's Gate into Blackwater Street. At that time the street pattern was quite different to today's layout and Cheetham Street formed a continuation of St Mary's Gate, roughly on the line of the present dual carriageway. St Mary the Baum Church stood on Cheetham Street. The steam tram route ran along Yorkshire Street turning right into Cheetham Street to terminate at Redcross Street. By extending the electric trams they could be linked into the reconstructed steam tramway at this point.

Having carefully considered the possibility, the Borough Surveyor said that it was feasible provided that a single track was laid on the north side of St Mary's Gate not less than 3ft from the kerb with level changes over about 140 yds. There would have to be no objections from property owners, lessees or occupiers on either side of the road but none were expected. An application for a Provisional Order for this section was lodged in October in the 1903/04 Parliamentary session.

More deviations from the deposited plans were approved in March 1903:

- single track in lieu of double track in Manchester Road from Crescent to Manchester Road with loops as necessary;
- single track in lieu of double track in Manchester Road from existing loop at Dane Street to top of Sparth Bottoms Road;
- a loop to be put in at junction of Oldham Road and High Level Road;
- the Terminus Triangle at Town Hall Square to be omitted;
- loops in Drake Street opposite to Water Street and Wellington Hotel to be extended as far as possible towards each other;

- single track in lieu of double track in Oldham Road from Canal Street to Queen Victoria Street with loops as necessary.

Two months later it was decided to retain double track in Manchester Road between Dane Street and the Castle Inn, as on the Parliamentary plans.

The River Roch from which Rochdale gets its name runs right through the town centre in front of the famous Town Hall. But most visitors would not realise it is there because it is culverted for a distance of 1,460 ft *(445m)* between Smith Street and the Esplanade, attracting the title of 'the widest bridge in the world'! There was a bridge across the river at the bottom of Drake Street, Wellington Bridge, but it was not wide enough or strong enough for trams. The plan to cover the river was put forward and readily approved by the Committee in May 1903. No doubt the evil smell of a highly polluted watercourse was an added incentive.

A number of road improvements were agreed to facilitate tramway construction. They included covering the river from Rochdale Bridge to Wellington Bridge, making a new street 15 yards wide *(13.7m)* from Bury Road to Spotland Bridge to give access to the new depot site, and a new street forming a continuation of Blackwater Street from Lord Street across the Manor Estate to the Esplanade. Many main roads were widened when the tramways were built to achieve the minimum 9ft 6in. *(2.9m)* required between the nearest rail and the kerb on double track.

Conversion of steam tracks

The Routes Sub-Committee had been busy deciding on the routes to be converted from steam to electric as well as those to be built new. They recommended the following routes:

- Littleborough Section: Wellington Hotel to Summit via Smith Street, Entwisle Road, Halifax Road and Todmorden Road;

- Cheetham Street and Yorkshire Street to Heybrook Corner;

- Whitworth Section: from Smith Street to Ending via John Street and Whitworth Road;

- Royton Section: from Wellington Hotel to Borough Boundary via Drake Street and Oldham Road;

- Drake Street from junction with Oldham Road to Castle Inn (Manchester Road);

- Milnrow Road from Oldham Road to a point 150 yds or thereabouts beyond Newbold Street;

- High Level Road, Lower Tweedale Street and Tweedale Street from Oldham Road to Manchester Road;

- Heywood Section, from Wellington Hotel to Borough Boundary via South Parade, Esplanade, Manchester Road and Bury Road (Marland). *('Bury Road' is now Bolton Road).*

These were all existing steam tram routes except the part of the Whitworth route between Smith Street and Yorkshire Street, Milnrow Road and the Tweedale Street route.

All the track reconstruction and new construction works were to be carried out by the Borough Surveyor with the following order of priority:

1. South Parade to Castle Inn.
2. Tweedale Street (completion).
3. Milnrow Road (completion).
4. Wellington Hotel to High Level Road.
5. Heywood Section as far as Borough Boundary.
6. Littleborough Section (including connection from Cheetham Street to Heybrook Corner.
7. Remaining routes to be determined.

Tenders were invited for all the necessary rails, fish plates, tie bars, sole and anchor plates, points and crossings, bolts and nuts, cement, overhead electrical equipment, rail bonds and cables. Messrs. Bayliss, Jones and Bayliss of Wolverhampton won the tender for 54 tons of tie bars and Walter Scott Ltd of Leeds won the supply of 2,400 tons of rails in 60 ft lengths for straights and 45 ft lengths for curves and 100 tons of fishplates. Leonard Cooper Junior, also of Leeds, won the tender for 2,100 combined joint and soleplates.

Supply of points and crossings went to Hadfield's Steel Foundry of Sheffield but special trackwork including the depot fan went to The Lorain Steel Company of London (presumably the same company that previously supplied rails from Philadelphia). More tenders invited were for wood paving and basalt lava setts. Messrs. Armstrong Addison of Sunderland won the supply of creosoted beech wood blocks for paving. Track laying on the new sections of tramway progressed during the summer on Milnrow Road and Tweedale Street, the latter being nearly complete by mid October.

Anyone involved in new light rail systems in British cities will know only too well that the cost and disruption of moving underground services is a major problem. On a smaller scale, the problem existed a century ago. The Tramways Committee wanted the Gas and Electricity Committee to share the cost of diverting the gas main in the Esplanade between Willow Bank and the iron bridge. Not surprisingly this was rejected and the Tramways Committee had to reluctantly accept bearing the whole cost. However when it came to laying ducts for the tramway feeders in Manchester Road, the Gas and Electricity Committee agreed to share the cost provided that extra ducts were included for their cables.

More changes to the plans

Yet more changes to the deposited plans were approved by the Committee when a long list of minor alterations to passing loops and single or double track lengths was submitted by the Tramway Routes Sub-Committee in January 1904. The following month it was decided to consider doubling tracks on other parts of the system. Plans for a double junction at the north east corner of the Tweedale Street and Manchester Road junction were approved.

On 22nd February the Committee agreed to these changes:

- double track in place of single track in Manchester Road between King Street South and the 'Windmill Inn' at Sudden;

- double track in place of single track in Smith Street and Entwisle Road between Duncan Street and George Street;

- double track in place of single track in Oldham Road between the 'Bridge Inn' and Canal Street with interlaced track over the Lock Bridge;
- double track in place of single track in Mellor Street between Bury Road and south side of No.1 Bridge over the River Spodden.

A proposal to build a connecting link along Wood Street between Oldham Road and Milnrow Road was not approved. It is difficult to see what operational benefit this would have been on its own. There was an earlier proposal for a link up Molesworth Street which could then have run along Wood Street to Oldham Road and the up High Level Road to reach the Station with the aim of providing a route from Yorkshire Street to the Station via Molesworth Street but this idea was not pursued. However the proposal to cover the River Roch to form the central station for the tramways was approved, creating the focal feature of Rochdale's tramways which is still there today in the form of The Butts. In March the Committee approved the plans for a Waiting Room and Ladies Conveniences to be erected on the river covering which was to become a familiar part of Rochdale's town centre landscape for the next few decades.

Track laying in Drake Street and Oldham Road continued throughout the spring of 1904. In May the Borough Surveyor was authorised to proceed with construction of the Heywood Section between the Town Hall and Sudden. This could only be done when the steam trams had ceased operation, an event which was forced on the Company on 10th June, much to the surprise and consternation of the good burghers of Heywood. Relations between the authorities were not close!

Relations with Littleborough Council seemed more cordial. When the Chairman of the Littleborough Tramways Committee asked on what terms Rochdale would undertake the reconstruction of the existing steam tramways, and the extension to Summit, the Rochdale Committee agreed to take on the work, subject to Littleborough agreeing to the pay the whole cost. Littleborough were however worried that they would lose their steam tram service as a result of the arbitration proceedings but were assured that Rochdale would do everything possible to keep them running until re-construction work commenced.

By 27th June 1904 the tracks along the Esplanade between Dane Street and the Town Hall were ready for inspection. This link was important as it would enable the Bury Road service to be extended into the town centre instead of terminating at Dane Street, now the site of Asda. In their customary efficiency, the Board of Trade confirmed that Major Druitt would make his inspection on 6th July, only nine days later. He must have been satisfied as passenger services began the same day.

In fact Major Druitt completed his report on 7th July and it was relayed by the Board of Trade to Rochdale Council on 11th July and reported to Committee on 18th July, less than a fortnight later. Once again, approvals had been given in rapid time. In his report the Major commented that

he had inspected "part of Tramway No 10, 1 furlong 5.5 chains in length, in the Esplanade, a double line commencing opposite the Town Hall and terminating by a junction with Tramway No.8 in Dane Street. The track is in good order and the overhead equipment similar to that already approved." He allowed a speed of 12 mph on the Esplanade, the highest speed yet approved on the system.

Work was progressing well on the river covering in the town centre, attracting crowds of people every day. Rochdale Observer reported on 6th July:

"There is general admiration for the arrangements, which will be as convenient for traffic as any tramway centre in the country. With the rails running on either side of the island platforms, the tram cars will arrive and depart with the minimum of congestion and the freeing

Tracks using grooved tram rail were set in granite setts as clearly shown in this view in Littleborough. Note that the eighteen inches either side of the rails, which was the responsibility of the tramway operator to maintain, is not differentiated in the pattern of the setts, as was often the case with tramways. (LHAS)

of South Parade for other traffic will diminish the present risk of accident. Cars from Drake Street will cross the river covering between the platforms, turning onto the line in The Butts by a curve."

Work was also progressing on the construction of the new road alongside the Car Shed which was to become Mellor Street. The Board of Trade were asked to inspect the Mellor Street route as soon as it was ready, and any other route sections that were completed by then. The inspection was fixed for July 20th. The Committee met at the Esplanade near the Town Hall and boarded a special tram to Mellor Street where Major Druitt made his official inspection.

The Major maintained his customary efficiency, submitting his report on 21st July recommending the Board of Trade to sanction the use of the tramway for passenger traffic. The route was a double track section, '3 furlongs 6.80 chains in length' *(740m),* linking the existing tracks at the junction of Bury Road and Bridge Street (now Mellor Street) with those at Spotland Bridge, thus uniting for the first time the two separated sections of Rochdale's electric tram routes. A speed limit of 12 mph was imposed, except round the curve at the bridge over the River Spodden which was 4 mph. A compulsory stop was required in Mellor Street before crossing Bury Road. The Norden service was diverted to operate via Mellor Street from 23rd July.

Track reconstruction was proceeding on a number of route sections and in August 1904, Royal Assent was given to the Rochdale Corporation Tramways Provisional Order allowing work to start on the Healey Section. Construction started at Cheetham Street. Meanwhile the Oldham Road route between High Level Road and King's Road was ready for inspection. By the end of August the routes to Sudden along Manchester Road and along Oldham Road to the Borough boundary were complete.

The Major returns for more inspections

Major Druitt returned to Rochdale yet again on 17th August to inspect the circular route from South Parade via Drake Street, Oldham Road, High Level Road, the Station, Tweedale Street and Manchester Road to The Butts. He approved the route subject to completion of the overhead equipment. He was not impressed with being asked to inspect the route before it was complete. The Board of Trade, when asked to arrange the inspection of Oldham Road, stressed that it must be complete in all respects and ready for use and they would require an assurance to that effect.

Speed limits were imposed on the circular route:

Lower Tweedale Street and Tweedale Street:	10 mph
Manchester Road:	12 mph upward 10 mph downward
Drake Street:	12 mph
except on the curve at The Crescent and between Milnrow Road and the Butts, descending:	6 mph
High Level Road:	12 mph
except round the curves into Oldham Road and into Station Yard:	4 mph
Oldham Road:	10 mph
except between Elbow Lane and Milnrow Road until road widening completed:	4 mph
On curve between Tweedale Street and Manchester Road:	4 mph.

Compulsory stops were made as follows:

Tweedale Street, before crossing Milkstone Road in each direction;

Drake Street, before crossing Water Street and at the bottom before crossing into The Butts;

Oldham Road, before crossing Milnrow Road on the downward journey.

Official records give 17th August 1904, the day of the inspection, as the start of service but other sources give 20th August or 27th August. As the overhead was reportedly not complete on 17th, a later date seems more plausible.

The inspection of the Oldham Road section between High Level Road and King's Road followed on 2nd September and it was opened for passengers the same day. Major Druitt specified a speed limit of 12 mph except for the section under the Lancashire and Yorkshire railway bridge which was limited to 8 mph. Compulsory stops were required at Crawford Street and before Woodbine Street inward. It is interesting to note the authority which had come to be invested in the Inspector who could authorise public operation on the spot, in advance of formal written authority from the Board.

The track connection between Blackwater Street and Cheetham Street via St Mary's Gate which had been proposed about 18 months earlier was finally approved and the necessary points and crossings provided. In September work began on reconstructing the section of tracks in Yorkshire Street between St.James's Church and Heybrook corner.

Completion of route sections were coming thick and fast. Another inspection took place on Wednesday 5th October covering three routes: the outer part of Oldham Road between King's Road and the Borough boundary, Milnrow Road to the terminus at Firgrove and Manchester Road between Tweedale Street and Sudden. Major Druitt had been promoted to Lieutenant Colonel, perhaps in recognition of his frequent successful trips to Rochdale! He arrived just before three o'clock and boarded a special single deck car which was waiting for him at the railway station.

The car proceeded along High Level Road to Oldham Road and then to the Summit Inn at Royton, presumably having reversed over the crossover in Drake Street. A small group including schoolchildren had assembled to welcome him. Alderman Cunliffe created a diversion by calling for three cheers to signify the occasion. There was considerable interest from onlookers along the other routes inspected.

Lieut.Col. Druitt recommended they be sanctioned for public use subject to a number of comments. Only single deck cars could be used on the Milnrow route because of the low railway bridges. Some guard wiring was not complete on Oldham Road and Manchester Road. Speed limits were 14 mph on Oldham Road except when passing Broad Lane outward where it was 4 mph. In Milnrow Road it was 8 mph from Oldham Road to Fishwick Street, 4 mph round the corner at Fishwick Street and then 12 mph to the terminus. In Manchester Road it was 10 mph outwards from Tweedale Street to Bury Road and 12 mph inwards.

Most corners at junctions were limited to 4 mph, a limitation commonly applied to tramways in Britain and which still applies today to some junctions on the Blackpool tramway.

Passenger service on all three lines began straight away, anticipating once again a favourable outcome from the inspection. At the Thornham boundary with Royton UDC the tracks met Oldham Corporation Tramways tracks which they had reconstructed from the former narrow gauge steam tramway. Oldham began electric operation on 1st November 1904 but cars did not stray across the boundary for another eighteen months. Through operation between Norden and Hathershaw began on 1st May, 1906.

The next inspection was arranged for 23rd November 1904 for the St.Mary's Gate, Cheetham Street and Healey Section. Once again Lieut.Col. Driutt approved the routes for passenger traffic, specifying speed limits as follows:

Spotland Road	8 mph
St Mary's Gate	4 mph
Cheetham Street,	
(St Mary's Gate – Toad Lane)	4 mph
Cheetham Street, (remainder)	8 mph
Yorkshire Street	8 mph
Whitworth Road	
(Yorkshire Street –	
Cronkeyshaw Common)	10 mph
Whitworth Road	
(Cronkeyshaw Common - Healey)	14 mph

As before 4mph was the limit round corners. A compulsory stop was imposed in Whitworth Street in both directions before crossing Princess Street.

Tenders for granite setts for the Littleborough conversion were accepted from five suppliers. A total of 4,000 tons were shared between quarries in Penmaenmawr, Carnarvon, Pwllheli, Keswick and Darlington. A lifetime later when Metrolink needed granite setts for Balloon Street in Manchester they came from Portugal!

More double track was envisaged when in January 1905 it was resolved to install double track instead of single track with loops on Bolton Road between Marland Old Road and the Borough boundary.

The next inspection took place on 26th January 1905 this time for the section of Yorkshire Street up to Heybrook. The Board of Trade's letter confirming his approval to the section for passenger operation was dated 31st January. The Littleborough route was still being operated by steam trams but the track was in poor condition. As late as January 1905, only months before steam tram operation ended, repairs were authorised to continue until 1st February.

Reconstruction and conversion of the steam tramway to electric traction began on 27th March 1905, beginning at the terminus at Littleborough Church. As the last steam tram to Littleborough did not run until 11th May it seems likely that the service was progressively cut back from Littleborough Church, as had happened with conversion of the Healey route the previous year.

The inspection of the Bolton Road section took place on 13th April 1905. In accordance with procedures, Lieut.Col. Driutt submitted his report in time to enable the Board of Trade to send the report approving the section and the certificate of fitness on 18th April.

The next inspection was arranged for 29th May 1905 for the Heybrook to Littleborough route. The opportunity was taken to re-inspect parts of the Norden and Bury Road routes to review speed limits. The Board of Trade reported on 6th June that the section had been approved with the following speed limits:

Halifax Road	14 mph
Corner between Entwisle Road	
and Halifax Road	4 mph
Yorkshire Street	4 mph
Entwisle Road to be considered when works complete.	
New Road, Featherstall Road	
and Church Street	10 mph

Existing speed restrictions were revised as follows (original speed limits in brackets):

Dane Street and Bridge Street	12 mph (8 mph)
Bury Road	14 mph (10 mph)
Spotland Road, Spotland Bridge	
to Hudson Street	12 mph ascending (8 mph)
Edenfield Road	14 mph (10 mph).

Steam tramway finally replaced

Reconstruction of the steam tramway to standard gauge electric traction was proceeding apace and in June 1905 work was in progress in Entwisle Road and Smith Street. New track construction on roads where steam trams had never run was under way on John Street, and Church Street and Todmorden Road in Littleborough. Lieut.Col. Driutt approved the John Street, Smith Street

Crowds surround the first tram to reach Summit on the extension from Littleborough. The date is shown as 10 August 1905 although official records give 12th August as the date of the Board of Trade inspection and the first passenger service. (LHAS)

and Entwisle Road tramways on 4th July with a strict recommendation that all cars used on John Street be fitted with track brakes on account of the steep gradient. It was also required that all cars stop in John Street and Whitworth Road before crossing Yorkshire Street. He subsequently imposed a compulsory stop downhill on John Street at Pagan Street (now spelt Pagen Street) where the gradient was 1 in 11.5 *(8.7%)*. John Street was to be the scene of some spectacular tram accidents.

Lieut.Col. Druitt also travelled to Littleborough to inspect the final sections of the route in Church Street including the triangle at Railway Street (Littleborough Square) and once more gave his approval. The inspection of the last section from Littleborough up to Summit was arranged for 12th August and public service began the same day. The extension was always operated as a separate shuttle, usually half hourly with one single deck tram, with more frequent service at weekends when it was a popular destination for day trips. Summit was the north easterly extremity of the south Lancashire standard gauge network that once stretched as far as Liverpool.

The speed of conversion from narrow gauge steam tracks to standard gauge electric tracks was quite amazing. The Royton route took under five months in 1904, the Heywood route four months, and the Healey route just two months towards the end of 1904. The Littleborough route took only **eighteen days** in May 1905. Clearly the Borough Surveyor was learning by experience and each successive conversion improved on the closure time needed.

Automation arrived in November 1905 when it was decided to purchase one Turner's Patent Automatic Point Shifter for a trial. This was installed at the junction of Oldham Road and Milnrow Road and must have been deemed a success as four months later, seven more point shifters were ordered, one being installed at the top of John Street on a trial basis. However two years later it was reported that the large magnet coils in the point controllers at the Butts and top of John Street had failed so spare coils were ordered.

Following a request to raise the speed limit, Lieut.Col. Druitt was back in Rochdale on 20th December 1905 to inspect the Sudden section to the Borough Boundary. He approved an increase from 12 mph to 16 mph, the highest speed approved so far on the system. The new route section from the Borough boundary to Heywood was inspected the same day and the first car ran through to Heywood at 4.35 p.m.

Another small section of double track in place of single track was proposed in March 1906 for about 130 yards on Bury Road opposite the Cemetery. Board of Trade approval was received within the month. It was completed in April at a cost of £444 10s 0d *(£27,100)*. In June 1906 Oldham Road was widened between Elbow Lane and Milnrow Road enabling double track to be constructed in place of the previous temporary track.

Track repairs already

Surprisingly, track repairs were needed after only a short time in use. In July 1906, barely four years after the first tram had run, the Borough Surveyor pointed out that

repairs were required to the permanent way in Dane Street, Bridge Street, Mellor Street and Manchester Road. He was given approval to proceed with the most urgent repairs up to a cost of £80 *(£4,882)*. A month later more track repairs were needed, this time in Whitworth Road, Oldham Road, Cheetham Street 'and other streets' at a cost of £85 4s 0d *(£5,200)*. Yet more repairs were needed by March 1907 when the Committee visited Littleborough and Summit by special car to inspect the track. Approval was given to spend up to £150 *(£9,153)*. Small sums continued to be spent at frequent intervals as repairs became necessary.

In August 1906 approval was finally given to the reconstruction of the tracks at the junction of Blackwater Street and St Mary's Gate. On 28th September the new tracks in Blackwater Street between St Mary's Gate and Lord Street were inspected and approved by Major J.W. Pringle, R.E. on behalf of the Board of Trade. After much debate the Committee resolved to operate the Spotland service to Lord Street instead of Cheetham Street, reverting to the situation when the route opened in 1902. The service began on 29th September 1906, producing a significant increase in revenue.

Keeping the tracks clear in bad weather conditions could be a major battle. The winter of 1906/7 saw two severe snowstorms which disrupted traffic and caused increased expenditure on salting. While the tramway had snowbrooms and snowploughs to remove snow from the tracks, and trams were in any event guided by their rails, other road vehicles sometimes took advantage of the cleared path, to the detriment of the trams for whom it had been cleared.

A further proposal to substitute double track for single track was made in January 1907 for a short section of Milnrow Road between Oldham Road and Walker Street *(this section is now Chichester Street)*. The proposal was deferred.

In July 1909 tenders were invited for the points and crossings required for the new street between Blackwater Street and the Esplanade. Somewhat surprisingly it was again won by an American company, Messrs. Lorain of Johnstown, Pennsylvania who also supplied the rails and fishplates.

Construction reaches Bacup and Milnrow

In January 1910 tenders were invited for materials to construct the Whitworth extension. The following month Mr George Law of Kidderminster was awarded the contract to construct the permanent way for the Whitworth Tramways. By May the work was well under way. Indeed construction was so rapid that in June Lieut.Col. Druitt was able to inspect the section between Ending and Church Street, Whitworth and give it his customary approval. On 20th July he inspected the next section to Station Road, Facit and gave provisional sanction for public operation. Thus Whitworth once again had trams after an amazing gap of nearly twenty years.

The next section to Lands Gate, Shawforth was approved in September, following confirmation from the Board of Trade on 9th August that the Bacup Light Railway Order 1910 had been made. Tenders for materials and construction were promptly invited. At the same time, the Clerk to Milnrow Urban District Council wrote stating that the Provisional Order for the Milnrow tramway had been confirmed and asking the Committee to proceed with construction as quickly as possible. Milnrow asked again in September for an early date but were told that construction of their section would have to wait until early 1911 because Rochdale were too busy with the Whitworth and Bacup construction. Tenders for construction of the Whitworth Tramways (No.2) and Bacup Light Railway were awarded on 15th February 1911 to Wm. Underwood and Company of Dukinfield with Walter Scott supplying rails and fishplates and Hadfield's supplying points and crossings.

Application was made to the Board of Trade in September 1910 for permission to lay double track instead of single track in Blackwater Street and part of Milnrow Road and Whitworth Road, near St James Church. The Board questioned the doubling of track in Blackwater Street and the matter was deferred. Consent was given to Milnrow Road but an inquiry was to be held regarding Whitworth Road. Meanwhile construction of the tramway in the new street Newgate was proceeding. Lieut.Col. Druitt inspected Newgate on 2nd November and gave provisional approval for operation. On the same day he held the inquiry into doubling track in Whitworth Road and gave approval to doubling between Yorkshire Street and Rope Street.

The new Newgate link was opened on 3rd November 1910 enabling the Spotland route to reach the Tramway Centre with all the other services. The track layout then took on the form which it was to retain for the rest of the life of the tramway. The track layout is shown in the Town Centre plan (inside back cover). The layout of the overhead was delightfully simple with only one facing frog at the bottom of Newgate. However the trolley poles on any trams not following a regular route had to be changed manually between the parallel wires on each side of the island.

More disappointment awaited Milnrow who in January 1911 learned that Rochdale intended to widen and raise the levels of Milnrow Road at Firgrove Bridge over the Rochdale Canal which would not allow work on the tramway to start until the roadworks were completed. Furthermore, Rochdale could not supervise works so far apart as Milnrow and Bacup simultaneously and therefore Milnrow could not be started until Bacup was finished. Milnrow protested at the delay and Rochdale responded by instructing the Manager to prepare specifications and quantities so that work could start as soon as practicable. Tenders were eventually invited in June 1911. George Law of Kidderminster was awarded permanent way construction with Walter Scott again supplying rails and fishplates and Hadfields the points and crossings. In August Mr. W. J. Gale of Kidderminster was appointed Assistant Engineer to supervise the works at a salary of £3 (£189) per week.

A new type of point controller was installed at the junction of Oldham Road and High Level Road and put into operation on 17th March 1911. Its main advantage was that no box or pillar was needed on the footpath. It gave satisfactory results.

Lieut.Col. Druitt inspected the Whitworth No. 2 tramway and the Bacup Light Railway on 26th July 1911 and provisionally sanctioned their use. (Some records show tram operation actually started on 25th July 1911).

Speed limits were specified as 16 m.p.h.in Market Street from Healey to Facit and 12 m.p.h. in Market Street between Church Street and Tong Lane, between Buxton Street and Land Gate and in Shawforth. Maximum speed through facing points was 4 m.p.h.

On the Bacup section speed limits were 16 m.p.h in Rochdale Road between Greenhill and the Borough boundary, 12 m.p.h. between St James's Street and Greenhill and 10 m.p.h. in St. James's Street. Bridge Street and all facing points were limited to 4 m.p.h.

The question of maintenance of the road within the statutory limits, normally between the running rails and for 18ins. each side, was always a subject of debate between tramway operator and highway authority (and still is with today's tramways!). A Joint Committee with the Paving etc. Committee recommended in September 1911 on the existing arrangements as follows:

1) The Borough Surveyor to be solely in charge of the upkeep of the paving and incidental work within the tramway limits, and have charge of the men on this work within the Borough.

2) The Paving etc. Committee to be paid the cost of such upkeep, except that the Paving etc. Committee will bear the cost of all setts required for renewals within the Borough.

3) The necessity for repairs or renewal of rails, points and crossings and similar work, or for any alteration in the method of packing and bedding of rail etc. to be determined by the Tramways Manager, the work to be carried out by the Borough Surveyor.

4) The maintenance of the tramway work within the districts of Norden, Littleborough, Wardle and the portion in Whitworth at Ending carried out under the 1900 Act, to be under the direction of the Tramways Manager.

5) The services of the Permanent Way Foreman to be transferred to the Tramway Depot during the winter period when repairs are suspended.

Lieut.Col. Druitt was back in Rochdale on 12th December 1911 to inspect Milnrow Tramways No. 1. He gave his provisional approval and trams began operating beyond Firgrove as far as Kiln Lane in Milnrow on the same day. Formal approval and sanction to use electrical power on this section was received from the Board of Trade on 23rd December.

Three months later on 1st March 1912 Lieut.Col. Druitt inspected the last section of the Milnrow route from Kiln Lane to Huddersfield Road, the Milnrow Tramways No.2. Again he provisionally sanctioned public operation and it was followed up with formal approval and sanction to use electrical power from the Board of Trade. This stipulated speed limits:

16 m.p.h.	Rochdale Road between Rochdale boundary and Whitehead Street.
14 m.p.h.	Newhey Road between Charles Street and Royds Street.
10 m.p.h.	Newhey Road between Royds Street and the terminus near Huddersfield Road.

MILNROW ROAD SCENES

The Milnrow route originally terminated at Firgrove because the canal bridge forming the boundary between Rochdale and Milnrow was too narrow. Combination bogie car No.33 of 1905 is ready to return to Bury Road via the town centre. An old steam tram body serves as a passenger shelter.
(Eric Fielding)

Tram Terminus, Firgrove.   809

Combination bogie car No. 35 waits at the Firgrove terminus at Newbold Street sometime between 1905 and 1911. The old steam tram body serves as a shelter for waiting passengers. The scene is deserted apart from one youth propping up the stone wall.
(Eric Fielding)

Another view of Firgrove terminus with Car 36 ready to cross the town to Bury Road. A group of children and adults join the crew for the photograph. In 1911 the route was extended to Milnrow and the following year to its final terminus in New Hey.
(Eric Fielding)

8 m.p.h.	Dale Street between Station Road and Charles Lane.
6 m.p.h.	Rochdale Road between Whitehead Street and Weston Street. Dale Street between Bridge Street and Station Road.
4 m.p.h.	Through facing points, whether fixed or movable. Rochdale Road between Western Street and Bridge Street. In Bridge Street. On the curve between Bridge Street and Dale Street.

Operation started on 1st March. This proved to be the penultimate extension of Rochdale's tramways and the last to be opened for another twelve years.

In September 1915 the Manager reported that a number of rail joints were had deteriorated, noting that some sections of track were already over ten years old. It was agreed that 350 rail joints should be welded. A year later in September 1916 the track in John Street was found to be in urgent need of renewal. As it was difficult to obtain new rails in wartime it was agreed to lift the little worn track in Cheetham Street which was not being used and relay it in John Street. New crossings for the John Street/Yorkshire Street junction from Titan Trackwork could not be obtained until early in 1919.

During the war years, maintenance of the permanent way became increasingly difficult with shortages of labour and materials. Only absolutely essential repairs were made resulting in a considerable backlog of work.

In January 1920 the manager reported that 260 yds *(238m)* of the single track in Bridge Street from the Bury Road corner to the Electricity Works needed renewing. He suggested it should be laid with double track and the Committee agreed. Ministry of Transport approval to double tracking was received in April 1920, despite objections from some frontagers. The Paving Committee wanted the Tramways Committee to pay the whole bill for re-paving the street as well as laying the track but the Tramways Committee thought the Paving Committee should make a fair contribution. A compromise was reached for the Paving Committee to pay for concreting the road outside the statutory 18ins. from the rails and the Tramways Committee paying for half the cost of lifting and relaying the setts in these areas. The total cost was £6,905 *(£208,920)* of which the Paving Committee met £1,457 *(£44,080)*.

The John Street/Smith Street junction was next to be renewed with rails and crossings supplied by Hadfields in March 1920. Pointwork also needed replacing on the Healey, Littleborough and Marland sections, this time Titan Trackwork being the supplier. During 1920/21 trackwork

was renewed along the whole of Dane Street and Blackwater Street curve in addition to John Street/Yorkshire Street and Whitworth Road and the points and crossings at Drake Street, the Esplanade and on the Littleborough Section. The single track along Bridge Street was relaid as double track.

Electric welding of rail joints across the system was completed in 1921 and the track was reported to be in very fair condition.

A length of 220 yds *(201m)* of double track in The Esplanade was renewed in 1923, the work being carried out before completion of the river covering scheme. The covering of the river from Drake Street to Weir Street required more track work. The sections of river covering are shown in Table 16.1 below. A length of track in Smith Street was removed and replaced with a temporary track during construction. The terminus for Littleborough and Bacup cars was moved to Duncan Street (which no longer exists). The tramway junction at Smith Street/John Street was re-laid at a cost of £2,491 14s 6d *(£92,400)*.

Table 16.1	River covering dates.			
Section	**From**	**To**	**Started**	**Completed**
1	Rochdale Bridge (Yorkshire Street)	Wellington Bridge (Drake Street)	May 1903	July 1904
2	Yorkshire Street	Newgate	April 1909	July 1910
3	Newgate	Town Meadows (Theatre Street)	June 1922	August 1924
4	Drake Street	Weir Street	September 1923	March 1926

Rochdale's last new tramway

In February 1924, Titan Trackwork won the tender for supplying special trackwork for the Maclure Road and Tweedale Street route. The Borough Surveyor prepared plans showing a typical cross section (see Fig 16.4) with some dimensions reduced from those of the initial designs in 1901. Granite setts were now 4in by 5in and the sand bed was only $3/4$ in. The statement of materials to be used specified:

The Rails to be B.S.S. No.1 (weight per yard 103.7 lbs) for straight track, and for sharp curves B.S.S. No.7c (weight per yard 109.7 lbs.).
Points and Crossings to be of Manganese Steel.
The Joints on the straight track to be Thermit Welded and one 4/0 Copper Bond fixed.
The Joints at the Points and Crossings to be made by B.S.S. Fishplates 2 ft long weight per pair 56½lbs, and fixed with 6 1in bolts and locknuts, also two 4/0 Copper Bonds to be fixed.
Cross bonds to be fixed 50 yards apart.
Mild Steel Tie bars 2 in x 3/8in at 7 ft. 6 in. centres on straight track and at 5 ft. centres on curves.
The Foundation to consist of Portland Cement Concrete of a minimum depth of 6 in.
The Paving to be of Granite Setts 5 in deep and the joints racked with chippings and grouted with a mixture of pitch and creosote oil.

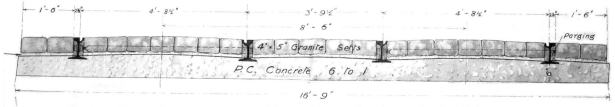

Fig 16.4 The track cross section used for the Maclure Road extension in 1924. It is little different from the original design except for slightly smaller setts. (MTMS)

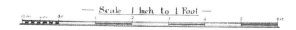

Not a lot had changed in nearly 25 years, indeed this form of construction would still be good today.

In July 1924 the Borough Surveyor submitted plans for the widening of Milnrow Road railway bridge including double tracking between Walker Street (now Chichester Street at this point) and Moss Street. The plans were approved.

Work to connect the Rochdale and Middleton tracks at Sudden, consequent upon the acquisition of the Middleton company, began on 14th July 1925. It cost £2,190. *(£66,260)*

On 3rd December 1925 the completed river covering at Smith Street was tested according to Ministry of Transport requirements and was found to be satisfactory.

In January 1927 a decision was taken to widen the bridges across the railway and the Rochdale Canal on Manchester Road at Castleton. The opportunity was taken to replace the single track tramway with double track over the bridges between the railway bridge and Albion Street. In June the Ministry of Transport agreed to meet half the cost of removing the existing track from its present position to the centre of the road, provided it was done at the same time as the bridge widening. Loan sanction for the Corporation's contribution of £2,623 *(£108,630)* and Ministry of Transport approval to the works under Section 24 of the Middleton Light Railways Order, 1896 were received in November 1927. The works were finally completed in October 1929 and the through tram service between Rochdale and Manchester resumed on 14th October.

More track reconstruction was needed to permanent way in poor condition. Renewal work began on Manchester Road on the Sudden section and a portion of the Castleton route, track in Smith Street and Entwisle Road, and on Whitworth Road from Cronkeyshaw Common to Shawclough Road at Healey.

New rails, fish plates, points and crossings were still being obtained by tender at not infrequent intervals. One such order in May 1927 called for the supply of 300 tons of rails and four tons of fishplates from Messrs.A. McBean & Sons with Titan Trackwork supplying points and crossings. Some of this investment would have a life of less than five years.

More track repairs

Manchester Road needed more repairs in January 1928. Track renewals were approved for the sections between Abbott Street and Kingsland, and between Samuel Street and Castleton railway bridge. In June The Borough Surveyor submitted plans and estimates for reconstructing the tramway from Sudden to the Borough boundary including doubling the track and the necessary overhead line equipment. It was necessary in some places to set the kerbs back to create the full 9' 6" required between the nearest rail and the kerb. Consent was needed under Section 24 of the Middleton Light Railway Order, 1898 to lay down a double line in lieu of single line at the locations indicated on the submitted plans. Approval was obtained in September 1928 and arrangements were made for the work to start in March 1929. Loan sanction for the works cost of £43,858 *(£1.83m)* was obtained in October 1928.

The track across Lock Bridge on Oldham Road, over the Rochdale Canal, was originally laid as interlaced track. In April 1929 the Borough Engineer recommended that it be re-laid as double track.

Despite the impending demise of the trams, at least on the Littleborough route, a budget item of £52,000 *(£2.13m)* was included by the Borough Surveyor in the list of highway the schemes to be submitted for Ministry of Transport approval in August 1929. It was earmarked for the 'reconstruction of such tramways as may be approved by the Council'. However, the Ministry replied that the cost of reconstruction of tramways was not eligible for assistance from the Road Fund. Undeterred, an application for the same sum was made to the Unemployment Grants Committee.

When the Borough Surveyor asked whether the Committee wanted to relay the tracks in Bolton Road which were affected by a road widening scheme, they decided not to take any action. They probably had in mind replacing the trams with buses to avoid the high cost of trackworks, as had been the case on the Littleborough route.

In December 1929 the Borough Surveyor and the Manager reported that the condition of the tracks on a number of roads in the Borough required maintenance to keep them in a usable condition for the remainder of the loan period. The list included:

Rooley Moor Road
Whitworth Road
Entwisle Road and Halifax Road
Oldham Road
Edenfield Road
Milnrow Road
Newgate and Yorkshire Street crossings
Drake Street
Tweedale Street

Together, these streets made up most of the remaining tram network. The estimated cost of repairs was £28,000 (£1.15m). The scheme was approved in principle subject to obtaining a grant from the Unemployment Grants Committee towards the cost. When the Ministry of Transport asked in April 1930 for further information about the application, the Committee deferred consideration. The Ministry also asked whether in the event of the re-construction of the tramway in Milnrow Road the Corporation would be prepared to undertake to construct the tramway loop near the Oldham branch Railway in the centre of the carriageway. The undertaking was given. However in September 1930 the Ministry indicated that the matter was being held without a decision. They had probably got wind of the impending tramway abandonment and may even have encouraged it.

The Royal Commission on Transport completed its work at the end of 1930 and was distinctly anti-tram, recommending that no additional tramways should be constructed, and that they should gradually disappear and give place to other forms of transport. Further information is included in Chapter 21.

The Committee subsequently tried to obtain grants from the Unemployment Grants Committee for the re-instatement of the roads after lifting tramway track which had been abandoned. This time the reply was that no further grants were being made for road or bridge works and the scheme was therefore no longer eligible.

In January 1930 the Borough Surveyor needed some used tram rails for repair work so permission was given to lift the disused tracks in High Level Road for that purpose. Later that year rails were removed from the Halifax Road route for repairs elsewhere.

A 'Celerity' Atlas No.2 Rail Grinder was purchased in January 1930 from the Equipment and Engineering Company. Hadfields supplied another 12 pairs of points and crossings in February 1930. Four miles of trolley wire was purchased from British Insulated Cables the following month. There was still no resolution on abandoning the tramway.

Track repairs continue as tramway heads for closure

In May the Borough Surveyor reported yet again on poor track condition and tenders for points and crossings were accepted for Tweedale Street, Dane Street, Spotland Road and Whitworth Road. In October 1930 approval was given to replace the points and crossings at the junction of Oldham Road and Milnrow Road.

As late as February 1931, the Borough Surveyor was authorised to carry out repairs to the tramways in Oldham Road between Kings Road and Healing Street, Oldham Road near Balderstone Mill, Manchester Road between the Presbyterian Church and Sparth Bottoms Road and Drake Street between Fleece Street and Water Street. Despite tram services being reduced to peak periods only, the Borough Surveyor was asked to repair the tracks at the Nursery loop and Oxford loop on Whitworth Road, on Bolton Road and in Milnrow near Kiln Lane.

The Borough Surveyor reported in November 1931 on the state of roads with tram tracks. The Committee resolved to carry out work:

The road gang have removed the tram rails and are re-instating the granite setts to form the new roadway. Littleborough, 1933.

1) On Class 1 roads -
Halifax Road, from Borough boundary to Heybrook: removing track, making good concrete foundation and surfacing with asphalt.

Entwisle Road and Oldham Road from Borough boundary to Balderstone Mill: removing track, making good concrete foundation and repaving using setts (after redressing) removed from Halifax road.

Edenfield Road from Dellar Street to Ings lane: covering road from kerb to kerb with one coat asphalt work.

Edenfield Road from Phyliss Street to Amy Street: removing track, making good concrete foundation and surfacing with asphalt.

2) On unclassified roads –
Yorkshire Street from George Street to Littlewood Street: covering road from kerb to kerb with one coat asphalt work.

Yorkshire Street from Littlewood Street to Heybrook: repairing paving and grouting the rails.

3) Grouting the rails in the following roads:
Spotland Road;
Oldham Road (part);
Bury Road;
Rooley Moor Road;
Edenfield Road (parts of).

Trams had already ceased running on most of these sections so grouting the rails must have been a cheaper option than lifting the track and re-paving. A total of £38,000 (£1.56m) was contributed by the Passenger Transport Committee towards the cost of making good the highways on removal of tramway rails after the abandonment of tramways.

In June 1932 the Paving Etc. Committee resolved to reconstruct the carriageway on Bolton Road between Springfield and Sudden by taking up the setts and laying mastic asphalt on a concrete foundation. On the next section from Springfield to the Borough boundary the track was removed and the granite sett paving re-instated.

Inability to maintain the tracks in good condition in the end forced the demise of the trams. Power supply and rolling stock could have been kept going for a few years more but the track was getting desperate. The heavy investment needed was beyond the resources of a relatively small town, even with a modest sinking fund. It was a familiar story, repeated for many similar sized systems across the country.

One of the 1926 batch of all enclosed double deckers (Nos.86-89) built by English Electric on a Preston 21E 4 wheel truck. It ran for only six years before withdrawal for scrapping. (Ian Yearsley)

17. Power supply and overhead.

How to generate the power

Before the Corporation had sought powers to construct an electric tramway under the 1900 Act, it had invited Alfred Dickenson of Birmingham to decide whether a separate power station should be erected for the tramways or whether to combine it with the lighting power station. It was estimated that the tramways would use seven times as much power as street and domestic lighting, the tramways using 164 units per hour. By 1930, domestic and industrial use of electricity was twenty times that needed for the tramway.

An early view of the Tramway centre sees an inspector with a junior crew member while open top Brush car No.27 waits at the island. The double trolley wires with no switches can be seen above the tram. The original tramway shelter had not then been replaced.
(Touchstones Rochdale)

Supply of current was problematic because the existing Corporation Electricity Works did not have enough capacity to work the whole tramway system. There was a prolonged controversy on whether to extend the works or build a separate generating station at the Sanitory Works on Entwisle Street, fuelled by burning the town's rubbish. Sadly this remarkably far sighted proposal, given today's environmental concerns over waste disposal and the need for conservation, was not developed.

The Borough Engineer read a letter from Mr Lacey, the consultant Electrical Engineer of Lacey, Clirehugh and Sillar of Westminster, to the Committee at its meeting on 4th February 1901. It specified the extra plant required at the Electricity Works within the next few years for the purposes of the tramway system:

'By October, 1901:
   One 400 kilowatts Steam Dynamo, erected in the existing building.

One boiler 8ft. by 30 ft. together with steam and exhaust pipes.
Condensing plant and accessories in the existing boiler house.
Tramway switchboard and engine-room connection.'

'By May, 1902:
   One 400 kilowatts Steam Dynamo, erected in the existing building, including foundations.
   One boiler 8ft. by 30 ft. together with steam and exhaust pipes, feed pumps, economisers, foundations, seatings, accessories in extension of boiler-house.'

A further report from Messrs. Lacey, Clirehugh and Sillar was sent on 15th February 1901 following a request from a joint meeting of the Tramways, Health and Electricity Committees on 5th February. The topic was the 'Utilisation of Refuse for the Generation of Electricity', as had been debated previously. It was an innovative concept that has often been proposed, even in recent times, but never implemented. When Metrolink was first planned for Manchester in the nineteen eighties, one suggestion was to re-instate the Bloom Street power station in the city centre to generate the necessary power, fuelled by waste products. It was not pursued.

The report examined the costs of providing new equipment at the Sanitory Works on Entwisle Road to enable all the refuse to be used as fuel to produce steam for electricity generation. Some refuse was being converted into manure but that process was to be discontinued because it was not cost effective. The costs of this method of generation compared with the alternative of increasing the output of the existing power station were little different, £8,026 (£532,000) per annum for generation from refuse and £7,916 (£525,500) per annum from the power station.

Mr Lacey estimated that 60 trams covering 1.5 million miles per annum would need 1.65 million units per annum. (In fact by 1907 there were 59 trams covering 1.2 million miles per annum using 1.89 million units per annum). He pointed out that with the large electrical load of the tramway, unit costs would come down with consequent benefits for other users in the town. The prospect of being able to sell cheap electricity to both business and domestic consumers was exciting. This argument won the day. The battle was entirely within the municipal empire as refuse was the responsibility of the Corporation's Health Committee and electricity production was under the Gas and Electricity Committee.

Overhead design begins

At their meeting on 18th March, 1901, the Committee resolved to ask Mr Lacey to prepare designs for poles and other matters relating to electrical equipment. His designs were considered at the meeting on 13th May and it was resolved that the Blackburn design be adopted but Mr Lacey was asked to advise on the type of poles to be used on The Esplanade, this being a sensitive area in front of the Town Hall.

The tenders for copper rail bonds from Felton & Guillaume were approved at the meeting on 27th May. At the same meeting, evidence of inter-Committee conflict emerged when the Gas and Electricity Committee advised that the switchboard for the tramways at the Generating Station should be provided by, and at the expense of, the Tramways Committee. The Committee responded that in their opinion the Gas and Electricity Committee should pay! Peace was

Committee on 19th August 1901 stating that satisfactory guard wires would be necessary at the points where the telegraph lines would be crossed by the trolley lines. In fact Section 24 of the Rochdale Corporation Act 1900, which authorised construction and electrification of the tramways, set out in considerable detail over more than two pages the provisions for the protection of Post Office telegraphic wires. It must be recalled that until comparatively recent times, the Post Office were solely responsible for all telephone equipment as well as postal services. In those early days, telephone wires were often strung between poles overhead rather than buried in the ground.

On 3rd February 1902 the tender was accepted from Messrs W T Glover for 18-way Doulton Conduits for tramway feeders, to be laid from the corner of Bridge Street to Manchester Road. This was a variation to their contract for cables.

Intending passengers crowd onto an open top car on Oldham Road at Kings Road. The attractive overhead poles with their finials, scrollwork and cast iron bases contribute to the pleasing simplicity of the overhead line equipment.

(Eric Fielding)

restored the next week when the Gas and Electricity Committee resolved to provide it at its own expense.

Another piece of the overhead jigsaw was earmarked with the acceptance of the tender from W T Glover & Co. of Manchester for feeder cables. Macartney McElroy and Company were awarded the contract for overhead equipment on "the extensions", i.e. those sections of tramway which had not had steam trams.

A further request to the Gas and Electricity Committee was considered at their meeting on 14th August. The Tramways Committee wanted the Electricity Department to provide for supervision of the electrical work of the overhead equipment, cables and bonding of the tramways. It was agreed, subject to payment of 20/- per week. (£1, £62.40). The Borough Electrical Engineer, Mr C. Clare Atchison, was duly appointed to supervise the electrical work for the tramway. His salary for this work was £50 per annum (£3,120). He was paid this sum until the overhead works were completed in March 1906.

The Post Office were concerned about the proximity of overhead wires to their equipment and wrote to the

Nobody likes having a large traction pole right outside their front door and Mr Turner of 181, Rooley Moor Road was no exception. He asked for the pole to be removed from outside his residence and the Committee agreed, subject to the cost of relocation being borne by Mr Turner.

Power supply was an issue in Littleborough where the Urban District Council asked if they could supply the necessary power for working the tramway in their district or any part of it. The Committee responded that they could not entertain the proposal. A separate sub-station was accordingly built in Littleborough and fed from Rochdale's power station.

Most of the overhead was suspended from span wires between poles or on bracket arms. The Borough Engineer recommended the 'flexible suspension' type of bracket arm construction. A few building fixings were used, known as rosettes, including one opposite the 'White Horse' public house in Rooley Moor Road, the premises of Messrs. John Kenyon Ltd. of Cloughfold who were paid 5/- per annum (£16.09) for the privilege. Another was on the north-east corner of Spotland Bridge for the sum of 1/- per annum, 5p (£3.22).

WAITING FOR THE CAR, MANCHESTER RD, ROCHDALE.   T. PINDER. PHOTO.

A typical side pole with cantilevered bracket arm supporting running wires in both directions, on Manchester Road at New Barn Lane. Finial, scrollwork and decorated pole base present a classic tramway image. The 4-wheel open top car appears to be being overtaken by a horse and cart!   *(T. Pinder)*

At the meeting on 26th May 1902 Mr Lacey was asked to prepare plans, specifications and estimates for the overhead equipment for all the remaining tram routes authorised by the Rochdale Corporation Act 1900, except the sections previously excluded, namely Spotland Road to Whitworth Road, Smith Street to Milnrow Road, Milnrow Road along Wood Street to Oldham Road and Drake Street along Richard Street and Station Road. It was agreed that all the poles would be painted green with maroon bands, similar to the pole at the corner of Bridge Street near the Gas Works. However at the June meeting Mr Lacey was asked to prepare alternative estimates and drawings for sectional poles and parallel bracket arms throughout the system.

Overhead telephone extensions were to be made to connect all section boxes and the termini at Bury Road, Norden and Rooley Moor Road, together with the temporary Coptrod and Bridgefold Car Depots, to the Electricity Works. The contract with Messrs. McCartney, McElroy & Co. was extended accordingly.

The first electrical inspection

On 9th June 1902 Mr A P Trotter's Report of his inspection of the electrical equipment on the Bury Road route on 15th May was read out by the Town Clerk. This was the same day that Major Druitt inspected the tramway. Mr Trotter noted that the swivel head trolley system was used and that the work was satisfactory and complete. His only criticism was the guard wiring which he considered was 'rather overdone'. A Post Office representative joined him on his inspection and it appears that wiring to protect

overhead telephone wires could have been done in a less obtrusive manner. He nevertheless recommended that the electrical working of the Tramway be sanctioned.

In March 1903 the Sub-Committee reported on their recommendations for the type and location of overhead line equipment, as shown in Table 17.1.

Centre pole construction was approved for The Esplanade between Manchester Road and Rochdale Bridge, each pole having an arc lamp fitted at the top and an incandescent lamp bracket on each side. In April 1904 this design was rescinded and instead span wire construction proposed. However it seems the original design was adopted as contemporary photographs clearly show centre poles with bracket arms and a large street lamp in a circular support on top of the pole. Ornate scrollwork on bracket arms was often applied with decorative finials and bases on the poles.

The overhead equipment for the remaining parts of the tramway was supplied by Messrs.J.G.White of London. The contract to supply all the high and low tension feeder cables, pilot cables and conduits for the whole tramway was awarded to W.T. Glover & Company of Manchester.

Frogs were not always fitted in the overhead, as for example at Spotland Bridge where the running wire from Mellor Street was only connected through to Edenfield Road. Trams leaving the depot to go up Rooley Moor Road had to stop to allow the conductor to transfer the trolley pole from one wire to the adjacent wire. The same applied in the opposite direction. The same principle was applied at the Tramway Centre where the minimum number of frogs was needed for the complex routing pattern.

An intriguing request came from Wardle Urban District Council who wanted to use the tramway poles in Halifax Road as sewer ventilators. The Committee responded that 'they could not entertain the suggestion'!

Table 17.1 Type of overhead equipment.

Street	From	To	Type
Smith Street	Wellington Bridge	John Street	Poles on north side
Entwisle Road	John Street	Church of Good Shepherd	Poles on south side
"	Church of Good Shepherd	Halifax Road	Poles on north side
Halifax Road	Entwisle Road	Smallbridge	Span construction
	Smallbridge	Todmorden Road	Bracket arms on north side
Todmorden Road	Halifax Road	Summit	Poles on west side
Milnrow Road	Newbold Street	Railway bridge	Bracket arms on south side
"	Railway Bridge	Oldham Road	Bracket arms on south side except north side at Railway Hotel
John Street	Smith Street	Yorkshire Street	Bracket arms on west side
Whitworth Road	Yorkshire Street	Ending	Bracket arms on west side
Yorkshire Street	Cheetham Street	West Street	Bracket arms on south side
"	West Street	Entwisle Road	Span construction
Drake Street	Wellington Bridge	Manchester Road	Span construction
Tweedale Street/ Lower Tweedale Street	Manchester Road	Railway Station	Bracket arms on north side
High Level Road	Railway Station	Oldham Road	Bracket arms on south side
Oldham Road	Drake Street	Platting Lane	Bracket arms on west side
"	Platting Lane	Dog and Partridge	Poles on west side
"	Dog and Partridge	Summit Inn	Span construction
Bury Road (Castleton Moor)	Heywood Market Place (St Luke's Church)	White Lion	Span construction
"	White Lion	Cemetery	Bracket arms on south side
"	Cemetery	Plough Inn	Bracket arms on north side
"	Plough Inn	Sudden	Bracket arms on south side
Manchester Road	Sudden	New Barn Lane	Bracket arms on east side
	New Barn Lane	Dunster Avenue	Span construction
	Dunster Avenue	King Street South	Bracket arms on east side
	King Street South	Dane Street	Span construction

NB It is assumed that 'poles' also referred to bracket arms.

This view of the cenotaph and the new Post Office, opened in 1927, shows clearly the centre pole overhead design on the Esplanade with integrated street lights.

(TMS)

The possibility of generating power from refuse was raised again in a report in the Rochdale Observer on 18th June 1903. However, the Rochdale Corporation Health Committee had decided to discontinue the manufacture of manure at the sanitary works on the recommendation of the manager because it was losing money. The Gas and Electricity Committee questioned this and asked what surplus power could be applied to generate electricity as more current would shortly be needed for tramway traction. It became a question of whether the manufacturing of manure should be continued or whether all the steam raised by the burning of the town's refuse should be applied to the production of electric current.

Messrs J.G. White had been criticised for poor performance but on 22nd July 1904 they sent a telegram stating that they hoped to complete the overhead equipment on the Circular route by 31st July. In fact it was still not complete when the Board of Trade inspection took place on 17th August.

In August 1904 the Borough Surveyor reported that he had made arrangements to fix rosettes to the walls of a number of buildings in lieu of traction poles. They included:

Rochdale Pioneer's Society premises, Oldham Road;
London City and Midland Bank;
Lancashire and Yorkshire Bank;
Manchester and Liverpool District Bank;
Messrs. Kelsall & Kemp Ltd's warehouse;
Messrs. J.R. Hartley & Sons office;
Mr. B. Hirst's shop, 13 South Parade;
Messrs. Orrell Bros.' shop, 5, Drake Street;
Mr. Boardman's shop, 10 Drake Street;
Messrs. Brierley & Hudson, The Butts.

Some further rosettes were substituted for traction poles while in other locations the reverse happened. In at least one instance, No.12 Drake Street, a request to provide a rosette in place of a traction pole was refused.

Where the overhead passed under railway bridges, arrangements were made with the Lancashire and Yorkshire Railway to provide wooden troughing attached to the underside of the bridge for the trolley wire.

Traction poles were sometimes also used to support electric street lights. In August 1904 the Committee even agreed to allow gas lamps to be placed on tramway poles in certain cases. The safety implications were not mentioned – they would have been doubly or triply insulated.

Poles were fitted with ornamental cast iron bases to reduce the starkness of their appearance and also to protect the lower part of the pole from corrosion. Wardle Urban District Council objected to the width because it was causing an obstruction on narrow footpaths. The Committee agreed to remove all the original wide bases and no more would be used on any routes. This was later rescinded and wide bases were used on some sections in Littleborough and on Halifax Road and Whitworth Road, but never in Wardle! The arguments raged on with some wide bases being removed. Eventually the Committee's patience was exhausted and they resolved that the poles in Wardle and Littleborough would be left without bases of any kind. Littleborough Urban District Council protested strongly but the Committee were unmoved. Two

years later they sold 500 unused pole bases to the highest tenderer, the Rochdale Britannia Iron Foundry Company.

In November 1904 one patent trolley reverser was ordered on trial but their use was limited.

Wires into adjacent districts

By October 1905 the overhead wiring had reached Littleborough but the design must have been faulty as the Manager reported that there was excessive sag in the wires. He requested permission to erect additional poles on the triangle terminus but the matter was referred to the Routes Sub-Committee. The problem was complicated by the risk of trolley poles of Summit and Rochdale cars overlapping each other but it was left to the Manager to find a suitable solution.

An early example of shared use of poles occurred when the Committee raised no objection to the Paving Committee affixing traffic direction signs "for the guidance of drivers of automobiles and other vehicles" to tramway poles at convenient points.

The Bacup Light Railway required rather more complex arrangements than previous sections. Not only was it not in Rochdale but the existing tramway operator was Rawtenstall Corporation. There was no track connection as they were different gauges, Rawtenstall being 4ft (1220mm). Agreement was reached for the supply of electricity to Rochdale Corporation with separate agreements between Rawtenstall and Bacup, and Bacup and Rochdale. The period of 30 years from September 1910 was more than enough as Rochdale's trams only lasted for another 22 years. The price was fixed at $1^3/8$d (36p) per unit for the first two years, $1^1/4$d (33p) for the next eight years, with revision after ten years from the date of commencement of supply. Thereafter revision would be every five years. Complex arrangements were also made to ensure that the payments passed between the three bodies. In addition to feeding the Bacup Light Railway, Rawtenstall agreed that Rochdale could take power for Whitworth No.2 tramway as and when required.

Construction and erection of the overhead equipment and feeder cables on the Whitworth, Bacup and Milnrow sections was all carried out by the tramways own staff. No doubt the acquisition of the motorised tower wagon greatly eased the task.

The total number of traction poles in Rochdale was given as approximately 2,000 in May 1912. No fewer than 1,400 of them needed painting. The trolley wire on the Norden section was renewed in 1915, by then being 13 years old.

In October 1917 the Manager proposed that the sub-station in Littleborough should be closed and replaced by a cable laid from Smallbridge to the Green Man Inn at Hurstead at a cost of £450 (£14,200). The Electricity Committee paid half the cost and it resulted in 'a considerable saving' to both Committees.

Probably one of the last building rosettes was fixed to the new Post Office building which opened in July 1927. It can still be seen clearly today on the restored frontage, along with another on the nearby Barclays Bank building, representing one of the last visible remnants of the tramways.

18. Depots

Four depots in four years!

The first tram depot in Rochdale was the steam tram depot in Entwisle Road which opened in May 1883 for the 3ft. 6in. gauge system. It was adjacent to the Corporation Sanitary Depot, still used as a refuse depot today. A four track tram depot was alongside a three track locomotive shed and four more tracks led into the workshops. It continued in operation until the final closure of the steam tramway on 11 May 1905. The depot was demolished and the site used for the public baths.

A depot is an essential requirement for any tramway but Rochdale's electric tramway had to operate for the first couple of years without one, at least a permanent one. The first steps to acquire land for the Mellor Street depot were not taken until the end of 1900. Part of the Bridgefold Estate between the River Spodden and the proposed new road to be called Mellor Street was to be purchased for the Car shed and Depot. The General Purposes Committee granted the Tramways Committee as much land as was needed for the depot, on terms to be agreed later. The Borough Surveyor was authorised to proceed with works to Spotland Bridge which formed part of the new works needed to construct the road and the tramway.

It was clear that the new depot would not be available in time for the first trams to use. An urgent request was sent on 4th March 1901 to the Improvement Sub-Committee asking them to negotiate at once to purchase properties in Lord Street and Henland with a view to the site being used as a temporary starting point for the cars of the Spotland section of the tramway. Lord Street was at the town centre end of the route, at the foot of Blackwater Street. This proposal did not materialise.

The Borough Surveyor submitted plans and elevations for the new Car Depot to the Committee on 27th May, 1901. They were approved but amendments were requested to the offices. Amended plans and elevations were agreed on 10th June. On 18th November the Committee visited the site for the proposed car depot on the Bridgefold Estate. They agreed the price to be offered for the land and approved the Borough Surveyor's plans for the car shed, special trackwork and offices. Three weeks later on 9th December the trackwork approval was rescinded and an alternative track layout substituted. To improve the access into and out of the depot, the Board of Trade were to be asked to sanction double track on the new street, Mellor Street, and extending the loop in Spotland Road onto Spotland Bridge. The Board of Trade Railways Department consent was given on 26th

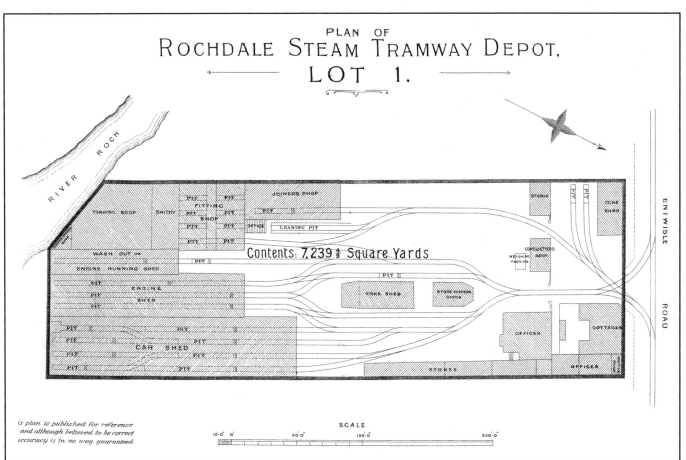

The layout of the steam tram depot on Entwisle Road, as it appeared on the sale plans when the system closed in 1905. (MTMS)

The main structure of the Mellor Street Car Shed is nearing completion but track laying has not yet commenced. This view was probably taken in early 1904.

(Touchstones Rochdale)

November, only eight days after the request was sent. Today it would probably take months!

It must have been obvious that the new depot would not be ready for the first trams. On 25th November, the Borough Surveyor was asked to prepare plans for a temporary car shed at Bridgefold, close to Spotland Bridge. They were duly approved on 9th December and tenders invited for a shed to hold four cars. The tender of The Pendleton Iron Works Company was accepted on 6th January 1902, another example of the speed which was typical of that era but unachievable in our modern world. The temporary car shed was built at the northern end of the permanent depot site although at that point they had not actually acquired it.

The Committee agreed to purchase the land for the depot from Bridgefold Estates on 3rd February 1902. It comprised 11,692 square yards *(0.98 Ha.)* between the site for the new road and the River Spodden. The cost of £32,000 *(£2.06m)* included work to pack the old colliery workings below the land. The Board of Trade approved a loan to cover the cost under the powers of the Rochdale Corporation Act 1900 with repayment over 30 years on the security of tramway revenue, the Borough Fund and the Borough rate.

The temporary depot at Spotland Bridge could only serve the Norden and Spotland routes. There was as yet no track connection to the Bury Road route. So it was that on 2nd April 1902 the Borough Surveyor was asked to make arrangements for the provision of another temporary car shed, this time at the Bury Road end of Mellor Street, at the junction with Bridge Street *(now the continuation of Mellor Street)*. In some reports it is referred to as Coptrod Depot. The Committee wanted to see the Bury Road section running as early as practicable.

Not only was the depot not ready but neither were the offices. Permission was sought from the Gas and Electricity Committee to house the tramways offices temporarily at the Electricity Works. Conveniently, the Borough Electrical Engineer, Mr C. Clare Atchison, was asked to act temporarily as Superintendent. The office accommodation was duly agreed for the sum of £20 *(£1,287)* per annum.

Terms for the insurance of the Coptrod Depot building and contents were obtained and the Borough Treasurer instructed to get a cover note. Total cover was for £3,000 *(£193,056)* comprising £2,600 *(£167,315)* for the three cars, £200 *(£12,870)* for the building and £200 *(£12,870)* for sundries. As the depot was already in use it seems the insurance cover was none too soon.

The temporary car shed at Bridgefold was completed in June 1902, just in time for the first trams to Norden and Spotland. Insurance for the Bridgefold car depot was arranged in June 1904 for £10,000 (£628,930) and a further £5,000 (£314,470) for the cars.

Work starts on permanent car shed

The permanent car shed was designed to accommodate 48 cars in the main shed and about ten more in the workshops. A special meeting of the Committee on 25th June 1903 accepted the tender of a local Rochdale contractor Messrs.W.A. Peters & Sons for the construction of the permanent car depot at Bridgefold. A separate tender was won by Peters for steel revolving shutters which were substituted for wooden folding doors. The post of Clerk of Works was advertised and Mr William Mallinson of 1 Riddle Street, Rochdale was appointed at a salary of 50/- per week (£154).

Messrs. W.A.Peters' contract was extended following meetings of the Car Shed Sub-Committee in February 1904 to include heating for the repair shed, workshop and paintshop and the foundations for the offices alongside the Car Shed. At the same time, the specification for the rails over the pits was changed from grooved girder rail to bullhead rail. Tenders were also sought for an overhead electric crane and Messrs. Bryce Limited of Manchester won the order for a 5 ton 3 motor crane.

Detailed matters continued to be approved as works progressed with more changes to the offices. The floor surfaces in the repair and paint sheds were specified as 5 in deep beechwood blocks on concrete foundations finished with creosote. The floor in the car shed bays adjoining the side walls at the entrance was to be concrete with a granolithic finish.

At last tenders were invited for construction of the new offices adjacent to the depot after many changes to the plans. The contract included terra-cotta work supplied by the Huncoat Brick and Terra-Cotta Company in Accrington. This attractive brickwork can still be seen today on the building in Mellor Street, now occupied by a potato merchant. The tender was won, perhaps not surprisingly, by Messrs W.A. Peters & Sons. The depot was nearing completion in July so construction workers could conveniently move from one contract to the next. The Car Shed became operational on 15th July 1904 and was reported as such to the Committee on 25th July.

The Borough Surveyor described the Car Shed as being built on a site of 11,692 sq. yds. (0.98 ha.) on land owned by the Corporation on the east side of Mellor Street. The shed was a lofty building 216 ft. (65.8m) long by 100 ft. (30.5m) wide with good natural light from the glazed roof. A single track connection with the double track in Mellor Street was provided at each end of the shed, forking into a fan arrangement into eight sets of lines in the main shed and two tracks into the repair and painting sheds on the easterly side. If one entrance was fouled by a car off the line, the other could still be used.

Continuous inspection pits were constructed under the tracks which were supported on steel stanchions with steel joists carrying the rails. The stanchions were fixed to solid concrete bases. The pits were open allowing maintenance staff to pass from one track to another across the shed. Spaces between the running tracks were filled with pitch pine planks except at each side where solid concrete was used between the last rail and the wall. Below the pit level was an open subway which linked to the lower level store rooms and repair shop so that motors could be removed from a car and taken on trolleys to the mechanics' shop.

The tram depot on the newly opened Mellor Street is fronted by the impressive tramway office with its terra cotta decoration, opened in July 1904. The tramway workshops opposite were not completed for another fifteen years.

The repair shop was 117 ft. (35.7m) long and the paint shop 45 ft. (13.7m) long on the river side of the shed. Off the repair shop were the general stores, mechanics', blacksmiths' and joiners' shops and messroom, foreman's room and toilets. Off the paintshop were the armature repairing shop and additional stores. All the buildings were constructed in brick with terra cotta features. The shed was designed to accommodate 56 cars of the 4 wheel type but this was reduced to 49 with the use of bogie cars. Expansion was considered feasible either on the same site or on the other side of Mellor Street.

On 18th July, three days after the new depot was opened, the Borough Surveyor was authorised to dispose of Coptrod Car Shed

The office building was also of red brick with terra cotta features including the imposing frontage to Mellor Street which still exists. It was a long narrow building having an extensive frontage but little depth. All the rooms faced the street and were accessed from a 5 ft. (1.5m) wide corridor.

The north end of the Mellor Street tram shed showing the depot track fan and the eight covered depot tracks. It was completed in 1904. The offices can just be seen on the right.
(Eric Fielding)

Single deck bogie cars 57 and 37 undergo major maintenance in the tramway workshop on Mellor Street while maintenance staff pose for the photographer. An equal wheel maximum traction bogie is in the left foreground. This building still exists.
(MTMS)

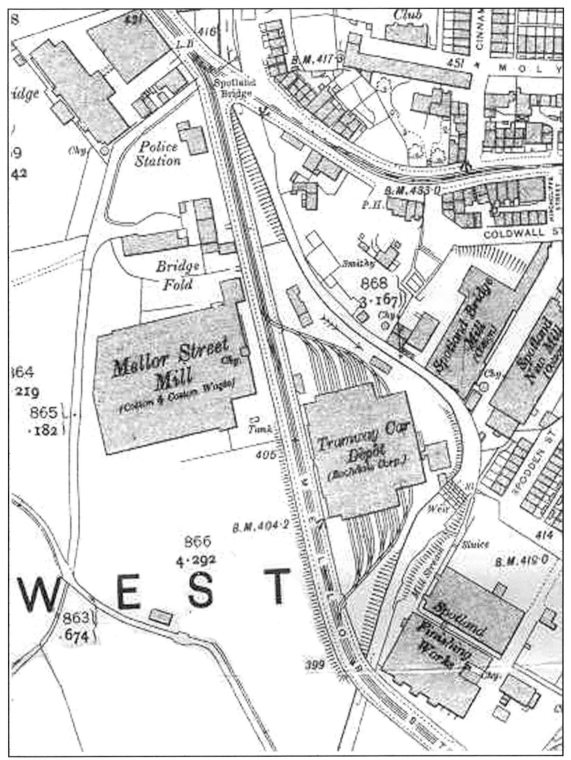

Rochdale tram depot in 1908. Also visible are the track layouts on Mellor Street, Spotland Road and Spotland Bridge. The tramway workshops on the west side of Mellor Street had not then been built.

(Reproduced from Ordnance Survey 1910)

Accommodation on the ground floor included:

- entrance hall;
- inquiry office;
- interview room;
- general office, 39 ft. by 18 ft. *(11.9m by 5.5m)*;
- inspectors' office, 15 ft 6ins, by 18 ft. *(4.7m by 5.5m)*;
- conductors paying in room, 22 ft by 18 ft. *(6.7m by 5.5m)*;
- draughtsmens' and cost clerk's office, 19 ft. by 18 ft. *(5.8m by 5.5m)*;
- traffic superintendent's office;
- general manager's office, with bay window;
- stationery store and office clerks' room 22ft. by 15ft. *(6.7m by 4.6m)*;
- lavatories for office staff;
- lavatories for motormen and conductors.

A large committee room was provided on the first floor, 39 ft long, 24 ft. wide and 15 ft high *(11.9m by 7.3m by 4.6m)* but it was soon used only for storage and issue of tickets. The Tramways Committee preferred to meet in the Town Hall which offered more munificent facilities. Other rooms included lost luggage, uniform store and more lavatories. There were three cellars for the low pressure water heating plant and storage with direct access into the car shed. The offices were lighted by electricity, still a relatively new method, and had 'telephonic communication' between every room in the offices, car shed and workshops, another innovation.

A dwarf brick wall, 2ft 6 ins. high, surmounted by wrought iron railings also 2 ft. 6 ins. high, completed the appearance of the building. It opened on 23rd June 1905. The whole complex of car shed , workshops and offices were considered to be well arranged and equipped. The Borough Engineer undertook all the design work with the Borough Electrical Engineer carrying out the electrical equipment and lighting and the General Manager the fitting out of the workshops. The total cost of depot and offices including all equipment was about £32,000 *(£2.00m)*.

A contemporary description of the interior of the car shed in the Rochdale Observer commented:

'Here one finds capacious pits from which the men are able to examine the trucks and underwork generally of the cars. Every time a car has been out it is thoroughly cleaned and on this work alone ten or a dozen men are engaged all night seven nights a week. Trifling repairs are carried out in the general car shed; where more serious work is required the cars go to the adjoining repair shed and are often literally taken to pieces. All kinds of repairs, the most serious as well as the most trifling, are done under the Mellor Street roof. There is the armature shop where all electrical repairs are done, the machine shop fitted with a couple of lathes and a couple of drilling machines, an emery wheel, a hydraulic press and a power saw, the blacksmith's shop with its two large forges, a Bunsen apparatus for shrinking on tyres, a paint shop, a joiners' shop, a sand drying apparatus and much else'.

Littleborough car shed proposed

By 1906 the expanding fleet prompted discussion of additional depot accommodation on a different site, with Littleborough as a favoured option. However the General Manager did not recommend it because it would entail duplication of some staff and tools, lack of proper control and extra lighting, heating, rents, rates and taxes. He concluded it was wrong in principle and produced figures to support his case. (Table 18.1 below).

Table 18.1	Estimate of the cost of a Car Shed at Littleborough.
Capital Account	
Shed to accommodate four cars	£500 0s 0d
Track, Special Work etc.	£250 0s 0d
Overhead Equipment	£ 50 0s 0d
Plant	£ 35 0s 0d
Total	£825 0s 0d
Revenue Account	
Interest and Sinking Fund	£ 49 10s 0d
Rent, Rates, Taxes and Insurance	£ 20 0s 0d
Staff	£195 0s 0d
Total	£264 10s 0d
Estimated Saving on present Working Expenses	
Wages	£ 50 0s 0d
Current	£ 70 0s 0d
Insurance	£ 6 0s 0d
Total	£ 126 0s 0d
Balance in favour of working from main depot at Mellor Street rather than small depot in Littleborough, per annum	£138 10s 0d

An interesting insight into the materials and equipment used in the depot is given by a list of tenders for the stores for the year ending 31st March 1908. The full list is set out in Table 18.2. Some names are still very familiar but most have long since disappeared. Nearly half the suppliers were in or near Rochdale and almost all within the north-west.

The Car Shed Foreman, Mr Galloway, handed in his resignation in January 1908. It was accepted with regret and an advert for his replacement placed in two tramway journals and 'The Manchester Guardian'. The salary was £3 *(£178)* per week. Fifty two applications were received. A short list of six candidates was interviewed and Mr E. Sidgwick of Stalybridge selected.

A car shed for Bacup

By May 1911 construction of the route to Bacup was well advanced. It was apparent that the distance from Rochdale meant that cars would have to leave very early and return very late if a similar level of service was provided as on the rest of the system. A 'dormitory' car shed was therefore proposed and plans drawn up by the

Table 18.2.   Tenders for stores for year ending 31st March 1908.

Supplier	Items
J. Hamilton, Rochdale	Weed brooms, buckets, glue, saw blades, bolts, washers, flat iron, steel chisel, bar iron, sheet iron, mild steel.
The Masul Metal Polish Co.	Metal polish
Raines, Porter and Seddon, Hull	Carso liquid soap, paraffin wax.
R. T. Butterworth, Rochdale	Trolley rope.
J. J. Smithies, Rochdale	Brass and iron wood screws, files, cotter pins, emery cloth.
Magnolic Metal Co.	Magnolic metal.
T. Tinsley, Rochdale	Bolts, set screws, nuts.
Pilkington Bros., St Helens	Glass.
Plomo Speciality Manufacturing Co., Birmingham	Patent spur gear composition.
W. Brierley Ltd, Rochdale	Section insulator ends, phosphor bronze, copper wire, bar copper, sheet copper, brass sleeves, bogie side castings, motor suspension bearings.
Fleming, Birkby and Goodall, Liverpool	Trolley wheels, forks, harps, graphite brushes.
J. W. Kirkham, Bolton	Axle box steps.
The Atlas Foundry Co., Rochdale	Brake shoes, fire bars, iron castings.
Schofield's Foundry, Littleborough	Malleable castings.
British Westinghouse Co., Manchester	Gear wheels, pinions.
Brierley and Kershaw, Rochdale	Springs.
Tempered Spring Co.	Elliptical springs.
Manchester Armature Repair Co., Manchester	Armature coils.
British Thomson-Houston Co.	Mica collars and cones.
P. R. Jackson and Co., Manchester	Vulcanite plates.
L. Andrew and Co., Manchester	Presspahn, Micanite cloth, binding wire, jacketing, insulating tapes, Micanite, scrap mica, Armacell paint, P.B. paint, ebonite plate, rubber sleeves.
Helsby Cable Co., Warrington	Ozokerite tape.
Le Corbone Co.	Carbon brushes.
Henley Telegraph Works, London	Pure para strip.
Premier Electric Lamp Co., Liverpool	Lamps.
Siemens Bros., London	Linen tape, rubber gloves.
General Electric Co., Manchester	Straight line ears, insulated bolts, globe strains, pull-offs.
Brecknell, Munro and Rodgers	Splicing sleeves, frogs, crossings, trolley standard springs.
Wm. Greenwood and Fletcher Bolton, Rochdale	Timber
Firth, Ray and Prosser, Rochdale	Linseed oil, paints, paint brushes, palette knives.
J. H. Isherwood and Co., Rochdale	Turpentine, white lead, gold size, dry white lead, paints, patent filling, ground pumice stone. brushes, mops, pencils.
Read and Co., Birmingham	Varnishes, black Japan, terebine.
E. Wrigley and Sons Ltd, Rochdale	Waybills, inspectors' sheets, linesmen's sheets, traffic books, official note paper, envelopes, wage books, abstract book.
E. Waide, Rochdale	Waybills, sundry reports, weekly returns, duty sheets.
Ormerod Bros., Rochdale	Mileage and summary sheets, accident report forms, committee report forms, Oldham daily returns, time sheets, envelopes, requisition form for stores.
J. D. Howarth, Rochdale	Inspectors' special report forms, Oldham traffic books.
Edwards and Bryning, Rochdale	Sub-committee report forms, sub-committee advice notices, Heywood traffic books.

Manager. In fact the Sub-Committee had visited Bacup on 4th October 1910 to inspect several suitable sites for a car shed. A 550 sq.yd. *(460 sq.m.)* site on Rochdale Road at Sheephouses, between Bacup and Britannia, was offered by Bacup Corporation, about a mile south of the town centre. The land was purchased for £70 *(£4,408)* and the Committee invited tenders for its construction.

Another Committee visit was made to Bacup on 29th May 1911 to inspect the Bacup Light Railway and the Sheephouses site, and progress on construction of the Whitworth No.2 tramway. By September the car shed work was in progress and it reached completion towards the end of 1911, opening for service on 1st January 1912. The depot only had two tracks and could accommodate just six trams, one of the smallest tram depots in Britain. It was also one of the highest at 949ft *(290m)* above sea level. The staff had to wait another six years before their partitioned-off mess room got a roof and a stove for heating.

Expansion and new workshops

By May 1912, the tramways were almost at their full extent and the Mellor Street Car Shed was getting full. An extension was considered and the General Purposes Committee were asked to reserve some vacant land on Mellor Street which the Corporation owned. Nearly two years later in January 1914 the Committee finally resolved to erect a workshop on the opposite side of Mellor Street and to purchase extra machinery. However before confirming the resolution a visit was made to Bolton Tramways Car Shed on 28th January to inspect their new workshop and machinery.

On 4th February 1913 the Manager and Mr Hathaway were authorised to prepare plans for the additional Car Shed and workshop accommodation at Bridgefold. They wasted no time and on 25th February Mr Hathaway's plans for the construction of the additional accommodation were approved application was made to the Board of Trade for loan sanction as follows:

Erection of additional Car Shed	
with workshops:	£12,625
Machinery:	£ 2,035
Trackwork:	£ 1,370
Street works:	£ 320
Lighting;	£ 400
Overhead equipment:	£ 250
Total:	£17,000 *(£918,545)*

The General Purposes Committee were asked to transfer the 8,000 sq.yds. of land, part of the Bridgefold Estate, for the purpose. The cost of the land at £1,125 *(£60,786)* was included in the construction cost.

Loan sanction was received from the Board of Trade on 14th September, after the outbreak of war. Tenders were invited for construction of the Car Shed and Workshops at Bridgefold in December 1914. Building work was awarded to Mr. J. E. Rangeley of Rochdale with reinforced concrete work going to Messrs. R. & T. Howarth of Rochdale and steelwork to Lambourne & Company of Manchester. The post of Clerk of Works for the new Car Shed was advertised at a salary of £3.00 *(£141)* per week. Mr. C. H. George was appointed and excavations began on 25th February 1915.

The site of the former steam tram depot on Entwisle Road had been acquired by the Cleansing Committee (who still occupy the site today). In February 1915 they resolved to install a tramway 56 yards in length with overhead power supply to be used by the water car and sweeping machines which the Tramways Department provided at an agreed fee. Titan Trackwork of Sheffield were awarded the contract for the track including the pointwork to join the existing track on Entwisle Road.

The contractors for the new Car Shed and Repair Shops, J. E. Rangeley and R. & T. Howarth, were ready to start work by July 1915 but in view of the war they offered to allow the payments due under architect's certificates to be held over until the conclusion of the war if interest on the sums was paid by the Corporation. Their offer was readily accepted but was withdrawn by the contractors the following month; perhaps they had begun to suspect that the war might be prolonged.

A deputation from the Committee met the Finance Committee in September 1915 to expedite the completion of the new Car Shed. It was already in course of erection but they wanted to roof the workshop area. The necessary funding was agreed. However a new development occurred later that month when the Rochdale Munitions Committee and the Ministry of Munitions asked the Committee to allow a portion of the building to be used as a national shell factory. They agree to let it rent free as long as they could be represented on the board of management. The Mayor and the Chairman were duly appointed to the board.

In order to reflect the change of use of the building, the Gas and Electricity Committee provided the lighting and power supply for the Car Shed but the Munitions Committee had to pay for the extra power needed for the manufacture of munitions. Titan trackwork of Sheffield was selected for the supply of rails and crossings for the new Car Shed.

The former steam tramway depot in Entwisle Road had passed to the Cleansing Committee when it ceased to be used for trams but a residual tramway presence remained in the form of a siding for the water car and snow brushes. In August 1917 the Cleansing Committee adapted part of the old joiner's shop on the westerly side of the old steam tramway depot to house their new petrol driven motor sweeper and watering car and a steam powered gully emptier. The tramway sweeping machine was still operational.

At the end of the war the Committee requested possession of the National Shell Factory as soon as possible for its original purpose of a tramway workshop. They took the opportunity to purchase some machinery suitable for use in a tramway repair shop and plant and stores from the old workshop were moved to the new one. At the Ministry of Munitions request, the Committee undertook the work necessary to re-instate the floor and building and they readily agreed, at a cost to be borne by the Ministry.

However, military use of the new Car Shed was not quite over. The Minister of Labour asked for part of it to be used as a training centre for disabled soldiers and were allowed the area intended for use as a paint shop for a period of not more than three years, with an extension of twelve months in April 1922.

Eventually in March 1920 the Committee purchased machine tools for the new Workshop. The list included:

1 heavy self-contained motor driven wheel lathe;
1 screwing and tapping machine;
1 sensitive drilling machine;
1 portable electric drill;
1 portable air compressor;
2 Crellins portable hydraulic pit bogies;
1 portable crane;
   twin melting pot for white metal and burner for tyre heating;
1 coke breaking machine;
1 15 h.p. motor for driving woodworking shop.

The Manager also tried to obtain second hand a 6in. sliding, surfacing and screw cutting lathe and a milling machine and a pneumatic power hammer and motor. The Borough Architect advised on strengthening the roof trusses to support an overhead runway and travelling crane and an office for the Works Superintendent was erected. The budget for the machinery was £4,500, (£107,640) rather higher than the original estimate of £2,035 (£48,680), an example of post war inflation, and Board of Trade sanction was sought to borrow the money. Approval was given in April.

Buses need a garage

The introduction of motor buses into the municipal fleet imposed new demands on space and maintenance facilities. The land for a bus garage was to have been acquired from Messrs. Davey, Kenyon and Company on the westerly side of Mellor Street but complications regarding the safeguarding of underground watercourses resulted in the sale being rescinded. An offer by Rossall Dalby & Parker, Auctioneers and Valuers of Rochdale, of a newly erected garage at Wardleworth Brow for the purpose of a motor bus garage was not pursued. In November 1925 the Borough Surveyor was asked to prepare plans and estimates for a purpose built motor omnibus garage to accommodate 20 vehicles.

Messrs. R. & T. Howarth of Crossfield Works, Rochdale were the successful tenderers in April 1926 Ministry of Transport sanction for a loan of £2,700 (£106,130) to supplement the sum authorised by the Rochdale Corporation Act, 1925 which gave the Corporation powers to run buses. Moves were made to obtain a petrol tank, pump and oil cabinets, but then in July 1926 the tender from Messrs. R. & T. Howarth was rescinded because of the land acquisition problems.

The Borough Surveyor prepared an alternative scheme for a bus garage and again the tender was awarded to Messrs. R. & T. Howarth. Such was the speed of expansion of the bus fleet that the Borough Surveyor had to submit plans for an extension to the bus garage in April 1927. By June loan sanction for the cost of £4,200 (£173,940) had been obtained and the contract for the extension was awarded to Messrs. R. & T. Howarth.

A further extension to accommodate another 20 or 25 buses was announced in January 1928. Plans tabled in February showed space for seven buses by extending the new bus garage to the entrance from Mellor Street. Alternative schemes showed an extension from the tramway repair shop to the existing entrance providing accommodation for 15 buses or roofing over the present entrance and a new entrance near the tramway repair shop providing for three buses. The Committee visited the site before deciding to go for the first option for seven buses, well short of the aim to provide for up to 25 extra buses. Loan sanction was sought for the £3,000 (£125,230) capital cost of the scheme. The contract for the works was again awarded to Messrs. R. & T. Howarth.

By August 1930 tramway abandonments and replacement by buses were gathering pace. Works costing an estimated £2,850 (£138,590) were necessary to the Car Shed:

1) to adapt certain bays on the easterly side of the existing Car Shed for the storage and washing of omnibuses for which purpose:

   a) the pits in this portion of the car Shed be covered with 9" by 4" pitch pine planks;

   b) the existing gangways be reconstructed in reinforced concrete;

   c) additional water supply points and lighting plugs be provided throughout the Car Shed;

2) to install a 10,000 gallon petrol tank and two supply pumps at the northerly end of the Car Shed;

3) to provide temporary storage accommodation for the disused tramcars at the most northerly end of the car Shed Yard;

4) to widen the gateways at the car Shed and at the entrance to the existing garage.

Loan sanction was sought to cover the cost.

In October 1930 it was agreed to install heating apparatus in the portion of the tram sheds that was being converted into a bus garage.

Abandonment of the tram routes to Littleborough, Norden and Bamford resulted in the withdrawal of 16 tramcars and the consequent loss of workshop staff. One fitter, one turner, two bodymakers, one wood machinist, one blacksmith and one blacksmith's striker were no longer required. The Manager was asked to reorganise and reduce the workshop staffing.

The final changes to convert the Car Shed to a bus garage were approved in June 1931 when the Omnibus Sub-Committee agreed to adapt the remaining bays in the Car Shed for omnibus accommodation. A screen was fitted to the engine shop in the garage. The cost came to £1,650 *(£89,260)* and as usual loan sanction was sought.

Changes were then needed to convert the workshops on the other side of Mellor Street. An exit door was cut into the former tramway workshop so that buses could enter or exit from either end. Trams, being double ended, could easily reverse within the depot but buses could not turn round inside the workshop. This doorway is still visible although it has not been used for many years. Other work included taking up the rails and covering the pits with 5" planking and the concreting of portions of four pits.

With the closure of the tramways in 1932, the buses entered into sole possession of the garage which continued in use for another sixty years with Rochdale Corporation Transport until 1969, then SELNEC Passenger Transport Executive until 1974, then Greater Manchester PTE until 1986, and finally GM Buses until closure in November 1991. The Tramway Offices can still be seen on Mellor Street although the depot behind them is not the original tram shed. It is now occupied by a local potato merchant. The workshops building across the road also still stands and was occupied until 2005 by textiles company Alexander Drew.

19. Parcels and freight.

Freight ideas not progressed

Tramways are usually associated with passengers but they can sometimes usefully carry freight or parcels as well. One interesting prospect for a freight tramway network was aired at a meeting in 1902 attended by the Chairman at Liverpool Corporation. A proposal to transport merchandise from Liverpool Docks to south Lancashire towns was discussed but the Committee did not feel able to make any decision until more information was available. In fact the concept was never developed.

In September 1906 the Manager tabled a report on developing parcels traffic on the tramway but the matter was deferred for further consideration. What could have been a fascinating development was a freight spur from the Manchester Road tramway. The Committee asked the Gas and Electricity Committee if they would like to include a tramway in the Provisional Order in 1906 to connect the existing tramway with the coal sidings of the Lancashire and Yorkshire Railway. It is not clear exactly where such a line would have run. The concept was not pursued.

Parcels on any tram

By 1912 parcels were being carried for delivery at any house, shop or other building immediately joining the line of route. Charges were 2d *(52p)* for parcels up to 14 lbs, 3d *(79p)* over 14 lbs and under 28 lbs and 4d *(£1.05)* over 28lbs and under 56 lbs, the maximum permitted. Any parcel which could not be delivered was returned to the Tramway Centre for collection.

Parcels were normally carried on trams between 9 am and 5.30 pm Mondays to Fridays, and between 9 am and 12 noon on Saturdays, but not on Sundays, holidays or during exceptional traffic or on Workmen's cars. Parcels could also be left at the left luggage office in the town centre for 1d *(26p)* per day.

An agreement was signed between Rochdale Corporation and the General Post Office on 10th March 1913 for the carriage of mailbags on trams, every day including Sundays at a price of £3 *(£182)* per annum for each ordinary mail bag. Special mail bags were carried at 6d *(£1.52)* per bag. The contract was deemed to have started on 1st January 1912, more than a year previously, and would run until 31st December 1916. It could be terminated on six months notice by either party.

An approach was made in July 1925 by Mr Henry Mattinson, General Manager and Chief Engineer of Manchester Corporation Tramways for an extension of their parcels service to Rochdale. The Manager recommended that the scheme should go ahead and it duly commenced on Monday 30th November. A delivery van was purchased for the purpose. The parcels travelled to and from Rochdale town centre and were redistributed by van.

Letter boxes on trams

A useful innovation was approved for a twelve month period in November 1924 when the Committee agreed to a request from the Postmaster in Rochdale to fix letter boxes on tramcars arriving in the town centre just before 8 p.m. Anyone wishing to post a letter could stop a tram at any normal tram stop to post their letter, especially useful in outer districts where the last collection from pillar boxes was 6 p.m. The Post Office paid for the boxes and maintained them.

Parcels were carried on trams between Manchester and Rochdale. This rare view of a Rochdale tram in Middleton, bearing the route number 17, is at Market Place looking towards Long Street. (Chas.Wilkinson).

20. Accidents will happen.

Steam tram and horse bus accidents

All transport systems are liable to accidents and although tramways generally had a good safety record, they did not escape alarming incidents.

In June 1884 a steam tram wearily struggling up Drake Street came to a halt, short of steam power, whereupon the driver reversed the car downhill in order to 'take another run at the hill'. Believing that the tram was in fact running backwards out of control, two women jumped screaming from the top deck, and sadly one of them died from her injuries. This incident highlighted the problem of tram locomotives that were not powerful enough to cope with the gradients.

In the days when brakes were not quite as efficient as today, relatively minor collisions were not uncommon. Open top Brush 4-wheel car No. 23 suffered substantial damage to the platform but the car body remained intact. *(MTMS)*

The following year saw two spectacular accidents on the Rochdale to Bury route, resulting in cars overturning due to excessive speed, fortunately without fatalities. In the first the crew had somehow mislaid the cotter pin that secured the coupling between the loco and its trailer. Failing to find it they used a piece of bell cord to fasten the coupling. Needless to say it did not last long and the trailer ran back on the gradient. In the panic to escape the conductor was pushed off the platform leaving nobody to apply the brakes. The car ran into a passing loop, narrowly missing another tram, derailed and fell onto its side. Lessons always have to be learnt: this one was easy – do not couple trams with rope!

The second was caused by a tram driver who was speeding to catch up time on his 50 minute, 7 mile journey to Rochdale. On entering the points, allegedly at 20 mph and with standing passengers on the top deck, it overturned. More lessons to be learnt!

Accidents did not only happen to trams. The Rochdale Observer reported an alarming fatal accident on 7th July 1903 when the Bacup to Rochdale horse bus belonging to W. Roberts and Sons Ltd of Bacup, a familiar sight at the time, was passing through Healey along Whitworth Road. A steam lorry belonging to John Bright and Brothers, well known in Rochdale, was a short distance in front and it may have startled the horses. They bolted across the road near the Gale Inn, the driver being thrown from his vehicle. A passing medic, Dr Dixon, administered brandy and water but could not save the driver or one of the horses.

Electric tram accidents

One of the first incidents with electric trams occurred on 29th September 1902 when a tram reportedly collided with a horse drawn cart. The owner, Mr Henry Stewart of 40, Redcross Street issued a summons against the Corporation for damage to the cart, depreciation in the value of the horse and loss of a quantity of eggs which he claimed were destroyed. The action was vigorously defended. The case was heard at Rochdale County Court on 15th May 1903 and the Corporation won the case with costs. Perhaps Mr Stewart had omitted to present the damaged eggs as evidence!

Serious injury was avoided on 15th September 1904 when a Spotland tram skidded off the tracks in Blackwater Street and ended up in Henland, a narrow alleyway leading to Newgate. The rails had become greasy after a water cart had sprayed the road. Blackwater Street was on a significant downward gradient and the tram approaching the terminus on the single track, just after five o'clock, could not stop. It slid across Lord Street beyond the end of the rails and hit a lamp post on the corner of Lord Street and Henland. Unfortunately the street lamp contained a gas pipe but quick witted PC Tomlinson, on duty nearby, immediately stopped the gas leak and informed officials at the gas works. Nobody was hurt and little damage done.

Fog was always a hazard for road vehicles and while trams were better off than most because the rails provided an infallible guide, accidents could still happen. On 16th November 1904 tram Nos. 34 and 35 collided in fog in Dane Street. Another collision between two trams occurred only two weeks later when Car No. 1 ran into the rear of Car No. 30 on Drake Street, this time without the excuse of fog. However when fog again affected the tramway in December, the tram drivers' skill was praised for avoiding accidents, as the Rochdale Observer noted on December 24th:

On 2nd November 1916 double deck workmen's car No. 45 from Rochdale to Bacup was derailed and ran away backwards. It crashed into a stone wall near the Co-operative store at Shawforth, ending up some eight feet above the field below. Over a dozen of the 30 or so passengers on board were injured but thankfully there were no fatalities. *(MTMS)*

Eric Fielding)

On 9th July 1904 a collision occurred between a tramcar and a cab owned by Mr Samuel Ogden who was injured and his cab damaged. An accident occurred on 12th July on Bury Road when a trolley head came off, slightly damaging a girl's clothing and leaving her with nervous shock. It could easily have been much worse. Another road accident with an electric tram was on 6th August when Car No. 6 collided with a cart belonging to Mr Wycherley near Midge Hall Lane. Another collision occurred two days later in Willbutts Brow on the Norden route between Car No.1 and a lorry belonging to the Lancashire and Yorkshire Railway. Yet another August accident on 11th was at Spotland Bridge between Car. No.4 and a mineral water cart belonging to Messrs Heywood & Co. of Royton. These were typical incidents in the early years of electric trams.

'After a week of dense fog, beating all records for the past 20 or 30 years, the welcome change last night to a clear atmosphere seemed to good to be true. Before the late change, yesterday was the worst day of all, though Tuesday ran it very close when fog hung over the town like a heavy pall. The tram system in Rochdale was seriously disorganised, as often it was impossible to see

The first John Street accident occurred on 14 February 1914. Single deck bogie combination car No. 63 ended up embedded in The Rochdale Equitable Pioneers shop on Smith Street. Twenty passengers and the driver were injured but amazingly there were no fatalities. The fragile body structure was extensively damaged but the more solidly built underframe and bogies were relatively unscathed.

(MTMS)

a car five yards away and the fact that a trying week has passed without accident is in itself testimony to the extreme care and caution displayed by the drivers and conductors. What made things worse was the fact that the fog was accompanied by 11 degrees of frost.'

Some accidents thankfully did not result in serious injury, or worse, but were still quite spectacular. One such occurred at lunchtime on 8th November 1905. A tram from Oldham Road was travelling slowly down the gradient on Drake Street behind a Threlfall's Brewery motor wagon. As it approached Water Street the wagon stopped suddenly. Driver Harold Haigh of Norden applied his brakes promptly but the rails were too greasy and the tram slid into the back of the wagon with considerable force. The Rochdale Observer for 11 November reported:

'Mr Haigh was struck on the chest and stomach by the rear portion of the wagon and a barrel full of beer rolled over him. The motor wagon was not much damaged'.

It does not report the damage to poor Mr Haigh!

The first fatal accident since the system opened occurred on 30th May 1906 when an elderly man, James Eccles, was knocked down by a tram. He died three days later on 2nd June. The motorman was exonerated from blame at the inquest.

Sliding down hills

Hills always presented a hazard to trams, especially steep hills. Rochdale, being in the Pennine foothills, has plenty of hills and trams went up quite a few of them. Sadly they sometimes came down even faster, with spectacular consequences, particularly the bogie cars whose rail adhesion was not of the best. John Street with a gradient of 1 in 11.5 (9 %) was the scene of more than one tram accident. On February 14th 1914, single deck bogie tram No. 63 operating the 7.50 pm journey from Tong Lane, Whitworth into Rochdale ran out of control and was derailed on the sharp right hand curve leading into Smith Street. It ran into a tramway pole and ended up embedded in the Rochdale Equitable Pioneers building on the corner of Smith Street and Molesworth Street.

Amazingly nobody was killed but 20 passengers and the driver were injured. Driver H. Sansome had stuck to his post until the moment of impact. His injuries prevented him from driving again and he was transferred to work in the repair shed. The Manager, Mr.G.Webster, visited the injured at home and relatives of those in the Infirmary and the Committee recorded their regret at the serious incident and expressed their sincere sympathy with the driver and injured passengers. The car body was extensively damaged, only two years after entering service. The Rochdale Equitable Pioneer's Society submitted a claim for goods damaged in the accident. A public inquiry into the accident was opened at Rochdale Town Hall by Lieut. Col. Druitt on Tuesday 24th February, concluding at the Infirmary on 24th March.

A different Co-operative store was the victim of another runaway accident on 2nd November 1916. The rear bogie of double deck workmen's car No. 45 from Rochdale to

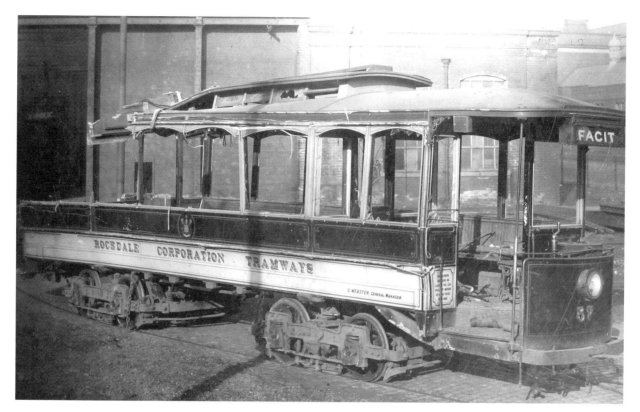

After the second John Street runaway crash on 9th February 1922, bogie tram 57 lies in a sorry state in the depot yard at Mellor Street. *(MTMS)*

Bacup was derailed going through the points. Whilst it was being re-railed, it ran away backwards. After travelling at a tremendous rate down the incline from near Britannia to the Co-operative store at Shawforth, it left the rails, crashed into a stone wall opposite the Red Lion, knocked over a tram pole and overturned, ending up on its side with a third of its length overhanging the wall, some eight feet above the field below. Over a dozen of the 30 to 40 passengers on board were injured but amazingly there were no fatalities.

Another potential hazard was road works, especially when tramway construction or re-construction meant digging up wide sections of carriageway, especially in the virtual absence of safety lamps. When the Littleborough steam tramway tracks were being removed to make way for the new tracks for electric trams, cab proprietor William Mitchell of Littleborough claimed damages for an accident which he alleged was due to the works being inadequately lighted and guarded. His claim was refused by the Committee.

While most accidents were between a tram and another vehicle or pedestrian, tram to tram collisions occasionally happened. One was on 27th January 1915 when a morning inbound car collided with an outbound car near the Gale Inn loop on Whitworth Road. The extensive use of single track with passing places made such accidents almost inevitable although speeds were usually low and sight lines good.

Despite the safety measures introduced to try to stop runaway trams on John Street, a very similar accident to the 1914 crash occurred on 9th February 1922, almost eight year later. Car No. 57, another eight wheel bogie single decker, got out of control whilst descending John

Street, leaving the rails on the curve into Smith Street. Once again it buried itself in the premises of the unfortunate Rochdale Equitable Pioneers Society. A total of 18 persons were injured, including the Borough Electrical Engineer, Mr F. H. Rudd. Major G.M.Hall from the Ministry of Transport inspected the scene of the accident on 17th February.

In his report, Major Hall found that there were no defects in the brake equipment or sanding gear. He stressed that it must be impressed on motormen that the utmost care and scrupulous observance of the regulations is essential for the safe operation of tramway traffic on severe gradients. Any failure to observe compulsory stops and speed limits should result in strict disciplinary action. He also advised that motormen should make frequent use of the track brakes and not only in emergency. The Manager responded by stating that any employee not complying with these regulations would be liable to dismissal.

Yet again the Rochdale Equitable Pioneers Society fell victim on 6th April 1925. This time the cause was a Sentinel steam lorry belonging to Messrs. John Taylor and Company, Pollard Street Brewery, Ancoats, Manchester which collided with single deck tram No. 40, the 4.20 pm from the Tramway Centre to Littleborough via John Street. The tram was ascending John Street towards Yorkshire Street but was hit by the lorry as it turned from Yorkshire Street into John Street. It ran backwards out of control, leaving the rails on the curve into Smith Street and once again ending up in the Coop premises. Tram 40 was extensively damaged at the front where it was struck and the controller and brake handle were completely out of action and the heavy underframe suffered badly.

Mr G. W. Stansfield who witnessed the incident said the result would have been much more serious but for the coolness and presence of mind of two people. The driver, Mr. Clifford Robinson, had been thrown off the tram by the impact at the top of the hill. The tram conductor, Mr. Samuel Beardsley, stayed at his post, wrestling with the trolley pole and the brakes to try to slow the car and shouting to passengers to lie on the floor. The policeman on point duty at the bottom of the hill, Constable Heaton, realised what was happening and stopped the traffic to leave the way clear for the runaway tram. Twenty four persons were taken to the Infirmary with 11 being detained. One of the Mellor Street recovery crew who removed the wrecked tram was Mr Sansome who had driven the tram that crashed in 1914, and who had also helped salvage the tram in the 1922 accident.

The Corporation held the lorry's owners entirely responsible and issued a writ against them. The Company declined liability. The Ministry of Transport intimated that it was unlikely that they would order an inquiry, suggesting that they did not consider the tramway to be at fault although they did request full details and plans. The Manager submitted his report in August but no further action was taken.

The last significant tram accident occurred on the Esplanade outside the Town Hall but this time it was Manchester Corporation double decker No. 990, approaching the town centre at the end of its long journey on route 17 from Manchester. The car collided with a trailer towed by a steam powered brewery wagon owned by Walker and Homfrey's Woodside Brewery in Salford. The wagon was turning right into Theatre Street and obviously it's driver did not appreciate how fast the tram was going. The front of the tram was badly damaged and Driver Harrop, of Miles Platting, had to jump backwards as his controller was knocked over by the force of the collision. Fortunately there were no serious injuries, not even to the barrels of beer which had toppled from the wagon and were scattered across the street.

21.The beginning of the end.

Track condition causes closures

By this time, much of the Rochdale system was rather worn single track with passing places, limiting speeds and capacity and making trams slow and noisy compared with the new buses. Manchester was still strongly pro-tram and opened a new line between Middleton and Heywood on 19th May 1928. They also re-constructed the former MET route between Middleton and Slattocks in double track. Rochdale could not match this generous scale of investment.

The influence of tramway managers, especially in the large undertakings, was immense. Henry Mattinson, General Manager of Manchester City Tramways, was very pro-tram and encouraged expansion of the network. It was to be short lived because when he died suddenly in 1928, his successor Stuart Pilcher was strongly pro-bus. Hence the joint Rochdale to Manchester route was destined to be short lived.

The increasing deterioration led to questions being raised at frequent intervals by the Urban Districts of Wardle and Littleborough about track along Halifax Road, New Road and Featherstall Road. Every time the matter was raised at the Committee it was deferred. Clearly the Committee could not make up their minds, or more likely some hard discussions were taking place behind closed doors on the future of the tramways. Lack of finance and the threat of bus competition no doubt influenced their deliberations.

Eventually the truth emerged at a Special Meeting of the Committee on 7th February 1929. Alderman Clarke admitted the question of the Littleborough route had been under consideration since December 1924. In November 1925 it had been recommended that the track should be reconstructed but from the Borough Boundary to Smithy Bridge Road would cost £17,000 (£4.38m) with another £30,000 (£7.52m) from there to Littleborough. At a meeting between Rochdale and Littleborough representatives, no objection was raised to amending the agreement to allow buses to be substituted for trams.

The Committee "having considered the question of relaying of the Tramways Track in the Urban Districts of Wardle and Littleborough, and the Chairman having referred to the present high cost of tramway track construction and altered conditions in methods of road transport since negotiations in connection with the Tramways Agreement with Littleborough commenced:

RESOLVED –
(1) That the Council be recommended to agree to the abandonment of the Tramway Track between the Borough Boundary at Wardle Lane and the Summit Terminus at Littleborough;

(2) That the Special Sub-Committee be authorised to re-open negotiations with the Littleborough Council with a view to the substitution of a service of omnibuses on this portion of the route, the variation of the Agreement

accordingly, and the taking of the necessary steps to effect the abandonment."

It was clear that in practice this meant the abandonment of the whole Littleborough route as the remaining section from Rochdale to the boundary at Wardle would not be economically viable on its own.

The crisis deepened with the publication of the accounts for the year ended March 31st 1929. The tramways had plunged to a loss of £10,040 11s 4d (£411,840) compared to a profit on the buses of £16,821 19s 6d (£689,970). Nevertheless the Department was striving to retain and win back passengers. Improvements to some trams were still being made including fitting top covers, high speed motors and transverse seats. The running time to Manchester was reduced from 70 minutes to 60 minutes and through fares were reduced from 9d to 6d. But these changes paled into insignificance in comparison with the worsening condition of the track and the financial picture.

Despite the state of the track and the impending demise of the tramways, experience gained in the development of Rochdale's tramways was recognised in April 1929. The Borough Surveyor, Mr. Sydney Morgan, was invited by the Institute of Municipal and County Engineers to sit on the British Engineering Standards Association Committee for preparing the British Standard Specification for Tramway Rails etc.

Nibbling away at the edges began to occur with buses substituted on some routes on Sunday mornings and trams curtailed to start at 1.30 p.m.. In August Spotland lost its Sunday morning trams in favour of buses and from August 4th this applied to all tram routes. Milnrow agreed to accept buses but Whitworth UDC, having by this time experienced buses, demanded the return of their Sunday trams.

Powers to abandon tramways

Paving the way for future abandonments, the Town Clerk recommended inclusion of the necessary provisions in a Bill to be promoted in the next Session of Parliament:

1) To enable the Corporation to abandon such tramways or light railways as the Corporation may from time to time decide, and to provide other transport service in lieu thereof.

2) To enter into agreements with any Corporation or Local Authority owning any tramways or light railways from time to time demised to or worked or run over by the Corporation with regard to the abandonment of any such tramways or light railways and the provision of other transport service in lieu thereof.

3) Restricting the running of Omnibuses on any route whether within or without the borough in competition with the transport services of the Corporation.

ROCHDALE CORPORATION PASSENGER TRANSPORT DEPARTMENT.

NOTICE.

ABANDONMENT OF TRAMWAYS & SUBSTITUTION OF MOTOR OMNIBUS SERVICES.

ROCHDALE, SMALLBRIDGE, LITTLEBOROUGH AND SUMMIT SECTIONS.

From Sunday, 19th October, 1930, the service of Tram Cars on the above routes will be withdrawn and substituted by a service of Motor Omnibuses.

For Fares, Stages and Time-Tables see other bills.

GEO. WEBSTER,
General Manager

The announcement of buses replacing trams on the Littleborough route on 19th October 1930. Similar notices were issued as tram replacement progressed. (LHAS)

A small change with great significance occurred on 16th October 1929. The name of the committee was changed from the 'Tramways Committee' to the 'Passenger Transport Committee'. While this was no doubt in recognition of the major role now being played by buses, it was also a sign that the days of the dominance of the tramways were coming to an end. The first meeting of the newly named Committee took place on 11th November, still under the chairmanship of Alderman Clark.

The following month on 5th December the Council decided to promote a Bill in Parliament to extend their omnibus powers, abandon the tramways and substitute bus services.

Accordingly, two Parliamentary Bills were promoted by Rochdale in 1930, the Rochdale Corporation (No.1) Bill and (No.2) Bills. The No.2 Bill contained clauses permitting the abandonment of certain tramways on omnibus routes. Heywood Corporation opposed the move and a Clause 28 had to be inserted to remove their opposition. Rochdale had to pay Heywood's ongoing capital costs for the tramway. The Bills were enacted as the Rochdale Corporation (General Powers) Act 1930.

The seriousness of the Transport Department's dilemma was highlighted by the accounts for the year ended 31st March 1930 which showed the buses continuing to make a comfortable profit of £16,217 6s 2d *(£788,630)* while the trams plunged deeper into the red with a deficit of £12,044 3s 0d *(£585,690)*.

In June 1930 the Manager put forward a proposal for the remaining part of the Littleborough tram route when the Wardle and Littleborough sections had been closed:

a) abandoning entirely the existing tramway service to Smallbridge

b) running a single deck bus or tramcar from the town centre along Entwisle Road, Yorkshire Street and John Street back to the town centre.

The following month the Committee agreed to abandon the tram service to Smallbridge but did not approve the replacement bus service, probably on the grounds that there were enough buses on the route already.

Original tram routes scrapped

The first major abandonment within the Borough, approved by the Committee in August 1930, included the two original trams routes to Bamford and Norden. It was precipitated by a decision of the Paving Etc. Committee to widen Edenfield Road which would have necessitated significant expenditure on the tramways. Track condition was another major factor. The recommendations were:

1) that the tramways between Churchill Street and Norden be abandoned and that a service of omnibuses be operated from the town centre to Norden (via Mellor Street);

2) that in view of the volume of traffic between the town centre, Spotland Bridge and Churchill Street, the tramways operating between these points (via Spotland Road) be retained;

3) that a half hourly omnibus service be operated between the town centre and Spotland via Spotland Road and that the tramway service from the town centre to Spotland be operated via Spotland Road during peak load periods only;

4) that the Bamford tramways be abandoned and that a service of omnibuses be substituted therefore.

This would leave Mellor Street without a tram service, the Norden route severely truncated and only a peak service to Spotland.

Taking advantage of the newly approved Rochdale Corporation (General Powers) Act 1930 the Town Clerk was authorised to apply to the Minister of Transport for consent to abandon:

a) The section of the Norden tramway from a point 80 yards west of Churchill Street to the terminus at Norden;

b) The Bamford tramway from the junction of Bury Road and Bridge Street to the terminus in Bury Road.

Notice was given "to the Road Authorities concerned of the intention to abandon the tramways so far as they were not within the Borough of Rochdale". This only covered Norden U.D.C. who duly approved the conversion to motorbuses.

Meanwhile, under the powers of the same Act, Littleborough Council were asked to seek the necessary consent to abandon the tramways in their district and to notify the County Road Authority. The Town Clerk applied to the Ministry of Transport for consent under the 1930 Act to abandon the existing tramway in Smith Street from John Street to Entwisle Road, Entwisle road for its whole length, Yorkshire Street from Whitworth Road, Halifax Road to the Borough boundary at Smallbridge and the existing tramway in Wardle U.D. Consent to all these abandonments was obtained in December 1930.

In fact the Littleborough route had been abandoned on 19th October 1930 in anticipation of consent and the replacing buses from Rochdale to Littleborough started the next day, as a through service to Summit, something the trams had never achieved. This was the first tramway closure, apart from the short section along High Level Road when Maclure Road opened.

A Special meeting of the Committee was held on 4th December 1930 to consider the Borough Surveyor's report on the condition of tramway track in the rest of the Borough. The Manager was asked to prepare a report showing the comparative costs of maintaining a tramway service and the substitution and maintenance of buses.

George Webster submitted a further report on tramway abandonment in December 1930 recommending that the whole of the Norden and Spotland routes be replaced by buses, rather than retain short workings to Churchill Street and peak only operation to Spotland. He also proposed abandoning the Thornham route beyond Balderstone. A replacement bus service would operate from the town centre to Thornham but with protective fares over the tramway as far as Balderstone. As with the Norden route it must have been obvious that this would be an uneconomic arrangement which would not last long. Not surprisingly, Mr Webster reported in May 1931 that revenue was poor on the remaining tramway to Balderston and recommended replacement by buses. It was approved by the Committee.

More tramway closures sought

The Town Clerk applied for consent under the 1930 Act to discontinue tramway operation on:

1) the existing tramway in Newgate, Blackwater Street, St Mary's Gate, Spotland Road and Rooley Moor Road;

2) the existing tramway from Spotland Bridge along Edenfield road to Savoy Street;

3) the existing tramway in Oldham Road between Broad Lane and the Borough boundary at Thornham.

Savoy Street is just on the Norden side of Churchill Street. Broad Lane was to become the terminus of the truncated route to Balderstone.

Consent to close the tramways in Edenfield Road from Spotland Bridge to Savoy Street, Edenfield Road from Savoy Street to the Norden Terminus and Bury Road from Bridge Street to the terminus at the Borough boundary was obtained in February 1931. Once again it was a bit late – these routes had already closed on 4th January. The following day, replacing buses ran on a revised network with a new service to Norden via Mellor Street to a terminus beyond the tram terminus at Hutchinson Road, still in use today. The Bamford circular was rerouted along Sandy Lane. An additional service operated between the Cemetery and Castleton via the town centre and Deeplish. Such changes demonstrated the greater flexibility of buses.

On 15th April the Manager announced that the last trams on the Spotland and Balderston to Thornham routes would run on Sunday 18th April. Consent to close the tramways in Newgate, Blackwater Street, St Mary's Gate, Spotland Road and Rooley Moor Road and Oldham Road between Broad Lane and the Borough boundary at Thornham was obtained in May 1931. They actually closed on 19th April and the circular route via the station ceased the same day. Again the replacing bus routes were restructured with a through service between Spotland and Brookside linked to the station circular, and a through Thornham to Norden service.

Conferences with the surrounding authorities followed in quick succession to discuss the state of tramway tracks, the arrangements for replacing trams with buses and the sharing of costs for the removal of disused tracks and the re-instatement of the carriageway. Conferences were held with Littleborough, Bacup , Whitworth, Milnrow and Heywood.

In February 1931 the Manager recommended the total abandonment of the Bacup route and the withdrawal of the express bus route over this section. A substitution bus route would replace both services. He also recommended the abandonment of trams between Sudden and Heywood Market Place and the substitution of a bus service and the total abandonment of the Milnrow route with replacement buses. The Committee agreed and authorised the negotiations to give effect to their decision. This effectively meant the end of Rochdale's electric trams as only the through route to Manchester was left untouched.

In May 1931 the Manager reported that revenue on the Bacup and Whitworth tramway was poor. Pending powers being obtained for the total abandonment of the route he recommended restricting the tram service to peak hours only with a Saturday service only from Rochdale to Healey in the afternoons and evenings. At other times buses would run. The Milnrow route received similar treatment in June with tram services reduced to peak periods only. A Special Meeting was held on 19th June 1931 to consider the Manager's report on the financial results of continuing tram operation on the Bacup and Whitworth and Milnrow routes, and the costs of bus substitution. The Committee resolved to "seek powers in the next Session of Parliament:

1) to enable the Corporation and the Whitworth Urban District Council to enter into an agreement with regard to the abandonment of the tramways through the Urban District of Whitworth now demised to or worked or run over by the Corporation, and the provision of other transport services in lieu thereof;

2) to enable the Corporation and the Milnrow Urban District Council to enter into an agreement with regard to the abandonment of the tramways through the Urban District of Milnrow now demised to or worked or run over by the Corporation, and the provision of other transport services in lieu thereof;

3) restricting the running of omnibuses within the Urban Districts of Milnrow and Whitworth in conjunction with the transport services of the Corporation."

The Committee further agreed to reduce the tram services on both routes to peak periods with substitute bus services at other times.

In July 1931 the Town Clerk applied to the Minister of Transport for consent to abandon the tramway in Bolton Road between Manchester Road and the Borough boundary at Heywood. A draft agreement had been received from Bury Corporation for tramway abandonment and the operation of replacement buses.

A forerunner of GMPTE

A hint of the possible future shape of public transport was glimpsed on 2nd October 1931 when the Chairman and Manager met representatives of neighbouring authorities to discuss the question of forming a Joint Municipal Passenger Transport Board for South East Lancashire. The matter was referred to all the General Managers to consider and a unanimously agreed proposal was put forward the following year but it was not pursued. This was the year before the London Passenger Transport Board was created in 1933, later to become known as London Transport, and nearly forty years before the creation of the SELNEC Passenger Transport Executive in Manchester which subsumed Rochdale's Transport undertaking. (SELNEC stood for South East Lancashire North East Cheshire). SELNEC became Greater Manchester PTE in 1974 and went on to re-introduce trams into Manchester in 1992.

The Committee was given strong endorsement for its policy of abandoning tramways by the Royal Commission on Transport's 1930 report:

"Our considered view is that tramways, if not an obsolete form of transport, are at all events in a state of obsolescence, and cause much unnecessary congestion and considerable unnecessary danger to the public. We recommend therefore (a) that no additional tramways should be constructed, and (b) that, though no definite time limit can be laid down, they should gradually disappear and give place to other forms of transport".

The Committee accepted the paragraph so far as it related to congestion. The Royal Commission Report is widely acknowledged as dealing a fatal blow to tramways in Great Britain which effectively set public transport back half a century, at least in the larger cities, in marked contrast to their continual development in the Netherlands, Germany, Switzerland and elsewhere.

The high costs of conversion

The high costs of the tram conversion programme, particularly the costs of acquiring the bus fleet, were having an impact on the Committee's finances. Estimated income for the year ending 31st March 1932 was £227,820 (£13.25m) with expenses of £181,488 (£10.56m) leaving a balance of £46,332 (£2.69m). However loan charges, rent of leased lines and other charges amounted to £58,176 (£3.38m), giving a deficit of £11,844 (£688,880). The Committee had asked the Finance Committee to make provision of £10,000 (£581,630) for the ensuing year for the general rate but the Finance Committee wisely increased this to £14,000 (£814,280).

Even this proved to be insufficient as the revised estimate for the net loss for the year was £13,642 (£793,460) to which had to be added the deficit brought forward from the previous year of £5,197 (£302,270) making a total deficit of £18,839 (£1.10m).

As all the tramways in and around the Borough were now earmarked for closure, it was agreed in March 1932 that negotiations be opened with Manchester Corporation to consider the abandonment of the joint through tram route to Manchester. The Manager of Manchester Passenger Transport Department responded in April agreeing to the abandonment and suggesting a single fare of 8d (£1.94) for the replacement bus service.

Rochdale's Manager made recommendation to a Special Meeting of the Committee on 29th April 1932 that all tramway services be abandoned, indicating the number of buses required to make the changeover. He also recommended that the Rochdale to Castleton via Tweedale Street route be abandoned at an early date. The Committee authorised the necessary steps to put the changes, including replacement of the through tram service to Manchester, into effect. They proposed borrowing £50,000 (£2.91m) for the new buses needed.

Another Special Meeting was held on 9th May when it was agreed that the abandonment of the Bacup and Whitworth tramway and the partial abandonment of the Milnrow route would take place on 15th May. As previously recommended the express bus service to Bacup was withdrawn at the same time. The date of abandonment was subsequently given as 14th May although trams continued to run to Newhey until 6th August 1932 because of a shortage of new buses. Ironically, in the last few months of operation it was possible to run double deck cars on the Newhey route as the bridges had been raised but the track was so poor that minor derailments were common.

On 2nd June 1932 agreement was reached with Bury and Heywood Corporations on the abandonment of the joint tram route and that replacement buses would commence on or about 3rd July 1932. Official records give the last day of tram operation as 2 July 1932 but some sources suggest that trams did in fact continue to run until 21st August because of a last minute hitch. The replacement buses were to be operated by Bury and Rochdale and the financial arrangements with Heywood were specified. The agreement allowed Bury to continue to operate to Heywood for another 12 months from 3rd July, or as agreed. In fact Bury trams continued to run to Heywood until February 1933, well after the Rochdale system had closed. Manchester trams continued to run from Middleton to Heywood until 1st May 1934.

At the same meeting the Town Clerk was authorised to apply to the Minister of Transport for consent to abandon the tramways in Smith Street, John Street, Whitworth Road to the Borough boundary at Healey, from the Healey boundary northwards for a distance of 274 yards, Oldham Road from Drake Street to Milnrow Road and Milnrow Road from Oldham Road to the Borough boundary at Firgrove.

Consent for the Whitworth route was received in July and for the remainder in August. The Whitworth route had in fact closed in May and the Milnrow route closed on August 6th.

Also in August the General Manager of Manchester City Transport Department wrote to say it would not be possible to provide a substitute bus service on the through Rochdale to Manchester tram service before the beginning of October. This extended the life of Rochdale's trams a little.

The final closures

The Town Clerk was authorised to seek consent from the Minister of Transport to the final list of closures in August 1932. They included the existing tramways in:

- South Parade, Drake Street and Manchester Road from Packer Street to to the junction with the Middleton Light Railway;

- the Esplanade and Manchester Road from Packer Street to Drake Street;

- Dane street, Bridge Street and Mellor Street from the junction of the Esplanade with Manchester Road to Spotland Road;

- Lower Tweedale Street and Tweedale Street from Maclure Road to Manchester Road;

- Maclure Road and Richard Street from Lower Tweedale Street to Drake Street;
- Manchester Road from Silk Street to the Borough boundary of Rochdale and Middleton.

Consent from the Minister of Transport was not received until December, posthumously, as the last tram had already run. The joint route to Manchester was the last to survive and finally closed on 12 November 1932, 30 years and six months after Rochdale's first electric tram had run from Dane Street to the Cemetery Gates, nearly 50 years since the first steam tram had run, but only seven years since the start of the Manchester route.

The closure of Rochdale's last tram went almost unnoticed. A brief report in the Rochdale Observer on 5th November commented that the Rochdale to Manchester route would be replaced by double deck buses running every ten minutes, starting on 13th November. They would stop at all 192 tram stops and take about 50 minutes, only ten minutes longer than the express buses which had only 26 stops. On the last day itself, the end of the trams justified a mere one column inch on page 9 in the Rochdale Observer!

A few days later on 25th November, Alderman Clark, Chairman of the Passenger Transport Committee, gave a talk to the Rochdale Reform Club comparing the problems of running trams with the ease of running the new buses. The Tramways Act of 1870 had made authorities liable for repair of the road between the tracks and eighteen inches either side, intended to cover use of the road by horse trams. But it was still in force even though there was practically no road wear resulting from electric trams. The £75,000 (£3.58m) to buy out the steam tramway had incurred a further £81,000 (3.86m) in interest for which they had no assets. The Corporation were liable for the cost of reinstatement of the road after the tramway abandonment totalling £54,000 (£2.58m). All this came to over £200,000 (£9.54m) which had to be paid by the travelling public. On the top of that was the outstanding debt for tramway track construction, the offices, and lease of lines in other districts which would not be paid off until 1940 .

In contrast, buses purchased in the seven years since bus operaton began had already repaid a third of their cost and some new buses were being paid for out of revenue. There was no long term liability on the buses as had proved such a burden on the trams. The fleet stood at 114 buses, 66 double deck and 48 single deck, and by 1939 their debt would have been written off.

Following the closure, the Manager was authorised to dispose of all the remaining tramway rolling stock and equipment including a quantity of underground cable. No records of tramcar sales were reported to the Committee except for one tramcar body which was donated to the Rochdale Corporation Passenger Transport Employees' Social Club for use as a pavilion.

Two months later, in February 1933, the Manager presented his financial estimates for the year ending 31st March 1933, the last year during which the tramways operated. The net deficit for the year was £17,008 (£952,810) with a deficit of £5,511 (£308,730) carried over from the previous year making the total deficit £22,519 (£1.26m). The tramway conversion programme had been an expensive process, particularly the high cost of purchasing replacement buses and the costs of the depot conversion works.

Nevertheless, the demise of the trams was even more rapid than their birth thirty years earlier, (as shown in the figures in Appendix J, Table 3). They made their last profit in 1927/28 while the fledgling buses were profitable from the start, even bailing the trams out for the next five years. But despite the financial success of the buses the trams continued to carry more passengers, had much higher load factors, brought in more revenue and had higher earnings per vehicle mile than their rubber tyred successors, right up until the last full year of tram operation.

The tramway centre with its distinctive shelters did not long survive the trams as a new town centre plan had been devised by Sir Henry Maybury. For a while the replacement buses followed the tram lines in an anti-clockwise direction, but eventually the tramway centre was replaced by a long central island, simplifying the traffic flow. Another large oblong island was proposed opposite the mouth of Newgate around which all the traffic would circulate in a clockwise direction. John Bright's statue was to be removed from its existing position. An omnibus station was to be constructed with a series of platforms in the large open space between the Town Hall and Packer Street. All buses would load and unload at the bus station. Vehicles leaving the station would travel round a circle 60 ft. in diameter to enter the Esplanade. Footpaths would be widened. A pear shaped island would be provided at the junction of Smith Street and Drake Street to keep opposing streams of traffic in their correct lanes and the junction would be controlled by "electromatically operated light signals".

The roundabout at the bottom of Newgate is still there but the bus station on the Town Hall Square was never built. Buses continued to terminate scattered around the streets on The Butts, South Parade and Smith Street for another 46 years until the new bus station was opened between Smith Street and Baillie Street.

The causes of decline of tramways

The decline of tramways in Rochdale was being mirrored in other towns around Lancashire. In a paper to a transport conference in Manchester, Stuart Pilcher, General Manager of Manchester Corporation Transport Department, discussed the causes of the abandonment of tramways which was continuing at a rapid pace.

"The electrification of tramways throughout Great Britain took place in the early part of the present century so that the original rolling stock and track of those early days are now obsolete and worn out. The cost of reconstructing the permanent way has been more than doubled since the war (the First World War) and arrears

of maintenance and renewals which accumulated during the war years and the immediate post-war period when supplies were restricted and prices rose to prohibitive figures, were never overcome. Further, the tramway was, and still is, heavily burdened with the duty of maintaining the pavement between the rails and 18 inches on either side.

In the years preceding the passing of the Road Traffic Act which introduced a uniform system of licensing and control of public service vehicles throughout the country in 1930, a great deal of wasteful competition was suffered by tramway operators at the hands of persons who, in many instances, ran unlicensed vehicles, operated only on the best paying routes, and who did not have to provide unremunerative services. The public, moreover, showed a distinct preference for the bus with its mobility and higher speed and ability to draw up to the kerb for passengers to board and alight. It should be noted here that the higher speed has the further advantage on most undertakings of enabling the bus to run at a lower operating cost than the tramcar. An additional factor of importance was the development of housing estates on the outskirts of the urban areas and the decentralisation of the population outwards which required the provision of additional bus services along principal roads with a consequent reduction in the loading of the tramways on the main thoroughfares. With the development in design of the pneumatic tyred vehicle, operators began to abandon tramways in favour of the motor bus or trolleybus which could run at a lower capital cost and operating cost, was more popular with the public, could maintain low frequency services to outlying districts, caused less obstruction to other vehicles, and which avoided the necessity for heavy expenditure on track and rolling stock renewals."

Many of these causes applied to Rochdale's tramway although it was the state of the track that was the over-riding cause. Not everyone would agree with Pilcher's pro-bus enthusiasm but he did accurately reflect the trends of the time. Rochdale's closure in 1932 took the total of abandoned Lancashire tramways to six; nine more closed by 1938 leaving only another nine to struggle on through the austerity years of the Second World War. In the late twenties there were over 600 route miles of tramways in Lancashire but when Rochdale trams finished it was down to less than 500 miles. By the late thirties it had shrunk to just over 330 route miles; by the end of the forties only Liverpool and Blackpool were left.

Rochdale Corporation Tramways
Opening and closing dates - Page 1

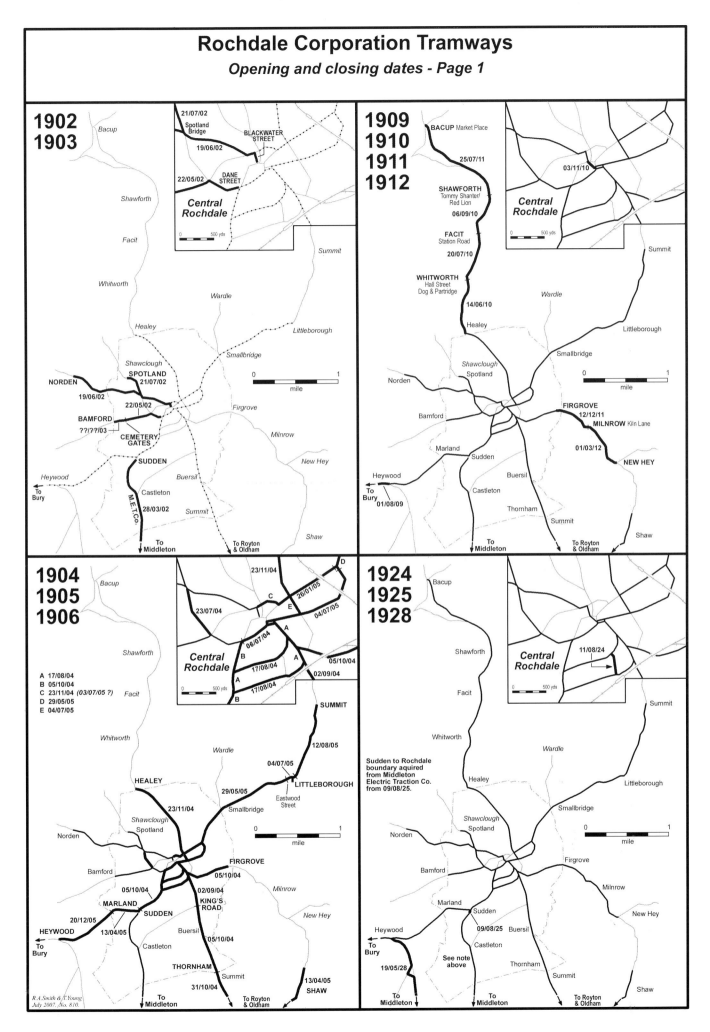

R.A.Smith & T.Young
July 2007. No. 810.

Rochdale Corporation Tramways

Opening and closing dates - Page 2

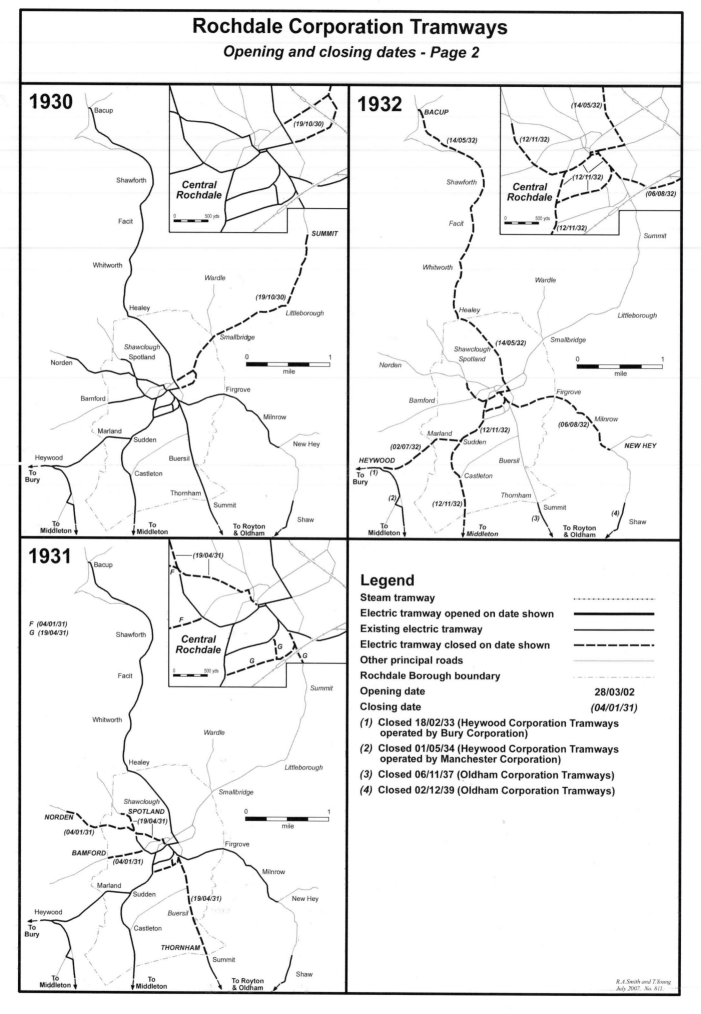

1930

Bacup
Shawforth
Facit
Whitworth
Wardle
Healey
Littleborough
Smallbridge
Shawclough
Spotland
Norden
Firgrove
Bamford
Milnrow
Marland
Sudden
New Hey
Heywood
Buersil
To Bury
Castleton
Thornham
Summit
To Middleton
To Middleton
To Royton & Oldham
Shaw

(19/10/30)
Central Rochdale
0   500 yds
SUMMIT
(19/10/30)
0   mile   1

1932

BACUP
(14/05/32)
(14/05/32)
(12/11/32)
Shawforth
Central Rochdale
(12/11/32)
(06/08/32)
Facit
(12/11/32)
0   500 yds
Summit
Whitworth
Wardle
Littleborough
Healey
Smallbridge
Shawclough
(14/05/32)
Spotland
Norden
Firgrove
Bamford
(12/11/32)
(06/08/32)   Milnrow
Marland
(02/07/32)   Sudden
NEW HEY
HEYWOOD
To Bury   (1)
Buersil
(2)
Castleton
(12/11/32)
Thornham
Summit   (4)
To Middleton
To Middleton   (3)
To Royton & Oldham   Shaw
0   mile   1

1931

Bacup
(19/04/31)
F
F (04/01/31)
G (19/04/31)
Shawforth
Central Rochdale
F
G   G
0   500 yds
G   G
Summit
Facit
Whitworth
Wardle
Healey
Littleborough
Smallbridge
Shawclough
SPOTLAND
NORDEN   (19/04/31)
(04/01/31)
Firgrove
BAMFORD
(04/01/31)
Milnrow
Marland
Sudden   (19/04/31)
New Hey
Heywood
Buersil
To Bury
Castleton
THORNHAM
Summit
To Middleton
To Middleton
To Royton & Oldham   Shaw
0   mile   1

Legend

Steam tramway	....
Electric tramway opened on date shown	————
Existing electric tramway	———
Electric tramway closed on date shown	– – – –
Other principal roads	———
Rochdale Borough boundary	
Opening date	28/03/02
Closing date	(04/01/31)

(1) Closed 18/02/33 (Heywood Corporation Tramways operated by Bury Corporation)

(2) Closed 01/05/34 (Heywood Corporation Tramways operated by Manchester Corporation)

(3) Closed 06/11/37 (Oldham Corporation Tramways)

(4) Closed 02/12/39 (Oldham Corporation Tramways)

R.A.Smith and T.Young
July 2007. No. 811.

22. Hello buses, goodbye trams.

Rochdale's first buses

Some municipalities bought buses very early on but Rochdale did not venture into this new mode until the mid-twenties. In September 1925 the Tramways Committee Sub-Committee attended the Exhibition at Olympia and had authority to purchase ten new buses. Their choice was a rather mixed fleet, just like the first trams a quarter of a century earlier:

- three chassis from Guy Motors Ltd of Wolverhampton with 30 -34 h.p. engines and 26 seater bodies;

- three Dennis 16 ft. wheelbase passenger chassis from Dennis Brothers Ltd. of Guildford with 60 - 70 h.p. engines;

- one Dennis 30 cwt chassis with 20 h.p. engine to be fitted with the Dennis standard box van body;

- three omnibus bodies from Strachan & Brown of North Acton, London, of the 26 seater type for one man operation, with emergency doors at the rear;

- three omnibus bodies, 33 seater type, with front and rear side entrances.

This totalled six buses rather than ten. The 30 cwt van was for the new parcels service to be operated with Manchester Corporation. The 33 seater bodies were delivered as 30 seaters.

A sub-Committee was set up in November 1925 to deal with all matters relating to motor buses.

The Manager's proposals for the first Rochdale Corporation bus routes were considered at a Special Meeting of the Committee on 30th November 1925. Five routes were suggested:

1) a half hourly service via Drake Street (starting near the Wellington Hotel) Maclure Road, Milkstone Road, Deeplish Road, Well-i'th'-Lane, Queensway, to Albion Street (Castleton), returning by the same route, requiring two omnibuses of the larger type;

2) a one hourly service (starting near Lancashire & Yorkshire Bank) via Newgate, Blackwater Street, St. Mary's Gate, Toad Lane, Falinge Road, into Shawclough, connecting with the Healey tramway at Lowerfold, requiring a one man operated omnibus;

3) a one hourly service between Rochdale and Wardle village, requiring an omnibus of the larger type;

4) a half hourly service between the tramway terminus at Bamford and Jericho requiring a one man operated omnibus;

5) a one hourly service between Shore Road and Pyke House, Littleborough, requiring a one man operated omnibus.

The trams finished without ceremony but at least the event was marked by a posed photograph of tram No. 80 with its replacing bus, Crossley Condor No.102. Tram 80 was the last tram on the last route, the No.17 to Manchester, on 12 November 1932. It was only seven years old. (MTMS)

These five services required a total of six buses, that is the whole fleet as then planned. All these routes were complementary to the tram network, apart from the Wardle route between Smallbridge and the town centre. Buses were still seen as a mode to reach the parts of town the trams could not reach, not as a replacement for them.

By January 1926 the Town Clerk had drawn up the Bye-laws for regulating the conduct of passengers on buses. The Manager prepared the fares, stages and stopping places for buses on six routes, now defined as:

Rochdale and Castleton;
Rochdale and Ending;
Rochdale and Wardle;
Rochdale and Jericho;
Littleborough and Shore;
Littleborough and Durn.

The first municipal motorbus service ran on 17th March 1926 half hourly between the Town Centre and Castleton via the Railway Station, Deeplish and Queensway. Rochdale was one of the last towns in the country to introduce buses. More routes quickly followed:

- Rochdale to Ending via Shawclough opened March 26th;
- Rochdale to Wardle via Smallbridge opened May 24th;
- Bury Road tram terminus to Jericho opened May 27th.

By April the Shawclough route was already overcrowded. A petition from residents of Shawclough and Lowerfold protested against the bus running through to Ending where passengers could transfer from the Whitworth trams. They suggested it should terminate at Lowerfold Chapel.

Rochdale buses beyond the boundary

In June 1926 approval to the operation of bus routes outside the Borough boundary was received from the Ministry of Transport. The routes were:

1) from the boundary between the Borough and the Urban District of Whitworth at Shawclough Road, along Shawclough Road to the tramways at Market Street, Ending;

2) from the centre of the Urban District of Littleborough, along Hare Hill Road and Shore Road to the village of Shore within the same Urban District;

3) from the centre of the Urban District of Littleborough, along Halifax Road and Blackstone Edge Road to Pyke House (Durn) within the same Urban District;

4) from the boundary between the Borough and the Urban District of Norden on Bury Road to the terminus of the Bury Corporation Tramways at Jericho, passing through the Urban District of Norden, the Township of Birtle-cum-Bamford (within the Bury Rural District) and the Borough of Heywood.

The first of these is intriguing as it would appear from the residents' objections that the service had actually commenced at least two months earlier. It would seem that when Rochdale reached agreement with Whitworth they went ahead without waiting for MoT approval. The residents repeated their overcrowding claims in July saying conditions were no better.

Buses began on the Littleborough routes to Clough Road, Shore and Hollingworth Lake on August 13th. A route from Rochdale to Turf Hill via Deeplish, Platting Lane and Broad Lane started on October 22nd. Approval was also received for the Wardle route from the Borough boundary on Halifax Road along Wardle Lane in the Urban District of Wardle to Wardle village.

There were still only six buses although the purchase of ten had been authorised. Prices were obtained from Dennis Bros. for four chassis and Strachan & Brown for the bodies, without inviting tenders. Their initial choice of vehicle had proved satisfactory, unlike many other early bus operators who experienced ongoing teething troubles. Their choice of routes was also sound; most still operate today.

The seriousness of the challenge presented by competing bus operators following the General Strike led to an Omnibus Sub-Committee meeting in August 1926 which was attended by members of Halifax Corporation and their Town Clerk and Tramways Manager. Halifax were seeking consent to run a bus service between Halifax and Rochdale via Sowerby Bridge, Ripponden, Blackstone Edge and Littleborough. They suggested that it be run in conjunction with Rochdale. Each authority would collect the fares on its buses over the whole route. Halifax offered to provide all the buses until Rochdale had obtained some

The first motorbuses were Guy and Dennis single deckers. No 6, DK3448 was a Dennis E type with Strachan and Brown 30 seat, two door body. It entered service 1926 but was not intended to replace trams, only to reach the parts that trams didn't reach.
(MTMS)

more vehicles. Halifax Corporation began operating the route on October 26th and Rochdale joined in on 22nd June 1927.

At the same meeting the Manager proposed a bus service between Hollingworth Lake and Shore via Dearnley and Littleborough. The necessary approvals were sought. Littleborough had already given consent to running buses along the main road between the Wardle boundary and Littleborough and up to Hollingworth Lake along Smithy Bridge Road. They had also given consent to Halifax for the new joint service.

Another joint service was approved in December 1926 between Rochdale and Shaw. Operators were Rochdale and North Western Road Car, starting on 17th August 1927.

Early bus operations had been quite successful and more routes were proposed including an extension at Hollingworth Lake from the Beach Hotel to the Fisherman's Inn. Ten additional buses were purchased, seven 32 seaters and three to be specified. Once again, Dennis supplied the chassis and Strachan & Brown the bodies.

More new bus routes started on 27th July 1927. A route to the south started at the Wellington Hotel and ran via Smith Street, Molesworth Street, Milnrow Road, Moss Street, St Peter's Street, Vavasour Street, Crawford Street, across Oldham Road into Durham Street and then to the railway station, returning to the town centre. A northerly route started from the town centre via Blackwater Street, St Mary's Gate, Spotland Road, Hudson Street, Heights Lane, Quarry Street, Whitehall Street, and along Mizzy Road into Fieldhouse Road, alongside Cronkeyshaw Common, and then Dewhirst Road to Syke Chapel, returning via the same route. While these bus routes did not compete directly with tram routes, there were some common sections and they did give better access to some residential areas which were a significant walk from a tram route. The former route became known as the 'Circular' bus route but was short lived, being withdrawn on 24th December 1927.

Express buses challenge the trams

A more direct challenge to the trams came from a proposal from Manchester Corporation Tramways who wanted to run an express bus service from Manchester to Rochdale, along Manchester Road and the Esplanade to terminate in the Town Hall Square. It was referred to the Special Licensing Sub-Committee of the Watch Committee who recommended approval. An express bus route had already proved successful between Heywood and Cheadle, (introduced on 11th April 1927 and extended to Gatley on 26 June), stopping only at tramway stage points with fares about double tram fares but faster journey times. From 24th October 1927 the through Rochdale to Manchester tram route was duplicated by a jointly operated express bus service every half hour, running through Cannon Street to terminate at Knott Mill.

Another famous Rochdale name appeared on the scene. Yelloway Motor Services run by Holt Bros. (Rochdale) Ltd started an express bus service in November 1927 between Rochdale and Manchester via Royton, Chadderton and Newton Heath. There were few stops and it was the fastest service between Rochdale and Manchester making it a popular choice. It lasted until 1944.

The expanding bus services needed more terminal space in the town centre. The Tramways Manager applied to the Watch Committee for carriage stands to be recognised as stands for motor buses on Packer Street from the District Bank to Fleece Street, for buses to Shawclough, Syke and Manchester, and on Smith Street from the Wellington Hotel to Weir Street for buses to Deeplish, and Castleton, Turf Hill, Shaw, Wardle, Hollingworth Lake, Blackstone Edge and Halifax. Bit by bit, buses were edging into previously exclusive tram territory. The application was granted.

In October 1927 tenders were sought for another eight buses. Approval for three was already obtained so the resolution was for another five. Loan sanction was sought for £15,800 (£654,330). The Dennis/Strachan & Brown combination was again chosen with seven 'E' type chassis and one 'F' type and eight single deck bodies fitted with 'Eco' destination indicators. Loan sanction was received on 20th January 1928.

Negotiations were opened with Todmorden Corporation for a through express bus route between Rochdale and Todmorden via Littleborough. Agreement was soon reached and 12th January 1928 set as the start date although in the event it started a fortnight later on 26th January.

Another express bus service was proposed which was to have a more direct impact on the trams. Discussions with Bacup Corporation lead to a scheme for a through express bus from Bacup to Manchester via Rochdale in co-operation with Manchester Tramways. This paralleled existing tram routes over most of its length. An application was lodged under Section 4 of the Rochdale Corporation Act, 1925. Ribble Motor Services lodged an objection.

The next joint bus service was between Rochdale and Bury via Jericho, starting on 19th December 1927. This was in effect an extension at both ends of the Jericho to Bamford route, taking in the sections previously exclusive to the trams of Bury and Rochdale. It was then only a matter of time before the tram routes at either end would succumb to bus competition.

A joint half hourly bus service was proposed in January 1928 between Rochdale and Ashton-under-Lyne via Royton, Oldham and Limehurst. Oldham provided two buses and Ashton and Rochdale one each, in proportion to the mileage in each area. This again paralleled tram routes over its whole length, including the former joint Rochdale to Hathershaw tram route. The service began on 22nd February 1928. Although competing with trams between Summit and Rochdale the buses were limited stop and charged higher fares.

In March 1928 the Manager reported that the entire bus fleet was in regular use and in the event of accident or breakdown it was difficult to maintain services. Authority was therefore given to purchase an additional five Dennis 'E' type single deckers with Strachan & Brown bodies using the reserve fund and without inviting tenders.

A public inquiry was fixed for 20th March 1928 to consider the Corporations's application to run express buses to Todmorden and Bacup. Approval to both routes was obtained from the Ministry of Transport in April. Bacup and Whitworth Councils asked for additional stops to be observed in their areas. Rochdale agreed to inaugurate request stops at these points, thus making the bus route rather less 'express' and a greater threat to the tram service.

Meanwhile the railway companies, who like the Corporations had been hit hard by the private bus competition sparked off by the General Strike, had secured controversial powers to operate their own bus services as a means of protecting their interests. In August 1928 they reached agreement with Rochdale and Halifax for the joint bus service between Rochdale and Halifax to be operated by the London, Midland and Scottish Railway. The costs of operating the service and the revenue collected were to be divided equally between the three parties. In addition the LMS would operate up to one third of the local bus service from Rochdale to Blackstone Edge but with protection given to the whole of the Corporation's tramway between Rochdale and Littleborough. 'Protection' in this context meant that the bus fares would be higher than tram fares and stopping places more limited. LMS took over the service on 10th December 1928.

An early attempt at integration which has still not been achieved today was recommended by the Manager in August 1928. He thought it desirable to extend as many bus services as practicable from the outer districts to the railway station so that residents from those districts could travel to the railway without change of vehicle. It was short lived for some routes with the Bury service being diverted to terminate at the town centre in April 1929.

Another bus service jointly operated with Manchester was proposed in August 1928 from Norden to Gatley via Bamford village, Hooley Bridge and Heywood. The Norden terminus was at the War Memorial on Edenfield Road. This service still exists in the form of the 167 bus route.

Improvements to the roads in Bamford allowed a circular bus route to be planned in November 1928 which ran along the first two tram routes in Rochdale. The half hourly circular service ran in each direction from the railway station running over the Norden tramtracks via Mellor Street and Edenfield Road to Bagslate Moor Road and Norden Road, returning via War Office Road and Bury Road. It followed the Bury Road tram route back into town. Buses ran every half hour in each direction, each bus making a return trip in the half hour. The route was approved by the Ministry of Transport on 8th January 1929 and began operation on 24th March. Departures via Bury Road were coordinated with the Bury bus service to give a 15 minute service to Bamford.

In December 1928 it was agreed that the LMS would operate a number of services jointly with the Corporation in addition to the Halifax service. They included:

Rochdale to Bury via Jericho;
Bacup, Rochdale and Manchester;
Rochdale and Todmorden;
Rochdale, Oldham and Ashton;
Rochdale and Shaw.

It is not clear why the Corporation should give up so much of their routes to a railway company so readily when they had previously been strongly opposed to any involvement. The strong threat of LMS bus competition may have demanded compromises to avoid losses.

Another five Dennis 'E' type chassis with Strachan & Brown bodies were ordered in January 1929, again without inviting tenders. They arrived in February, being numbered 31-35 in the fleet and bringing the total number of buses to 35.

A Dennis single deck bus with Strachan and Brown bodywork, a type that became familiar in the late twenties.

The Crossley Condor double deck bus became the favoured tram replacement vehicle Over 60 were purchased between 1930 and 1932 (MTMS).

Strachan & Brown invited the Corporation to exhibit one of their new buses at the Commercial Motor Show at Olympia. The invitation was accepted and it was agreed to purchase the vehicle that was exhibited and that in the special circumstances tenders be not advertised. The Show was held from 7th to 16th November, 1929.

The three Guy buses obtained in 1926 had remained the only Guys in the fleet, all subsequent purchases being from Dennis. In April 1929 it was decided to dispose of these three vehicles and write off the debt from the profits on bus operations. They were eventually sold to Messrs. Foster & Seddon of Pendleton, Salford.

In April 1929 the Manchester to Rochdale bus service, joint with Manchester, was extended to Littleborough to provide a through service from Littleborough to Manchester. It was extended to Altrincham on 16th May, creating a 22 mile cross conurbation route. In August approval was given for a route proposed by the Manager of Bolton Tramways from Rochdale to Bolton via Sudden, Marland, Heywood, Heap Bridge and Bury. It was to be operated by the three municipalities and began on 31st October 1929.

On 12th August an express bus route started between Rochdale and Bolton via Jericho and Bury. It was very short lived as in October 1929 it was withdrawn and the half hourly Rochdale to Bury via Jericho service re-instated.

Buses and trams galore!

By the end of the twenties the public transport scene in Rochdale was extremely colourful. As well as trams from

Rochdale, Bury and Manchester buses could be seen from seven municipalities (Rochdale, Ashton, Bolton, Bury, Manchester, Oldham and Todmorden), three company operators (Ribble, North Western and L.M.S.) and the independent Yelloway. Barely five years after the first Ribble bus ran, this was rapid progress indeed.

The first double decker to enter the bus fleet was recommended by the Manager in February 1930 who obtained quotations from Leyland Motors, Crossley Motors and Dennis Bros. for chassis and from Leyland Motors and Strachans of Acton for bodies. The tender of Crossley was accepted for a complete vehicle including 50 seat body and chassis. Messrs Northern Auto. Electric Services supplied lighting equipment. It was a lowbridge Crossley Condor model and became No. 37 in the fleet and was in effect the prototype tram replacement bus.

Buses had begun to extract passengers from the tramways, especially the express services, but they faced problems of their own in 1930. The 1930 Road Traffic Act introduced bus regulation and gave the new Traffic Commissioners wide powers to specify what could be run. They considered that traffic congestion in Manchester would be alleviated if the cross city routes were split to terminate on the fringe of the city centre. The Littleborough-Altrincham service was cut back to terminate at Cannon Street on 13th July 1931 and the Bacup-Flixton service suffered the same fate. The Norden-Gatley service was cut back to terminate at the new Parker Street bus station at Piccadilly Gardens on 25th October 1931.

Buses replacing trams resulted in a mix of public transport vehicles as described in a history of Castleton:

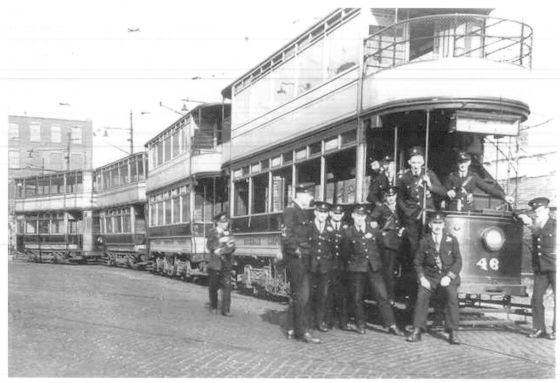

Four months after the last tram ran in Rochdale, Car 46 of 1905, still with open balcony and platform, heads a line of cars awaiting scrapping. Drivers and conductors have all had to transfer to buses but still seem to retain some affection for the trams. The last two fully enclosed cars were only seven years old when scrapped.

(MTMS)

"Journeys (from Castleton) to the other districts of Rochdale had become more convenient since the arrival of the new buses in the March of 1926. They were to replace the old and noisy tramcars which had served people over the years. The change over from tramcar to the omnibus was to happen in stages and therefore public transport was not affected in any way. This changeover period meant that for a given period main road traffic through the village had a mixture of buses, horse-drawn carts, motorised vehicles, tramcars and the tandems (popular at the time) not forgetting the bicycle. It was as though we had a 'traffic cocktail' with its many concoctions."

Buses win through

The Omnibus Sub-Committee recommended in May 1930 the purchase of 5 double deck and 6 single deck buses, subject to the Rochdale Corporation (No.2) Act receiving Royal Assent. Permission was sought from the Ministry of Transport to borrow £20,000 *(£972,580)* for the purchase. The order was increased by three double deckers in July following the decision to replace trams to Smallbridge with buses. Another £2,000 *(£97,260)* loan sanction was sought.

The decision to abandon the Norden and Bamford tram routes required three more double deck and three single deck buses. The order for Crossleys was increased accordingly. This brought the total orders to 11 double deckers and 9 single deckers. Loan sanction was sought for the additional cost of £9,150 *(£444,950)* for the extra six vehicles.

More tram replacement buses were needed and quotations were sought from Crossley and Dennis in December 1930. Crossley again won the tender to supply 6 six cylinder double deck and 6 six cylinder single deck buses. Loan sanction was sought for the cost of £18,060 *(£878,240)*. It was granted in February 1931, repayable over eight years.

An innovation for Rochdale was introduced in February 1931. The trams had never had route numbers, except for the joint route 17 to Manchester, and neither did the early motor bus routes. But it was decided that a system of numbering bus routes be introduced and that illuminated indication signs displaying the numbers of the routes and the destinations be fitted to all the buses.

Another innovation was the decision in April 1931 to purchase a diesel engine from Crossley Motors. To date all buses had been fitted with petrol engines which were then the norm. Oil engines were still in their infancy but the Manager wanted to try one out. Rochdale's forward thinking gained national recognition when Crossley Motors asked if they could exhibit a Rochdale diesel engined double decker at the Commercial Motor Show at Olympia in November. The Committee readily agreed and subsequently agreed to purchase the vehicle which became No. 82 in the fleet. The economy and easier maintenance of the diesel engine ensured that it quickly became the norm in place of the petrol engine.

Twelve more double deckers were ordered in May 1931. The order was split between Crossley Motors and Dennis Bros.and included for:

• 6 double deck diesel engined Crossley chassis with Crossley bodies;

- 3 double deck petrol engined Crossley chassis with Crossley bodies;

- 3 double deck Dennis 'Lance' petrol engined chassis with English Electric bodies.

Loan sanction for the total cost of £21,290 *(£1.15m)* was received in January 1932. By March 1932 the bus fleet reached 79 buses, 48 single deck and 31 double deck, of which 8 were diesel engined. A year later this had risen to 114 buses including 66 double deck with 43 diesels.

Another 12 buses were required to cover the partial abandonment of the Bacup and Milnrow tram routes. Of the three types purchased with the last order the diesel engined Crossleys had performed most efficiently and so another 12 of the same type were ordered. Loan sanction for the £24,695 *(£1.44m)* cost was obtained in June 1932. This covered these twelve vehicles plus the one extra exhibited at Olympia, 13 buses in total.

The final batch of tramway replacement buses were ordered in May 1932 to cover the rest of the Bacup and Milnrow routes, the through route to Manchester and the Castleton via Tweedale Street route. A total of 23 double deck diesel engined Crossley Condor chassis were supplied by Crossley Motors with one spare diesel engine. Ten 50 seat bodies were supplied by Crossley and thirteen 50 seat bodies by English Electric. The total cost was £43,515 *(£2.53m)* and loan sanction was sought from the Ministry of Transport. In the meantime a bank overdraft was arranged. The Crossley bodied buses became Nos. 95 to 104 in the fleet and the English Electric buses were 105 to 117. Loan sanction was obtained in November 1932.

It had taken less than ten years from the first abandonment to Littleborough in October 1930 to complete the conversion of Rochdale tramways to buses. By August 1932 only the long joint route to Manchester remained. It lingered on until the final closure on 12th November 1932. Rochdale's electric trams had lasted just 30 years.

Many Lancashire municipalities had obtained their buses from the Lancashire based Leyland Motors but Rochdale had obtained all their vehicles to date from Guy, Dennis or Crossley. In August 1932 Leyland Motors offered to supply a Leyland Titan 8 litre oil engined double decker on loan for a period of six months as a demonstration vehicle. It would be painted in Rochdale's colours of brown and cream. The Committee declined the offer.

The expansion of Rochdale's bus network was rapid. In 1933 the fleet comprised 114 'motor omnibuses', mainly of Dennis and Crossley manufacture, operating on 22 routes. Forty eight were single deck and sixty six double deck. The total income for the year ended 31st March 1933 was £189,000 *(£9.22m)* with expenses of £142,649 *(£6.96m)*, a gross operating profit of £46,359 *(£2.26m)*. The policy of tram replacement with buses was vindicated.

Rochdale had decided that buses were more suited to its needs and the two year conversion programme was initiated that culminated in the last tram running in November 1932. The high costs of replacing worn out equipment together with low traffic density on many routes made the decision almost inevitable. The joint route to Manchester survived the longest and Manchester Corporation continued to operate trams in its own area until

The tracks and the wires remain in the Town Centre but now only buses are to be seen. Dennis Lance 1 double decker No 81 with English Electric bodywork is about to depart for Thornham on what is now route 9. On the other side of the island 2-door Crossley Alpha single decker No.62 takes on passengers. The anti-clockwise traffic circulation that the trams followed is still operating but soon to be replaced with more conventional (for motor vehicles) clockwise circulation.

1949. But the replacement buses on the through route took traffic away from the remaining Manchester trams and in effect hastened their demise as well.

The new buses were reported to be very successful, turning the previous loss on the trams into a comfortable profit. A major factor was that they achieved an average speed of 11 mph compared to only 9.55 mph for the trams. A 15% reduction on the 65 minutes journey time to Manchester was a major improvement in productivity as well as attracting more passengers. The trams had been hampered by slower local trams carrying the heavier shorter distance traffic as well as the single line with passing places on parts of the route. By 1935 the last trams on Rochdale Road in Manchester had gone.

The Tramway Centre with its anticlockwise circulation was not suited to bus operation. The Butts and the Esplanade were remodelled to provide a wide dual carriageway with a central island and alternative terminal arrangements had to be found for the tram replacement bus services. An earlier plan to build a bus station in the Town Hall Square had never been approved and an alternative location was investigated on the old cattle market, where the Police Station is today. That was considered too far from the town centre. In August 1933 Mr Webster recommended on-street bus stands strung out along The Esplanade, Newgate, South Parade, The Butts, Fleece Street, Packer Street and Smith Street. Despite various attempts to provide a proper bus station, that situation continued for another 45 years until the present bus station was opened in 1978. Now that is under threat of moving further away from the town centre.

Rochdale's influence spreads far and wide

George Webster had seen the development of Rochdale trams from the earliest days and had been General Manager from 1913 until the closure of the tramways. He continued in post until 1936 when he was succeeded by George Cherry.

Links with trams continued well beyond 1932. Long after the last tram had disappeared from Rochdale's streets, a succession of Transport Managers looked after Rochdale's all-bus fleet but went on to manage electric vehicles. Chaceley Humpidge was manager of the Transport Department from 1942 to 1951. He then became manager of Bradford City Transport where he greatly expanded the trolleybus network and helped the restoration of a Bradford tram which ran on some depot track. He arrived in Sheffield as manager in 1961, just too late to prevent the last tram running in 1960. He was always convinced that trams had a place in modern urban transport and when a plan was unveiled to bring back trams to Sheffield in 1967 he was enthusiastic about the possibility. Sadly he died in 1972, long before his dream of building a tramway to Mosborough was finally realised in 1994. But he did achieve another ambition after retirement - ordination as a priest in the Church of England.

Next was Mr J.C. Franklin who was manager for only three years from 1951 to 1954. Joe Franklin had been Chief Engineer for the Salford Corporation Tramways just after the war where out of a fleet of 57 trams, only 15 were operational. He had always wanted to manage a tramway but arrived too late to see Rochdale's trams. His dream came true in 1954 when he went to manage Blackpool's famous tramway, Britain's first electric tramway and destined to become the only original street tramway left in Great Britain. Joe Franklin was a dynamic manager who introduced many innovations including double deckers to Fleetwood, illuminated tram tours, trailer car operation and one man trams. He managed the Blackpool Tramway for 20 years until his retirement in 1974.

Another ex-Salford Manager, Ronald Cox, took over from Joe Franklin in 1954. He had been Traffic Superintendent at Salford under Charles Baroth and continued Rochdale's line of strong managers who took pride in the stylish and well maintained fleet. Ronnie Cox left in 1962 to manage Bournemouth's transport including a large fleet of electric buses. He had run trolleybuses early in his career in his native St Helen's and new trolleybuses were being delivered to Bournemouth but they were destined to have a short life. Ronnie's stay in Bournemouth was also short as he was appointed General Manager of Edinburgh City Transport in 1964 and in 1973 became the first Director General of Strathclyde Passenger Transport Executive in Glasgow. The managerial skills he developed in Rochdale were taken through to one of the largest transport undertakings in Britain.

23. Memories live on.

Rochdalians recall their trams

The trams are long gone from the streets of Rochdale but they are not forgotten. Even after nearly three quarters of a century, some people still remember them, sometimes with nostalgia, sometimes with curiosity. Fifteen years after the last tram ran, Mr Hacking of Gale Street remembered vividly standing in town on a wet November night and seeing one of the old bogie trams clonking its way in from Bacup. "Its driver was covered in snow, wearing his queer little 'temmy' and great leather mittens and looking more like a returned arctic explorer. The bus driver was such a pitiful object in comparison!"

The last tram route was the long through service to Manchester and Mr Astles of Castleton remembers travelling on the tram through to Manchester although he was only seven when the last one ran. He recalls the driver swinging the pole round on the trams that only ran to Castleton, ready to reverse for the return trip to Rochdale. Meanwhile the conductor would walk through the tram, upstairs and downstairs, reversing the seats which were designed to face the direction of travel. This was on the newer trams; some older ones had fixed side seats downstairs which did not need to be reversed.

Eric and Ana Midgely of Spotland were 18 when the trams finished and they remember them well. On one occasion Eric had gone to Littleborough for a special event. The tram was waiting for them in the Square for the return journey home. His mother called to him to go upstairs because it was full downstairs. Eric obeyed but the tram was open top, like many of Rochdale's trams, with no protection from inclement weather and he was fearful of the effect of the heavy downpour on his Sunday best clothes.

Eric also recalls the accident on John Street in April 1925, one of the many tramcar assaults on the Cooperative store. A friend's father was among those injured and he was taken to the hospital for a visit. Eric's most vivid memory of that day was being given 2d *(30p)* to go and buy a comic!

Jesse Parkes of Passmonds remembers paying a halfpenny *(10p)* for a child fare on the tram along Entwisle Road. She recalls that the Smallbridge route was one of the first to be replaced by buses.

Retired Rochdale teacher Jack Crabtree lived on Huddersfield Road in New Hey as a young child where his grandparents kept a confectioner's shop. He remembers watching the trams at New Hey and one occasion when a tram left the terminus heading for Milnrow but broke down after only about 200 yards. There was great excitement when tramway maintenance men appeared with their electric arc welding equipment to effect the repairs. He later moved to Manchester Road in Castleton, just before the trams finished, and recalls the single track line which branched into a double track loop at Chesham Avenue where Castleton trams terminated.

Grandchildren of tramway workers can still be found around Rochdale. Barbara Tomlinson, a Rochdale osteopath, is the granddaughter of tram conductor Jesse Howarth. He was known as 'Mr Please and Thank You' because he never missed an opportunity to utter these words and was highly regarded as a 'gentleman conductor'.

David Simpson's grandfather worked as an apprentice and then a tram driver. He served in the First World War and was one of those who returned to work again on the trams. He received his 25 year certificate and like many tram drivers, retrained to drive buses, finally retiring at 65.

Shirley Smith's grandfather, Richard Bentley, was the Deputy Manager during the changeover from trams to buses in 1932. He had been appointed Chief Traffic Assistant in 1913. She recalls that when it was snowing, ham and eggs would be provided by sympathetic residents at Littleborough to revive the tram crews. Shirley's husband Norman continued the family tradition of service to Rochdale as a Councillor for 31 years, retiring in 2004.

Working in transport sometimes carried on through the generations. Arthur Hodgson of Sudden spent his life as a Rochdale fireman but his grandfather Charles Hodgson was a steam tram driver. His locomotive was No.51; they always kept to the same engine. When the steam trams finished Charles became an electric tram driver and took charge of Rochdale's unusual Water Tram which was based at the cleansing department's depot on Entwisle Road. This had been the steam tram depot so Charles was returning to his previous workplace. Arthur's father, Ernest Hodgson, also worked on the trams and then moved to buses, initially for Rochdale Corporation Transport Department and latterly for SELNEC PTE (South East Lancashire North East Cheshire Passenger Transport Executive), precursor of GMPTE. He retired in the seventies.

Anecdotes about trams abound. Richard Greenwood remembers a family going into town and mother leaving the children with father while she did the shopping. Father astutely gave the children a halfpenny each and put them on the circular tram. This allowed him just enough time to down a couple of pints before recovering the children and meeting mother!

An eye-witness account

Life is reputedly full of coincidences. Over forty years after meeting Kevin Petrie, father of one of my college friends, David Petrie, I discovered that not only had he lived in Rochdale but he had been something of an amateur historian with a keen interest in tramways. Amazingly he not only recorded experiences with Rochdale trams but one of his neighbours was George Webster, Tramways Manager from 1913 until their closure in 1932. An extract from his unpublished local history offers some fascinating insights from an eye witness. He moved from London to Rochdale in about 1916 and lived at 237 Edenfield Road, on the Norden tram route.

"237 was about a mile from the centre of Rochdale and trams went past the house up to Norden, about half a mile beyond our house. As I first remember it there were two types of trams in use: single-deckers, necessary because of a number of low bridges in the town, and open top double-deckers where the trolley was mounted on a stout upright tube on the upper deck. The seats had backs which could be moved to face either way. Downstairs the cabin was closed in but the end platforms were open, the driver and conductor being exposed to the weather. Roofed in double deckers were the same, fully closed in vehicles appearing about 1920 or 1921. Trolley poles, the means of contact with the wires, now generally replaced by pantographs, were spring-loaded and had a rope with which the conductor could hold them down when turning round at the terminus. The lines had junctions and crossovers involving points; when these were facing they had to be operated by a little lever that the driver carried. A thing that, so far as I know, you do not see now, at least not on the new Manchester trams, was a gridded platform slung under the drivers section at the end of the tram. If a tram ran over someone he landed on that grid instead of getting under the wheels and motors. I saw an article in a paper once by someone who had that experience and emerged from the platform, quite unharmed.

"Trams were of great interest to Conal and me. This was firstly because we had an instinctive interest in engineering and secondly because we lived opposite to the tramways manager, a Mr. Webster and a friendship sprang up which allowed us to be taken on to the driving platforms from time to time and work some of the controls under the strict supervision of the driver. There was a rather casual attitude in those days and, of course trams did not need steering; also there was little traffic about. I cannot see it happening now!

"The arrangement of the tramway station at the Town Centre was unusual. The river had been bridged for a

hundred yards or so, as I shall explain later, leaving a flat wide area on which the Town Centre station was built. It consisted of an oval, paved with flags in the middle of which was a building housing offices, a waiting room and conveniences. Because one boarded the tram on its left hand side the tracks were crossed over so that the left hand side of the tram was against the central reservation and passengers could change trams without getting into the traffic, which flowed on either side of the island. The sketch below illustrates this.

"Tramways were laid along all the main roads. The one that concerned us, primarily because we lived on it, was that that went to Norden (north valley). Others went to Spotland (River Spod valley area), Whitworth and Bacup to get to Rossendale, to Littleborough and Summit where one met a Todmorden bus, to Milnrow (pronounced "Milthrer") and Newhey, to Thornham where there were trams to Royton and Oldham and to Sudden (south valley). The road split here, one branch going to Manchester through Castleton, Middleton (whose church was the mother church of Manchester cathedral) and the other to Heywood with its connection to Bury. When we first came to Rochdale, Middleton trams met the Rochdale trams at Sudden, but later the lines were connected up and trams went right through to Manchester. In the thirties the (Manchester) trams were replaced on many routes by trolley buses and later by diesel buses. The town must have spent a fortune on new rolling stock.

"I have mentioned the bridges at the town centre. The town was built round the river Roach and in olden days there used to be bull baiting with dogs on the bank of the river. One day a bull got loose and chased the onlookers up a narrow ginnel, now an archway, into Yorkshire Street; so the archway is now called Bull Brow. In the nineteenth century there were three bridges, one at the east end, the bottom of Drake Street, a footbridge in the middle leading from near the

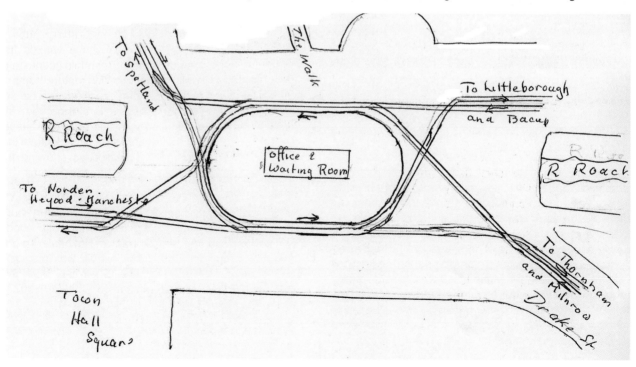

152

bottom of Drake Street to a passage way through the buildings on the north side, known as "The Walk", and one leading from the Town Hall Square to the bottom of Yorkshire Street.

Sometime in the early years of the last century it was decided to cover over a section of the river Roach between the two road bridges making a flat open space between the bottom of Drake Street and just beyond the bottom of Yorkshire Street giving access to Lord Street if I remember rightly, leading to Blackwater Street and Spotland Road. Blackwater Street got its name from an underground river that flows beneath it. The contractor doing this brought his plant in and put it down on the riverbank where he was going to work. A local warned him of the danger of doing this, but the contractor took a look at the insignificant stream and ignored the warning. Then there was a really wet day, not an uncommon thing in Rochdale followed by a flooded river and all the contractor's works were washed away; it broke him. The bridge thus built became, as I have said, the central tram station.

The tram controller handle used to drive Rochdale's first electric tram on the Bury Road route can be seen in the Touchstones Local History Museum on the Esplanade. (A.P. Young)

The valley was fairly narrow and the sides hilly. On the north side Blackwater Street and John Street were steep hills, too steep to ride a cycle up. John Street was the site of two accidents to trams whose brakes failed and the tram could not take the right hand bend at the bottom and crashed into a shop window. Drake Street on the south side was not as steep, but further along there were 204 steps leading to the parish churchyard on a flat area at the top of the hill. Dad once challenged me to run up those steps with my mouth shut; I couldn't. In the twenties the bridge was extended eastwards to the bottom of John Street and westwards to a point

level with the far side of the Town Hall giving access to the new post office, a handsome building, which was built opposite to the Town Hall about the same time. The cattle market was closed; it had become redundant by then. In the same period the area in front of the railway station was developed by building a new Catholic church and a new Fire Station there. The church is a fine domed building which was lined with white plaster in those days, but has since, I have heard, been covered with mosaics."

Tramway memorabilia and artifacts

Few signs of Rochdale's tramways remain today apart from the splendid Tramway Offices, complete with terra cotta sign over the doorway. A short length of tramway track in granite sets has been preserved in Yorkshire Street, between West Street and George Street near the Town Head roundabout.

An attractive tiled mural in the pedestrian subway under Constantine Road leading towards the Bus Station shows historic transport in Rochdale including a steam tram and an electric tram. They have been joined by a tiled artist's impression of Metrolink trams on Drake Street. Another tram painting can be seen in the entrance to the Wheatsheaf Hotel in Littleborough with steam and electric trams and a steam train. The Oxford public house on Whitworth Road has a tram on its pub sign in the correct colours of brown and cream. At first glance it looks quite authentic but although it shows Whitworth Road on the blind it has a large route number display showing 81. Rochdale trams did not have route numbers (except the 17 to Manchester). The location was once well known as 'the Oxford loop', a passing place on the long single track climb up to Healey.

There are many other pubs and restaurants which have various framed photographs of Rochdale scenes on their walls, many of which feature trams. Most of their customers will never have seen a Rochdale tram but there is still a fascination with this form of transport. A number of books on old Rochdale include photographs of trams and streetscapes showing tracks, overhead wires, shelters and other tramway items.

The Touchstones Local History Museum is a rich source of information on all aspects of Rochdale's history, not least its tramways. On display is a polished metal and wood tram handle from the first electric tram in Rochdale from Dane Street to Cemetery Gates. The handle was presented to Mrs Duncan, the wife of the Chairman of Rochdale Corporation Tramways Committee, on 22 May 1902.

Another link with tramway connections is Rochdale's twin town of Bielefeld in Germany. It was an early example of twinning being set up in 1953. While Rochdale abandoned its trams, Bielefeld not only retained them but modernised and extended their network, even building tram tunnels through the city centre.

A glimpse of Rochdale's trams can be seen in the amazing films taken by Mitchell and Kenyon in 1903 when moving pictures were in their infancy. One sequence was taken on a tram moving along Spotland Road, up Edenfield Road past St. Clement's Church, through Passmonds and into the terminus at Norden. An extract is included in the video of 'Trams in and around Manchester'.

Although no full sized trams exist from Rochdale, some modellers have produced fine scale reproductions which illustrate clearly what they were like. Eric Hall of Rochdale has built a number of different types, mainly in 1/24 scale. Ashley Best who now lives in Kent built an amazingly accurate model at 1/16 scale of single deck tram No. 43. It took twelve years to build.

They got it wrong!!

Sometimes errors creep into publications which otherwise are useful and informative documents. Here are a few examples.

" A rare sight of a policeman on point-duty directing traffic into Drake Street just after trams had given way to trolley-buses in 1932 although the tracks and overhead remain."
'*More Memories of Rochdale*'. True North Books. 1998.

Trolleybuses ran in Oldham, Ashton-under-Lyne and Manchester and even in Ramsbottom, but never in Rochdale.

"At the time gaslamps were the only form of light available on all main roads. In later years the overhead

cables for the electric tramcars were taken down as the electricity was fed via the tramline - something new at the time." '*Castleton - A History*'. James J Connolly. 1999.

Current collection from the rails is an interesting concept to avoid the need for overhead wires. Conduit trams, taking their power from a central 'third rail' below the road surface, did run in Blackpool until 1899 and in London until 1952 but never in Rochdale. A few towns tried the 'stud contact' system where electrical studs in the road were only energised as a tram passed over them but it was short lived. A modern version, electronically controlled, was introduced in Bordeaux, France in 2004.

"No. 36 single deck tram built 1904 and used until the Second World War on the Bury Road route".
'*Postcards of Old Rochdale*'. Cliff Hayes. Nostalgia Ink. Bolton.

Bury Road trams ceased in 1931, eight years before the start of the Second World War. Trams ceased altogether in Rochdale in 1932.

Getting dates of events wrong is very common, even in supposedly authoritative documents. Several dates given in Cliff Taylor's excellent booklet on Rochdale Trams (Ref 32) are known to be wrong even though he was acknowledged as an authority on Rochdale tramways. In the Castleton History (Ref 38) the first tram from Middleton to Castleton is given as being in 1898 and only as far as Trub. Records show that the first tram service from Middleton did not start until 28th March 1902 and then ran through to Sudden.

It is inevitable that in a book of this kind, some errors will have crept in. Some dates will no doubt be disputed. The author retains full responsibility.

above) In the porch of the Wheatsheaf Hotel a fascinating mural depicts electric and steam trams in Littleborough Square with a variety of horse drawn vehicles and a steam train in the station. Artistic licence is in abundance –tram types, tram liveries, track and overhead layout are all somewhat fanciful but the atmosphere it creates is evocative of the era. The artist was Tony Peel in 1995.

above) A detail from Tony Peel's Littleborough mural shows a steam tram trailer with a trolley pole!

left) A detail from Tony Peel's Littleborough mural shows an open top double deck tram No. 4 en route to Summit. But Rochdale's trams were never blue!

A tramway rosette can be seen on the front of the recently restored Rochdale Crown Post Office building on The Esplanade.

A tramway rosette can be seen on the front of the Barclays Bank building on The Esplanade.

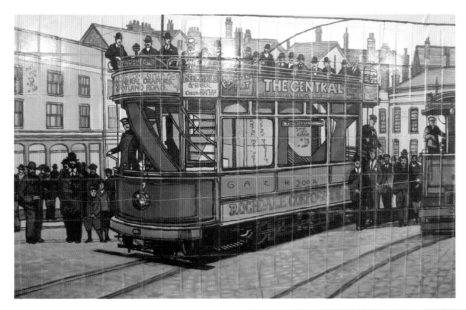

A mural in the pedestrian subway under Constantine Way includes electric tram No.7. The subway links the former tramway centre part of town to the bus station.

The mural in the pedestrian subway under Constantine Way includes a steam tram loco and trailer which used to operate along Smith Street, a few yards away.

Trams on the Bacup route sometimes turned at the 'Oxford loop' and the Oxford pub recalls the fact on their sign. The tram colours are fairly accurate but Rochdale never had a route 81 !

A last vestige of Rochdale's tram track can still be seen in Yorkshire Street, near George Street, complete with granite setts.

Tram rides can be made on former Hull tram 96 at Heaton Park Tramway Museum. It is just possible that its Brill 21E truck originated with Rochdale Corporation Tramways.

This extremely accurate 1/16th scale model of Rochdale Brush bogie combination car No.43 was made by Artist and modeller Ashley Best. It won first prize in a national competition.

Eric Hall's excellent 1/24th scale model of tram No. 87 gives a good impression of a typical Rochdale double decker in the latter days of the system.

'Another of Eric Hall's scale models, Rochdale Corporation Tramways open top number 24 is seen at Rochdale Railway Station; integration before the word was invented!
(Eric Hall)

The 'Phase 3' Metrolink extension to Oldham and Rochdale approved in 2002 included street running routes through Oldham town centre and the extension from Rochdale station to Rochdale Bus Station, as shown in dashed red on this plan. Most of the route is a conversion of the existing heavy rail Oldham loop line to light rail, with some additional stations. It branches off from the existing Bury Metrolink line at Collyhurst (in blue). The Government withdrew funding approval for the Oldham Rochdale line in 2004 but when it was conditionally approved again in 2006 it was termed 'Phase 3a' and did not include the two town centre extensions, only the conversion of heavy rail line, as in solid red. Funding for 'Phase 3b' was deferred to a later stage when it would be subject to a TIF bid which must include congestion charging. The bid was submitted in July 2007.

(GMPTE)

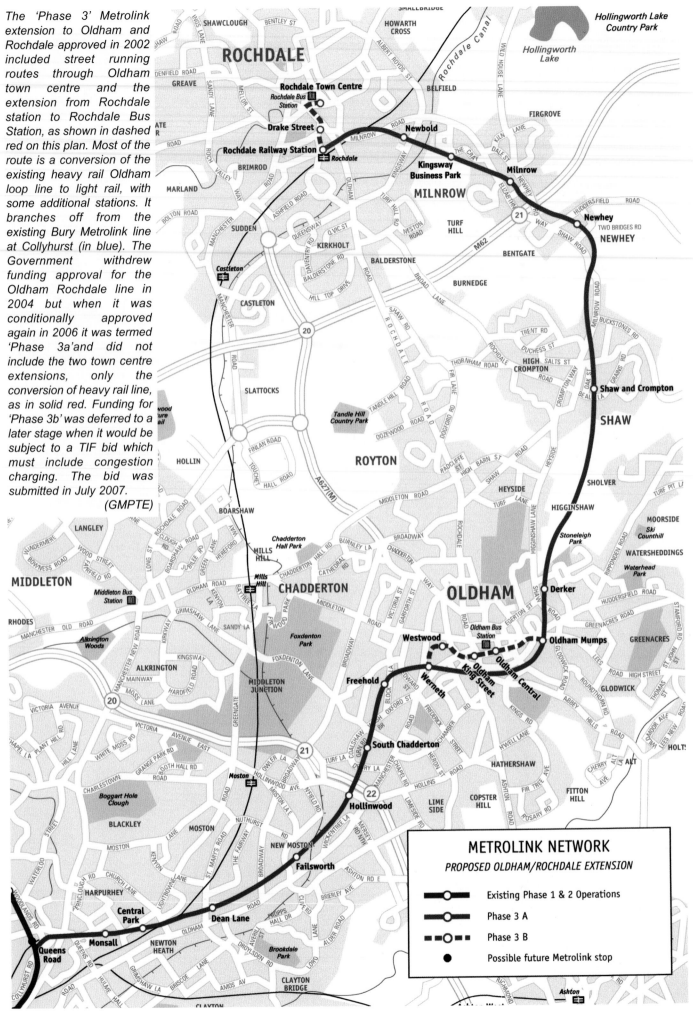

METROLINK NETWORK
PROPOSED OLDHAM/ROCHDALE EXTENSION

- Existing Phase 1 & 2 Operations
- Phase 3 A
- Phase 3 B
- Possible future Metrolink stop

160

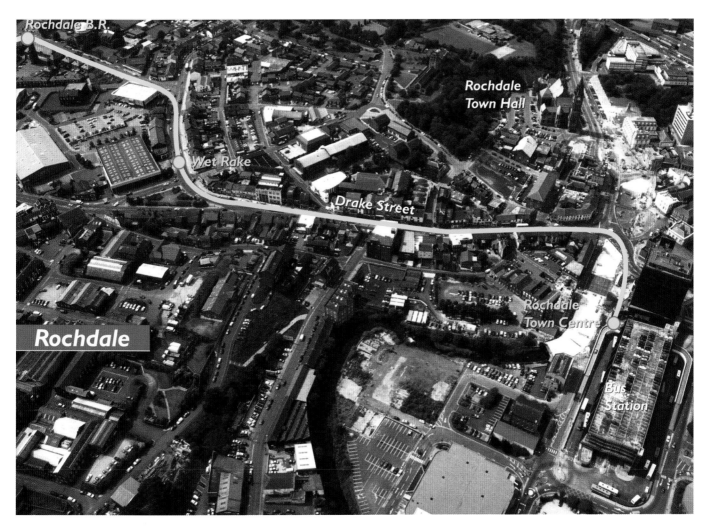

Initially Metrolink will terminate near Rochdale Rail Station on Maclure Road (top left). When funds permit, it will be extended through Wet Rake (now renamed 'Drake Street') and down Drake Street to the Bus Station (bottom right). By then the bus station will have been moved to a smaller site on the other side of Smith Street. *(GMPTE)*

The billboard on Drake Street announces that Metrolink is coming, but doesn't say when!

An artist's impression of Drake Street with Metrolink trams running into the town centre. Part of the street will become tram and pedestrian only.

Land was cleared in 2005 to make way for the Wet Rake Metrolink Station on Drake Street. The artist shows how it will look.

Metrolink tram 2201 emerges at the foot of Drake Street as it approaches the town centre, at least in the imagination of the artist. Steam trams ran down here in 1883 and electric trams took over in 1904.

24. Trams come back again.

GMPTE have been trying to bring Metrolink to Rochdale for over 20 years. This brochure was produced nearly ten years ago. *(GMPTE)*

When the last tram crawled back to the depot in 1932, nobody expected to ever see trams on the streets of Rochdale again. Maybe they were right but plans to bring trams back onto Greater Manchester's streets did come to fruition in 1992 when the first street running tramway to be built in Britain for forty years opened in Manchester. Metrolink is now an accepted part of that city and has proved enormously popular and beneficial to the local economy. It has raised the profile of Manchester and enabled it to justifiably claim to be a European and 'world class' city.

Not surprisingly all the towns around want their own Metrolink line and Rochdale is no exception. Plans to bring trams to Rochdale were first drawn up in 1983 when a feasibility study recommended converting the Oldham Rochdale loop line to light rail. It would have terminated at the existing Rochdale Station so would not have improved access by rail into the town centre, a distance of about ³/₄mile (1 km). It was soon realised that the ability of light rail to run on street opened up the possibility of leaving the railway alignment and continuing along Maclure Road and Drake Street to terminate alongside the Bus Station.

A long process of preparing plans, consultation with the Council and property owners and many others finally resulted in an agreed scheme. Parliamentary powers to convert the Oldham Rochdale line were obtained by GMPTE in 1990, when the first phase of Metrolink was under construction in Manchester. The following year powers were obtained to extend the line from Rochdale Station down Maclure Road and Drake Street to the Bus Station in the town centre.

A lengthy period of planning, negotiation with government and endless discussions on methods of procurement ended in 2000 when tenders were at last invited for the construction of the line as part of the 'big bang' expansion of Metrolink. Also included in the package were lines to East Manchester and Ashton and Wythenshawe and Manchester Airport with a possibility of adding in the line to East Didsbury and a line to the Trafford Centre if funding could be found. Funding for the three line expansion was approved by the Government in 2002 but was unexpectedly withdrawn in July 2004. By then consortia of contractors, tram builders and operators had spent millions of pounds on preparing detailed tenders.

Some work on the tramway to Rochdale actually began in 2004 at the North Manchester Business Park, now known as 'Central Park'. A spectacular 'Gateway Transport Interchange' has been built with a cable stayed roof suspended from an elegant pylon, together with a massive concrete finback bridge to take the trams over the main Rochdale railway line at Newton Heath. Sadly there will be no trams for at least five years.

Meanwhile preparatory work has been undertaken in Rochdale including the demolition of properties on Drake Street to make way for the Metrolink station at Wet Rake.

The Government changed its mind yet again in July 2006 when conditional approval was given for 'Phase 3a' of the expanded network. This included the Oldham Rochdale line as far as Rochdale Station but not the extra street running section to the town centre. That will be the subject of a further grant application under 'Phase 3b'. However it will include the bridge over the main Calder Valley line and the ramp down High Level Road, which will be closed to road traffic, and a temporary terminus on Maclure Road outside St John's Church. All being well therefore, trams will return to Rochdale's streets for a very short length after a gap of nearly eighty years.

Over £100million was earmarked for work to the existing Metrolink tram system in 2007. Tracks to Altrincham and Bury, some over 50 years old, were renewed, stations inproved and eight new trams ordered for delivery in 2009. Costing £17million, these 'Flexity Swift' trams built by Bombardier are similar to the K5000 trams operating successfully in Cologne in Germay. GMPTE hope to be able to order at least another 28 trams of the same type for Phase 3a extensions, including those that will run to Rochdale.

GMPTE began the long procurement process for Phase 3a in early autumn 2007 and intend to start construction in 2008, including the conversion of the Oldham-Rochdale line, subject yet again to final government approval to the funding. Target date for trams arriving at Rochdale Station

(Maclure Road) is 2011. The future of the street running section into Rochdale town centre is less certain as it is dependent on a major Transport Innovation Fund (TIF) bid for govenment funding submitted by GMPTA in July 2007. Nevertheless it is intended to extend the trams to the town centre by 2012. A condition for approval is the inclusion of the controversial congestion charging scheme. As well as further Metrolink extensions, the TIF bid includes upgrading of bus and rail services, new interchanges, park and ride schemes and other traffic improvement measures.

Rochdale Council regards the Metrolink extension into the town centre as crucial to its regeneration plans for the centre. Once again, trams may help to invigorate the urban area, bringing people in large numbers to shop, do business or enjoy leisure time in the town. When the first new tram glides down Drake Street, it will have taken thirty years since the initial plans were drawn up, about the length of time that the first generation of trams lasted on the streets of Rochdale!

Trams returned to the streets of Greater Manchester on 27th April 1992 when Metrolink 1007 burst through the wall at Victoria Station to run through the city centre to G-Mex. Powers to run trams into Rochdale town centre had been obtained in October 1991.
(A.P.Young)

The K5000 tram built by Bombardier for the city of Cologne in Germany is the type shortly to appear on the streets of Manchester. They will eventually run to Rochdale.
(Mark Terry)

A spectacular tram interchange complete with integrated bus stands at Central Park will one day serve trams to Rochdale. It was completed in 2006 at a cost of £35million, including a concrete flyover across the main Rochdale railway line. Sadly it is not likely to see a tram until 2011. (A.P.Young)

25. Finale.

Rochdale's short lived tramway was nevertheless a fascinating story of municipal enterprise and engineering innovation. It served the town well for a generation and helped to form the urban area as we know it today.

But Rochdale proved to be yet another example of Britain's habit of investing in high quality public transport only to throw it away long before it is life expired. Some of the newer trams were only four years old when sent for scrap and some top covers saw less than two years service. The vast sum spent by Manchester Corporation on relaying the Castleton route was abandoned after only four years, and their newly built route to Heywood lasted only six years.

Will we ever learn from our experiences? The chaotic progress of Metrolink extensions is not a good omen…..

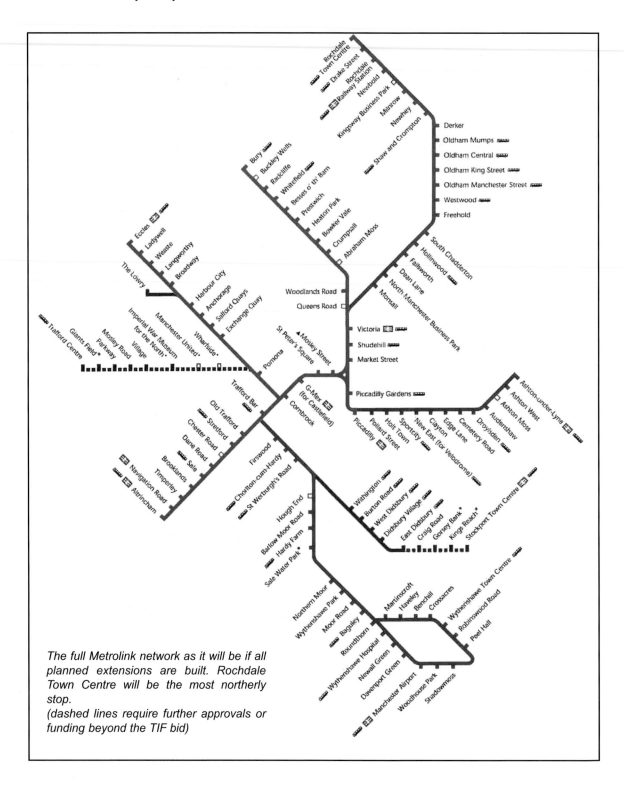

The full Metrolink network as it will be if all planned extensions are built. Rochdale Town Centre will be the most northerly stop.
(dashed lines require further approvals or funding beyond the TIF bid)

Appendices

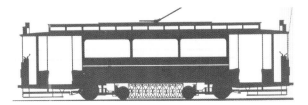

APPENDIX A
ACTS OF PARLIAMENT

Rochdale Tramways Order 1881.
Authorised construction and operation of steam tramways in Rochdale and Wardle.

Tramways Orders Confirmation (No.3) Act, 1881.
Confirmed Rochdale Tramways Order 1881.

Manchester Bury Rochdale Tramways (Extension) Order 1882.
Authorised extensions to steam tramways in Rochdale.

Tramways Order Confirmation (No.3) Act, 1882.
Confirmed Manchester Bury Rochdale Tramways (Extension) Order 1882.

Manchester Bury Rochdale Oldham Steam Tramway Act 1884.
Dissolved old steam tram company and authorised new company; authorised further extensions to steam tramway.

Manchester Bury Rochdale Oldham (Extension of Time) Act 1885.
Allowed extensions of time for some works to be undertaken.

Manchester, Middleton and District Tramways Act, 1885.
Authorised construction and operation of tramways in Middleton.

Manchester Bury Rochdale and Oldham Steam Tramways Act 1887.
Allowed some extensions of time, abandonment of some lines and provisions for Rossendale Valley Tramway.

The Middleton Light Railways Order, 1898.
Authorised construction and operation of electric tramways in Middleton.

Rochdale Corporation Act 1900.
Authorised acquisition of Tramways Undertaking and construction and operation of electric tramways in Rochdale.

Middleton Corporation Tramways Tramways Order 1900
(Confirmed by the Tramways Orders Confirmation (No.3) Act 1900) authorised construction of further tramways in Middleton.

Littleborough Urban District Council Tramways Order 1901.
Authorised construction of tramways in Littleborough.

Tramways Orders Confirmation (No.2) Act 1902. (Heywood Corporation Tramways Order 1902).
Authorised construction of tramways in Heywood.

Tramways Orders Confirmation (No.1) Act, 1904.
Confirmed Rochdale Corporation Tramways Order.

Wardle Urban District Council Tramway Order1904
Authorised construction of tramway in Wardle.

Tramways Orders Confirmation Act, 1906.
Confirmed Rochdale Corporation Tramways Order. (Royal Assent 4th August 1906).

Rochdale Corporation Act 1908.

Heywood Corporation Act 1909.
Specified running powers for Rochdale and Bury Corporations.

Whitworth Urban District Council Tramway Order 1909.
Authorised construction of tramways in Whitworth.

Bacup Corporation Light Railway Order, 1910.
Authorised construction of tramways in Bacup.

Milnrow Urban District Council Tramways Order 1910.
Authorised construction of tramways in Milnrow and Newhey.

Statutory Rules and Orders, 1911. No. 918. Tramway. Whitworth U.D.C. Tramways. 15th September, 1911.
Specifies regulations and byelaws for electrical power and operation of tramway in Whitworth.

Statutory Rules and Orders, 1911. No. 917. Railway. Bacup Corporation Light Railway. 19th September, 1911.
Specifies regulations and byelaws for electrical power and operation of tramway in Bacup.

Statutory Rules and Orders, 1912. No. 476. Tramway. Milnrow Urban District Council Tramways. 26th April, 1912.
Specifies regulations and byelaws for electrical power and operation of tramway in Milnrow.

Tramways Provisional Orders Act, 1923.
Confirmation of Orders for Rochdale and Leicester Corporation Tramways. Authorised construction and operation of tramway from Lower Tweedale Street along Maclure Road to Drake Street.
1 furlong 5.32 chains in length of which 1 furlong 3.65 chains is double line and 1.67 chains interlacing line. (Interlaced from Woolpack Inn to Drake Street.)

Statutory Rules and Orders, 1925, Nos. 616 to 623 inclusive.
Codes of Regulations and Bye-laws in regard to use if electrical power on the Rochdale and District Tramways; Bacup Corporation Light Railway; Whitworth Urban District Council Tramways; Milnrow Urban District Council Tramways.

Rochdale Corporation Act 1925.
Granted powers to run motorbuses.

Heywood and Middleton Light Railways Order 1927.

Rochdale Corporation (General Powers) Act 1930.
Powers to abandon tramways in Rochdale, Wardle, Littleborough, Norden, Heywood, subject to providing replacement buses, and giving notice to UDC's. Powers to run buses extended from 'five miles from Rochdale Town Hall' to 'five miles from the boundary of the borough'. Protective clauses included for Todmorden Corporation, Ribble M S, North Western Road Car and LMS Railway.

Bacup Corporation Act 1931.
Powers to abandon tramways in Bacup.

Rochdale Corporation Act 1932.
Powers to abandon remaining tramways and those in Milnrow and Whitworth.

Greater Manchester (Light Rapid Transit System) Act 1990
Powers to convert the Manchester to Oldham and Rochdale railway line to Metrolink light rail.

Greater Manchester (Light Rapid Transit System) Act 1991
Powers to construct and operate Metrolink tramway extension from Rochdale Station to Rochdale Town Centre.

APPENDIX B
THE TRAMWAYS COMMITTEE AND CHIEF OFFICERS

The Paving, Sewering and Scavenging Committee
(later The Paving, Sewering and Building Committee, commonly referred to as 'Paving Etc. Committee')

Chairman Councillor Turner

The Tramways Committee

First met on 23rd November 1900	Councillor Duncan elected first Chairman.
Chairman:	
November 1900 – November 1903	Councillor Duncan
November 1903 – October 1912	Councillor Wilson Dunning
	(Mayor 1908-10)
	(Alderman Dunning from November 1911)
November 1912 – November 1913	Councillor Joseph P Fielden
November 1913 – June 1925	Alderman James Taylor (died in service)
July 1925 – October 1929	Alderman H. Clark

Passenger Transport Committee

November 1929 – November 1933	Alderman H. Clark (served until 1938)

(Note: RCT brochure gives Chairmen as:

1902-08   Councillor Duncan
1909-1912   Alderman Dunning
1913-1914   Councillor J G Fielding)

Tramways Committee Members
(Passenger Transport Committee from November 1929).

1900/01

Alderman Petrie, Alderman Ashworth
Councillors Barraclough, Chadwick, Cunliffe, Duncan, Dunning, J. Taylor, Eastwood, Redfern, S Turner, Walker.

1901/02

Alderman Petrie, Alderman Ashworth, Alderman Topper
Councillors Chadwick, Cunliffe, Duncan, Dunning, J. Taylor, Eastwood, Redfern, Walker.

1902/03

Alderman Petrie, Alderman Ashworth, Alderman Topper
Councillors Chadwick, Cunliffe, Duncan, Dunning, J. Taylor, Eastwood, Redfern, Smith, Walker.

1903/04

Alderman Petrie, Alderman Cunliffe, Alderman Topper, Alderman S Turner.
Councillors, Dunning, Fielden, Howarth, J. Taylor, Eastwood, Redfern, Smith, Walker

1904/05

Alderman Cunliffe, Alderman Topper, Alderman S Turner.
Councillors, Clark, Dunning, Fielden, Holden, Howarth, Redfern, Shaw, Smith, J. Taylor, Walker

1905/06

Alderman Cunliffe, Alderman Topper.
Councillors, Clark, Diggle, Dunning, Fielden, Holden, Howarth, Redfern, Shaw, Smith, J. Taylor, Walker

1906/07

Alderman W Cunliffe, Alderman O Topper
Councs. H Clark, W Davidson, S Diggle, J P Fielden, J H Holden, J H Howarth,
C Redfern, W W Shaw, J Taylor, J Walker.

1912/13

Alderman Taylor
Councs. Clark, Davidson, Diggle, Dowell, Holden, Howarth, Pilling, Richmond, Swire, Walker, Wilby.

1921/22

Alderman Cunlife, Clark, Howarth
Councs. Crossley, Hardman, Holt, Hutton, Richmond, Wilson, Dutton, Wycherley, Turner, O'Doherty.

1922/23

Alderman Cunliffe, Clark, Diggle, Howarth
Councs. Crossley, Hardman, Holt, Hutton, Richmond, Wilson, Dutton, Wycherley, Turner, O'Doherty.

1923/24

Alderman Clark, Howarth
Councs. Crossley, Hardman, Holt, Hutton, Richmond, Wilson, Wycherley, Turner, O'Doherty, Stevenson, Topper.

1924/25

Alderman Clark, Howarth
Councs. Crossley, Hardman, Holt, Richmond, Wilson, Dutton, Turner, Stevenson, Topper.

1925/26

Alderman Clark, Howarth, Taylor
Councs. Ashworth, Crossley, Dutton, Hardman, Hill, Holt, Lancaster, Nicholson, Richmond, Stevenson, Topper, Turner, Wilson

1926/27

Alderman Clark
Councs. Ashworth, Crowder, Dutton, Hardman, Hill, Holt, Lancaster, Nicholson, Richmond, Stevenson, Topper, Wilson

1927/28

Alderman Clark
Councs. Ashworth, Crowder, Dutton, Hill, Holt, Lancaster, Nicholson, Richmond, Stevenson, Topper, Wilson

1928/29

Alderman Clark, Richmond
Councs. Ashworth, Crowder, Dutton, Hardman, Hill, Holt, Lancaster, Nicholson, Scarr, Stevenson, Topper, Wilson

1929/30

Alderman Richmond.
Councs. Ashworth, Crowder, Dutton, Fairhurst, Hardman, Heywood, Hill, Holt, Jackson, Scarr, Topper, Tweedale.

1930/31

Alderman H Clark.
Councs. Ashworth, Bottomley, Dutton, Fairhurst, Heywood, Hill, Holt, Jackson, Parker, Dr. Scarr, Topper, Tweedale.

Tramways Managers

May 1902 - June 1904	C. C. Atchison. (Electrical Engineer)
June 1904 - June 1913.	J. S. D. Moffet Assoc.M.Inst.C.E., M.I.Mech.E. (some RCT documents say ' Moffett')
June 1913 – 1936.	George Webster, M.Inst.T., O.B.E.. (appointed 16.7.13). (previously Traffic Manager and Chief Clerk from 1904)

Transport Managers in the post-tram era

1936-42	George A. Cherry.
1942-51	Chaseley T. Humpidge.
1951-54	Joseph C. Franklin.
1954 -62	Ronald Cox.

Chief Engineers

A. R. Williams.

Borough Surveyors (also referred to as Borough Engineers)

2 February	1871 - 1881	Thomas Hewson
6 October	1881 - 1918	Samuel Sidney Platt.
5 September	1918 - 1921	Henry Yarwood.
3 March	1921 -	Sydney Hubert Morgan.

Borough Electrical Engineers

October 1900 – November 1918	Mr. C. C. Atchison
January 1918 - ?	Mr. F.H.Rudd

Town Clerks

1856 – 1894	Zachary Mellor
1894 - ?	James Heap
1904 – July 1935	Henry Hickson, OBE.

APPENDIX C
MONTHLY MILEAGE AND PASSENGER FIGURES FROM 1906 TO 1918

Year	Month	Mileage	Passengers*	Heywood pass.	Total passengers
1906	January	87,505	658,813	51,422	710,235
	February	77,133	577,811	45,958	623,769
	March	91,064	696,369	60,630	756,999
	April	93,367	773,715	71,542	845,257
	May	93,311	744,599	66,380	810,97
	June	97,869	892,403	83,947	976,350
	July	94,991	855,504	78,000	933,504
	August	95,214	871,051	79,604	950,655
	September	92,067	858,275	77,797	936,072
	October	94,046	796,487	66,098	862,585
	November	89,436	712,451	59,585	772,036
	December	90,319	725,444	60,058	785,502
1907	January	93,645	716,630	60,524	777,154
	February	85,184	660,131	55,321	715,452
	March	100,307	873,603	79,889	953,492
	April	95,923	775,683	66,828	842,511
	May	101,307	888,990	66,380	955,370
	June	97,860	827,982	75,962	903,944
	July	100,768	895,230	78,738	973,968
	August	103,560	935,298	84,601	1,019,899
	September	97,942	879,516	79,674	959,190
	October	99,238	848,581	74,886	923,467
	November	95,264	820,271	71,537	891,808
	December	96,152	806,129	70,324	876,453
1908	January	93,075	725,301	63,032	788,333
	February	90,592	749,715	66,885	816,600
	March	94,948	791,044	74,205	865,249
	April	99,171	869,407	83,013	952,420
	May	100,426	921,383	88,880	1,010,263
	June	99,303	895,531	83,214	978,745
	July	100,717	899,112	81,662	980,774
	August	102,963	957,200	95,412	1,052,612
	September	96,121	833,650	79,732	913,382
	October	98,206	864,149	79,665	943,814
	November	91,724	748,804	68,036	816,840
	December	94,708	779,263	70,975	850,238
1909	January	96,470	766,624	68,254	834,878
	February	87,326	697,481	63,809	761,290
	March	96,532	751,083	69,043	820,126
	April	98,614	893,133	81,011	974,144
	May	99,479	881,621	80,009	961,630
	June	99,767	855,232	75,897	931,129
	July	101,476	899,359	78,890	978,249
	August	100,671	900,374	87,535	987,909
	September	971,153	837,642	79,649	917,291
	October	101,794	884,755	80,434	965,189
	November	95,218	729,584	64,281	793,865
	December	95,484	763,264	62,761	826,025

*Note : Passengers carried in Rochdale and all adjacent districts except Heywood

Year	Month	Mileage	Passengers*	Heywood pass.	Total passengers
1910	January	98,297	755,707	69,613	825,320
	February	88,616	693,361	58,412	751,773
	March	104,480	872,130	79,330	951,460
	April	97,336	791,564	64,722	856,286
	May	101,770	896,202	75,488	971,690
	June	102,010	876,301	70,578	946,879
	July	111,870	984,520	77,766	1,062,286
	August	112,203	930,890	74,875	1,005,765
	September	-	-	-	-
	October	114,562	940,978	79,867	1,020,845
	November	109,240	816,225	63,134	879,359
	December	114,790	932,483	74,291	1,006,774
1911	January	111,275	845,788	68,456	914,244
	February	102,170	758,856	58,826	817,682
	March	113,358	862,917	67,734	930,651
	April	114,516	965,673	78,524	1,044,197
	May	114,430	959,649	77,964	1,037,613
	June	116,384	980,943	74,582	1,055,525
	July	122,072	1,052,611	83,231	1,135,842
	August	132,490	1,117,457	91,310	1,208,767
	September	129,089	1,021,898	76,317	1,098,215
	October	129,907	992,819	76,191	1,069,010
	November	125,371	912,840	68,058	980,898
	December	131,925	1,039,449	76,723	1,116,172
1912	January	-	-	-	-
	February	120,012	858,185	62,558	920,743
	March	-	-	-	-
	April	122,502	1,000,960	74,599	1,075,559
	May	-	-	-	-
	June	138,057	1,078,707	74,517	1,153,224
	July	142,008	1,156,219	76,536	1,232,755
	August	143,856	1,140,276	78,196	1,218,472
	September	137,522	1,047,388	75,836	1,123,224
	October	140,676	1,085,400	73,986	1,159,386
	November	136,233	1,030,677	68,199	1,098,876
	December	140,975	1,100,213	73,187	1,173,400
1913	January	138,746	1,042,177	67,716	1,109,893
	February	125,838	942,684	63,428	1,006,112
	March	-	-	-	-
	April	-	-	-	-
	May	-	-	-	-
	June	130,114	1,126,032	74,649	1,200,681
	July	142,472	1,228,815	80,460	1,309,275
	August	-	-	-	-
	September	138,945	1,159,869	76,771	1,236,640
	October	-	-	-	-
	November	139,623	1,136,388	73,187	1,209,575
	December	144,927	1,135,382	71,803	1,207,185
1914	January	145,720	1,116,979	68,715	1,185,694
	February	141,976	1,088,911	68,913	1,157,824
	March	-	-	-	-
	April	146,261	1,212,285	79,118	1,291,403
	May	150,048	1,217,958	76,256	1,294,214
	June	146,841	1,176,556	75,137	1,251,693
	July	150,015	1,242,354	73,920	1,316,274
	August	-	-	-	-
	September	136,957	1,157,267	82,955	1,240,222
	October	-	-	-	-
	November	129,323	964,740	63,281	1,028,021
	December	136,823	1,048,798	68,218	1,117,016

Year	Month	Mileage	Passengers*	Heywood pass.	Total passengers
1915	January	135,139	1,059,313	68,555	1,127,868
	February	122,594	918,126	59,774	977,900
	March	-	-	-	-
	April	136,284	1,110,525	76,774	1,187,299
	May	138,412	1,280,440	89,067	1,369,507
	June	132,373	1,132,257	75,769	1,208,026
	July	141,507	1,248,197	82,000	1,330,197
	August	-	-	-	-
	September	133,245	1,172,571	84,143	1,256,714
	October	136,578	1,171,244	78,877	1,250,121
	November	-	-	-	-
	December	134,364	1,129,936	72,511	1,202,447
1916	January	130,561	1,176,387	80,541	1,256,928
	February	119,540	981,016	64,657	1,045,673
	March	129,534	1,061,975	69,743	1,131,718
	April	134,894	1,281,181	87,937	1,369,118
	May	131,651	1,176,715	81,067	1,257,782
	June	132,709	1,209,607	83,404	1,293,011
	July	135,197	1,315,889	88,699	1,404,588
	August	-	-	-	-
	September	130,034	1,261,162	88,565	1,349,727
	October	130,924	1,195,473	82,411	1,277,884
	November	125,386	1,082,411	70,955	1,153,366
	December	123,641	1,107,545	70,944	1,178,489
1917	January	127,596	1,091,008	70,606	1,161,614
	February	-	-	-	-
	March	130,428	1,148,378	74,303	1,222,681
	April	129,102	1,403,111	91,039	1,494,150
	May	132,303	1,330,935	95,301	1,426,236
	June	131,821	1,447,146	108,591	1,555,737
	July	132,712	1,470,135	111,328	1,581,463
	August				
	September	129,584	1,439,334	104,711	1,544,045
	October	131,441	1,353,673	93,552	1,447,225
	November	126,772	1,301,284	87,411	1,388,695
	December	122,230	1,324,916	91,845	1,416,761
1918	January	125,574	1,301,788	86,432	1,388,220
	February	-	-	-	-
	March	130,544	1,473,374	104,650	1,578,024
	April	125,456	1,403,111	100,402	1,503,513
	May	135,418	1,702,532	123,040	1,825,572
	June	125,962	1,485,976	104,121	1,590,097

APPENDIX D
ROCHDALE CORPORATION TRAMWAYS. HINTS TO PASSENGERS

(from Official Guide, Published by Edwards and Bryning, 1906)

1. Do not attempt to board or leave a moving Car.

2. Before boarding a Car at any Stopping Place or Terminus, allow all passengers to alight who desire to do so.

3. On approaching the Stopping Place at which you wish to alight, endeavour to notify the Conductor in time to avoid being over-carried, and as far as possible be in readiness to leave the Car immediately it stops.

4. Have your fare in readiness and tender the exact amount if possible. Giving change, especially for coins of high value, delays the Conductor.

5. If under the necessity of tendering a coin of high value which the Conductor may not be able to change, give him your name and address, and forward the fare as early as possible to the tramway Offices, Mellor St..

6. Your ticket must be kept available for inspection on demand throughout the whole journey.

7. No smoking allowed inside Double Deck cars, or in the central portion of Single Deck Combination Cars.

8. Spitting and depositing remnants of food or fruit in or upon the Cars is strictly prohibited.

9. Do not interfere with any part of the Car or its equipment.

10. Consider the convenience of fellow passengers in the matter of seating accommodation, ventilation, etc.

11. Inspectors and Timekeepers will afford you all information as to routes, etc.

12. The employees of the department are instructed to extend the utmost civility and courtesy to passengers, but it should be borne in mind that they have arduous duties to perform, in which they can be largely assisted by tolerant consideration on the part of passengers.

13. Enquire for all property left on the Cars at the Tramway Offices, Mellor St., Tel. No. 48.

14. Remember that the Cars are run solely in the interests of the travelling public, and that the convenience, safety and rapid transit of passengers can be largely assisted by general regard to the foregoing hints.

APPENDIX E
TRAMWAY ROUTES AND SERVICES

Table 1 Steam and electric tram start and close dates.

Section	From	To	Traction	Operator	Started	Closed	Notes
	Rochdale Town Centre (Wellington Hotel)	Buersil	Steam	MBR&O	07.05.83	13.04.04	
	Rochdale (Cheetham Street)	Healey (Ending)	Steam	MBR&O	01.11.83	24.09.04	Last steam tram on Healey route
	Heywood	Hopwood	Steam	MBR&O	xx.03.84	19.12.91	
	Heywood	Hopwood	Steam	HCT	22.12.04	20.09.05	
	Heywood	Bury	Steam	MBR&O	xx.03.84	xx.03.04	Bury-Heap Bridge suspended
	Bury	Rochdale via Heywood	Steam	MBR&O	30.05.84	10.06.04	Extension of Bury-Heywood
	Healey (Ending)	Whitworth	Steam	MBR&O	11.07.84	22.07.91	
	Whitworth	Facit	Steam	MBR&O	xx.04.85	22.07.91	Extension of Rochdale-Whitworth
	Royton	Littleborough via Rochdale	Steam	MBR&O (RCT from 13.10.04 to 11.05.05)	01.03.85	13.04.04 30.05.04 11.05.05	Last tram to Royton Last tram Royton-Summit. Last tram to Littleborough
	Rochdale (Cheetham Street)	Littleborough via Yorkshire Street	Steam	MBR&O (RCT from 13.10.04 to 11.05.05)	xx.10.86	11.05.05? or 08.05.05?	M-Sat pm (Market days) Cheetham St to Heybrook opened 01.04.89 ?
	Bury boundary (Heap Bridge)	Rochdale boundary (Cemetery Road)	Steam	HCT	20.12.04	20.09.05	Cut back to Heywood Summit 21.08.05 Cut back to Heywood town centre 15.09.05
Bamford	Manchester Road (Dane Street)	Bury Road (Cemetery Gates)	Electric	RCT	22.05.02	04.01.31	At this stage it was not possible to get any nearer to the town centre because of steam tram gauge. Extended to The Butts 06.07.04

Section	From	To	Traction	Operator	Started	Closed	Notes
Norden	Blackwater Street	Norden (Industry Street)	Electric	RCT	19.06.02	04.01.31	At this stage it was not possible to get any nearer to the town centre because of steam tram gauge. Rerouted to The Butts 23.07.04
Spotland	Spotland Bridge/ Rooley Moor Road	Spotland (White Lion)	Electric	RCT	21.07.02	19.04.31	Rerouted to Cheetham St. 23.11.04 Rerouted to Lord St 29.09.06
Bamford	Bury Road (Cemetery Gates)	Bury Road (Dog & Partridge Inn)	Electric	RCT	xx.xx.03 ?	04.01.31	c.800yds. extension Also known as Bamford.
Norden/ Bamford	Dane Street (Manchester Road)	Town Centre via Esplanade	Electric	RCT	06.07.04	04.01.31	
Norden	Mellor Street (Bury Road)	Spotland Road (Spotland Bridge)	Electric	RCT	23.07.04	12.11.32	New depot accessed from Mellor Street.
Norden	Norden (Industry Street)	Esplanade via Mellor Street	Electric	RCT	23.07.04	04.01.31	Replaced route via Spotland Road to Blackwater Street.
Circular	The Butts	Circular via Drake Street, Oldham Road, High Level Road, Tweedale Street, Manchester Road and Drake Street	Electric or 20.08.04? or 27.08.04?	RCT	17.08.04	19.04.31	
Thornham	The Butts (Drake St/Oldham Road, White Lion Hotel ?)	Oldham Road (Kings Road)	Electric	RCT	02.09.04	19.04.31	Kings Road (now Kingsway).
Thornham	Oldham Road (Kings Road)	Thornham Summit (Boundary Royton UDC)	Electric	RCT	05.10.04	10.04.31 (Broad Ln) 19.04.31 (rest)	Opened Thornham to Oldham by Oldham Corporation 01.11.04
Milnrow	The Butts? (Drake Street)	Firgrove via Milnrow Road (Newbold Street) (MUDC boundary)	Electric	RCT	05.10.04	06.08.32	Canal bridge was actual boundary.
Marland	The Butts ? (Drake Street)	Sudden (Manchester Road/ Bolton Road) via Manchester Road or Drake Street	Electric	RCT	05.10.04	02.07.32	Meeting here Middleton E.T. cars.

Section	From	To	Traction	Operator	Started	Closed	Notes
Bacup	Cheetham Street	Healey (Ending Rake, Whitworth UDC boundary.)	Electric	RCT	23.11.04	14.05.32	First part of Bacup route.
Spotland	St Mary's Gate	Cheetham Street	Electric	RCT	23.11.04	02.11.10	
Littleborough	Cheetham Street	Heybrook (Entwistle Road)	Electric	RCT	26.01.05	19.10.30	Steam cars to Littleborough via Entwistle Road continued until 11.05.05
Marland	Sudden (Manchester Road/ Bolton Road)	Marland (Heywood boundary)	Electric	RCT	13.04.05	02.07.32	Steam cars from boundary to Heywood until 20.09.05.
Marland	Sudden (Manchester Road/ Bolton Road)	Marland (Heywood boundary)	Electric	RCT	13.04.05	02.07.32	Steam cars from boundary to Heywood until 20.09.05.
Littleborough	Cheetham Street/ Yorkshire Street	Littleborough (Eastwood Street)	Electric	RCT	29.05.05	19.10.30	Cheetham Street to Yorkshire Street/ John Street closed 03.07.05 ?
Littleborough	The Butts/South Parade	Littleborough via Smith Street, John Street, Entwistle Road, Heybrook	Electric	RCT	04.07.05	19.10.30	Extended from Eastwood St to Littleborough Square.
Bacup	The Butts/South Parade	Whitworth Road	Electric	RCT	04.07.05	14.05.32	Town centre terminus changed from Cheetham St to The Butts
Summit	Littleborough Square	Summit (Todmorden Road, Summit Hotel)	Electric	RCT	12.08.05	19.10.30	Shuttle service, (1 car only) Littleborough Square to Summit.
Marland	Marland	Heywood Centre via Rochdale Road, York Street	Electric	RCT/HCT	20.12.05	02.07.32	Joint service with Heywood Corporation
Norden/ Thornham	Norden	Hathershaw (Oldham) via Thornham, Summit, Royton, Star Inn	Electric	RCT/OCT	01.05.06	26.12.16	Joint service with Oldham Corporation
Marland	Rochdale (Butts)	Bury (Kay Gardens, via Heywood, Wham Bar, Heap Bridge, Heywood St)	Electric	RCT/BCT	01.08.09	02.07.32	Joint Service with Bury Out via Drake Street In via Manchester Road (Heywood service extended?)
Bacup	Healey (Ending Rake, Market Street)	Whitworth (Hall Street, Dog & Partridge)	Electric	RCT	14.06.10	14.05.32	Part of Bacup extension
Bacup	Whitworth (Hall Street)	Facit (Station Road)	Electric	RCT	20.07.10	14.05.32	Part of Bacup extension

Section	From	To	Traction	Operator	Started	Closed	Notes
Bacup	Facit (Station Road)	Shawforth (Tommy Shanter/ Red Lion)	Electric	RCT	06.09.10	14.05.32	Part of Bacup extension
Spotland	Newgate	Town Centre	Electric	RCT	03.11.10	19.04.31	New road, extension of Blackwater Street. Spotland service terminus moved from Cheetham St to Tramway Centre
Bacup	Shawforth (Tommy Shanter/ Red Lion)	Bacup (Market Street) via Britannia, Sheephouses.	Electric	RCT	25.07.11	14.05.32	Meeting Rawtenstall system. (no track connection).
Milnrow	Firgrove (Newbold Street)	Milnrow (Kiln Lane)	Electric	RCT	12.12.11	06.08.32	
Milnrow	Milnrow (Kiln Lane)	New Hey (Huddersfield Rd) via Dale Street, New Hey Road, Huddersfield Road.	Electric	RCT	01.03.12	06.08.32	Last route extension until 1924.
Circular	Oldham Rd/High Level Rd	High Level Rd/Maclure Road	Electric	RCT	17.08.04	15.08.24	Replaced by Maclure Road (see below)
Circular	Drake St/Maclure Rd	Maclure Rd/Tweedale St.	Electric	RCT	11.08.24	19.04.31	
Castleton	Sudden	Castleton Borough boundary (Chesham Ave)	Electric	MCT	09.08.25	12.11.32	Trial run on 07.08.25 by Manchester.
Castleton	Rochdale Town Centre	Manchester (High St) (via Sudden)	Electric	RCT/MCT	09.08.25	12.11.32	Route 17 (only service to carry route number). Out via Manchester Road In via Drake Street. Short workings to Chesham Av.

179

Table 2 Electric tram services operated at the maximum extent of system in 1929.

Service	Route	Short workings	Car types
Bamford – New Hey	Bury Road (Dog & Partridge), Bridge Street, Dane Street, Esplanade, Town Centre, Drake Street, Milnrow Road, Rochdale Road, Dale Street, New Hey Road.	Town Centre to Athletic Grounds (Milnrow Road) for football traffic. Also Saturdays to West Street.	Single deck; double deck to Athletic Grounds for short time before closure. Westinghouse brake cars only. Double deck cars to New Hey for a short period.
Norden – Thornham	Edenfield Road, Spotland Bridge, then EITHER Spotland Road, St Mary's Gate, Blackwater Street, Newgate, OR Mellor Street, Bridge Street, Dane Street, Esplanade to Town Centre, then Drake Street, Oldham Road, Thornham Summit. (Connection with Oldham Corporation trams to Oldham and Hathershaw. Previous through service to Hathershaw joint with Oldham Corporation withdrawn by 1916).	Spotland Bridge or Town Centre to King's Road	Double deck balcony and fully enclosed
Spotland – Sudden	Rooley Moor Road, Spotland Bridge, Spotland Road, St. Mary's Gate, Blackwater Street, Newgate, Town Centre, Drake Street, Manchester Road.	Town Centre to Spotland (for Turner Bros.), Town centre to Sudden (for Dunlop). Sudden to Middleton.	Double deck balcony a fully enclosed.
Circular	Town Centre, Drake Street, Maclure Road, Lower Tweedale Street, Tweedale Street, Manchester Road, Esplanade. (Former route via High Level Road replaced by Maclure Road route, 1924).	Town Centre to Railway Station (when required).	Double deck open top.
Rochdale – Littleborough	Smith Street, John Street, Yorkshire Street OR Entwisle Road, then Halifax Road (Rochdale), Halifax Road (Wardle), New Road, Featherstall Road, Littleborough Square.	Rochdale to Smithy Bridge Road (Easter and holidays).	Double deck all types, also single decks. Double decks via Entwisle Road, single decks via John Street.
Littleborough – Summit	Littleborough Square, Church Street, Todmorden Road.	None.	Double deck open top, single deck. Latterly through workings from Summit to Rochdale.

Service	Route	Short workings	Car types
Rochdale - Bury	Town Centre, Drake Street, Maclure Road, Lower Tweedale Street, Tweedale Street, Manchester Road, Bolton Road, Rochdale Road East, York Street, Market Street, Bridge Street, Bury Street, Bury New Road, Rochdale Road, Heywood Street, Spring Street, Frederick Street, Market Street (inbound), The Rock, Clough Street, Rochdale Road (outbound).	Rochdale to Heywood	Double deck fully enclosed; open top and balcony cars on short workings to Heywood.
Rochdale – Bacup	Smith Street, John Street, Whitworth Road, Market Street (Whitworth), Market Street (Facit), Market Street (Shawforth), Rochdale Road, St. James' Street. (Terminus formerly in Bridge Street, cut back to foot of South Street.)	Rochdale to Healey. Rochdale to Facit.	Single deck. Double deck open top (extras). Some fully enclosed.
Rochdale – Manchester (High Street)	Town Centre, Drake Street, (outbound), Manchester Road, Esplanade (inbound), Manchester Road, Rochdale Road, Long Street, Manchester New Road, Rochdale Road, Shudehill, Nicholas Croft, High Street.	Rochdale to Castleton. Rochdale to Middleton.	Double deck fully enclosed Joint service with Manchester Corporation Tramways.

Driver and conductor stand by their charge, an open top 4-wheeler bound for Summit, a remote terminus on the road to Todmorden

Table 3   Rochdale Bus Routes in tramway era.

Route	Date opened	Last tram ran	Notes
Castleton	17.03.26	12.11.32	
Healey	26.03.26	14.05.32	
Wardle	24.05.26	-	
Bury	27.05.26		Jericho only. Extended to Bury 19.12.27.
Clough Road, Shore and Hollingworth Lake	13.08.26	-	Some reports give 20.08.26 for opening
Turf Hill	22.10.26	-	
Halifax	22.06.27	-	Abandoned 10.12.28.
Syke	26.07.27	-	
Shaw	17.08.27	-	
Manchester	24.10.27	-	Express route, withdrawn 12.11.32, same day as trams.
	13.11.32	12.11.32	Tram replacement bus service.
Todmorden	26.01.28	-	
Ashton-under-Lyne	21.02.28	-	Limited Stop, abandoned 18.02.39.
Bacup	05.03.28	14.05.32	Express route, withdrawn 14.05.32.
Belfield	09.12.28	-	
Bamford Village	23.03.29	04.01.31	Trams only to Dog & Partridge.
Bolton	21.10.29	-	Through running discontinued 17.09.39.
Littleborough & Summit	19.10.30	19.10.30	Same day as trams withdrawn.
Norden	04.01.31	04.01.31	Same day as trams withdrawn.
Bury Road	04.01.31	04.01.31	Same day as trams withdrawn.
Spotland	19.04.31	19.04.31	Same day as trams withdrawn.
Circular (Molesworth Street, Railway Station etc.)	19.04.31	19.04.31	Bus circular route different to tram route.
Thornham	19.04.31	19.04.31	Same day as trams withdrawn.
New Hey	15.05.32	06.08.32	Same day as trams withdrawn.
Bacup	15.05.32	14.05.32	
Heywood & Bury	03.07.32	02.07.32	
Castleton boundary	13.11.32	12.11.32	

Note: Dates have generally been taken from official minutes and annual reports but in some cases other sources including press reports give different dates.

182

APPENDIX F
TRAMWAY ROLLING STOCK
FLEET LIST

Fleet No.	Type	Trucks	Motors	Controllers	Brakes	Body	Seating	Entered service	Withdrawn	Notes
1	SD comb. 8-wh (Southport type)	Brill 22E Max. Traction	DK 35A 2 x 35 hp	Dick Kerr DB1-B	Hand slipper & magnetic slipper	ER&TCW	42 ?	1902	1919	Body known as Southport.
2	DD OT balc. 8-wh	Brill 22E Max. Traction	DK 35A 2 x 35 hp	Dick Kerr DB1-B	Hand slipper & magnetic slipper	ER&TCW	36/30 ?	1902	1919	Originally air brakes.
2 (second)	DD OT 4-wh	Brush Radial	Brush Conaty 2 x 25 hp	Brush HD2 1002B	Hand slipper &	Brush ?	26/22	1925	1931	Built 1905. Ex-METC. Originally Middleton No.11.
3	DD OT balc. 4-wh	Brill 21E Single truck	DK 25A 2 x 25 hp	Dick Kerr DB1-B	Hand slipper & magnetic slipper	ER&TCW	34/22	1902	1932	EE top cover 1930.
4	DD OT balc. 8-wh Enclosed platforms	Brush D equal wheel bogies	GE 58-4T 2 x 35 hp	BTH B18	Hand slipper rheostatic & mechanical slipper	Milnes	36/30	1902	1930	
5	DD OT balc. 8-wh Enclosed platforms	Brush B reversed max. traction bogies	GE 58-4T 2 x 35 hp	BTH B18	Hand slipper & magnetic slipper	Milnes	36/30	1902	1930	Brush D Equal wheel bogies to McGuire pattern fitted later
6	DD OT balc. 8-wh Open platform	Brush D equal wheel bogies	GE52-6T 4 x 25 hp	BTH B6	Hand slipper & magnetic slipper	Milnes	36/30	1902	1930	Originally fitted with Brill 27G equal wheel bogies?
7 - 9	DD OT balc. 4-wh	Brill 21E Single truck	DK 35A 2 x 35 hp	Dick Kerr DB1-B	Hand slipper & magnetic slipper	ER&TCW	4/22	1902	1930	Originally air brake
10	DD OT balc. 4-wh	Brush AA Single truck	Brush 1002 2 x 25 hp	Brush 3A	Hand slipper & magnetic slipper	Brush/EE	33/22	1903	1932	Hexag dash & enc platforms 1928. EE top cover 1930.
11	DD OT balc. 4-wh	Brush AA Single truck	Brush 1002 2 x 25 hp	Brush 3A	Hand slipper & rheostatic	Brush/EE	33/22	1903	1932	Hexag dash & enc platforms 1928. EE top cover 1930.
12	DD OT balc. 4-wh	Brush AA Single truck	Brush 1002 2 x 25 hp	Brush 3A	Hand slipper & rheostatic	Brush/EE	33/22	1903	1925	

Fleet No.	Type	Trucks	Motors	Controllers	Brakes	Body	Seating	Entered service	Withdrawn	Notes
12 – 15 (second)	DD OT balc. 4-wh	Brush Radial Conaty	Brush 1002B 2 x 25 hp	Dick Kerr DB1-B	Hand slipper & ?	Brush	26/22	1925	c.1931	Built 1905. Ex-METC 12 – 15 in 1925.
13 - 14	DD OT balc. 4-wh	Brush AA Single truck	Brush 1002 2 x 25 hp	Brush 3A	Hand slipper & magnetic slipper	Brush/EE	33/22	1903	1925	
15	DD OT balc. 4-wh	Brush AA Single truck	Brush 1002 2 x 25 hp	Brush 3A	Hand slipper & rheostatic	Brush/EE	33/22	1903	1925	
16	DD OT balc. 4-wh	Brush AA Single truck	Brush 1002 2 x 25 hp	Brush 3A	Hand slipper & magnetic slipper	Brush/EE	33/22	1903	1931	
17	DD OT balc. 4-wh	Brush AA Single truck	Brush 1002 2 x 25 hp	Brush 3A	Hand slipper & magnetic slipper	Brush/EE	33/22	1903	1930	
18	DD OT balc. 4-wh	Brush AA Single truck	Brush 1002 2 x 25 hp	Brush 3A	Hand slipper & rheostatic	Brush/EE	33/22	1903	1930	
19	DD OT balc. 4-wh	Brush AA Single truck	Brush 1002 2 x 25 hp	Brush 3A	Hand slipper & magnetic slipper	Brush/EE	33/22	1903	1932	Converted to engineering car 1927. Numbered 1.
20	DD OT balc. 4-wh	Brush Conaty Radials	Brush 1002 2 x 25 hp	Brush 3A	Hand slipper & magnetic slipper	Brush/EE	33/22	1905	1932	EE top cover 1930.
21 - 28	DD OT balc. 4-wh	Brush Conaty Radials	Brush 1002 2 x 25 hp	Brush 3A	Hand slipper & magnetic slipper	Brush/EE	33/22	1905	1931	24 Decorated car 1918. Platforms vestibuled.
29	DD OT balc. 4-wh	Brush Conaty Radials	Brush 1002 2 x 25 hp	Brush 3A	Hand slipper & magnetic slipper	Brush/EE	33/22	1905	1932	Hexag dash & enc platforms 1928. 1928 Carnival car. EE top cover 1930.
30	SD combination 8-wh	Brush D Equal wheel bogies	Brush 1202 2 x 35 hp	Brush 3A	Hand slipper & magnetic slipper	Brush/EE	38	1905	1931	
31	SD combination 8-wh	Brush D Equal wheel bogies	Brush 1202 2 x 35 hp	Brush 3A	Hand slipper & magnetic slipper	Brush/EE	38	1905	1930	
32	SD combination 8-wh	Brush D Equal wheel bogies	Brush 1202 2 x 35 hp	Brush 3A	Hand slipper & magnetic slipper	Brush/EE	38	1905	1931	
33 - 37	SD combination 8-wh	Brush D Equal wheel bogies	Brush 1202 2 x 35 hp	Brush 3A	Hand slipper & magnetic slipper	Brush/EE	38	1905	1930	

Fleet No.	Type	Trucks	Motors	Controllers	Brakes	Body	Seating	Entered service	Withdrawn	Notes
38	SD combination 8-wh	Brush D Equal wheel bogies	Brush 1202 2 x 35 hp	Brush 3A	Hand slipper & magnetic slipper	Brush/EE	38	1905	1931	Vestibuled in early 20's.
39 - 41	SD combination 8-wh	Brush D Equal wheel bogies	Brush 1202 2 x 35 hp	Brush 3A	Hand slipper & magnetic slipper	Brush/EE	38	1905	1930	
42	SD combination 8-wh	Brush D Equal wheel bogies	Brush 1202 2 x 35 hp	Brush 3A	Hand slipper & magnetic slipper	Brush/EE	38	1905	1926	
43	SD combination 8-wh	Brush D Equal wheel bogies	Brush 1202 2 x 35 hp	Brush 3A	Hand slipper & magnetic slipper	Brush/EE	38	1905	1931	
44 - 49	DD OT balc. 8-wh	Brush D Equal wheel bogies	Brush 1202 2 x 35 hp	Brush 3A	Hand slipper & magnetic slipper	Brush/EE	33/22	1905	1932	EE top covers 1930.
50	SD combination 8-wh	Brush D Equal wheel bogies	Brush 1202 2 x 35 hp	Brush 3A	Hand slipper & magnetic slipper	Brush/EE	38	1906	1930	
51	SD combination 8-wh	Brush D Equal wheel bogies	Brush 1202 2 x 35 hp	Brush 3A	Hand slipper & magnetic slipper	Brush/EE	38	1906	1926	
52 - 54	SD combination 8-wh	Brush D Equal wheel bogies	Brush 1202 2 x 35 hp	Brush 3A	Hand slipper & magnetic slipper	Brush/EE	38	1906	1931/32	52, 54 enclosed in 20's.
55	SD combination 8-wh	Brush D Equal wheel bogies	Brush 1202 2 x 35 hp	Brush 3A	Hand slipper & magnetic slipper	Brush/EE	38	1906	1926	
56	SD combination 8-wh	Brush D Equal wheel bogies	Brush 1202 2 x 35 hp	Brush 3A	Hand slipper & magnetic slipper	Brush/EE	38	1906	1930	
57	SD combination 8-wh	Brush D Equal wheel bogies	Brush 1202 2 x 35 hp	Brush 3A	Hand slipper & magnetic slipper	Brush/EE	38	1906	1931/32	
58	SD combination 8-wh	Brush D Equal wheel bogies	Brush 1202 2 x 35 hp	Brush 3A	Hand slipper & magnetic slipper	Brush/EE	38	1906	1930	
59	SD combination 8-wh	Brush D Equal wheel bogies	Brush 1202 2 x 35 hp	Brush 3A	Hand slipper & magnetic slipper	Brush/EE	38	1906	1931/32	Enclosed in 20's.
60 - 69	SD combination 8-wh	Brush D Equal wheel bogies	Brush 1218 2 x 42 hp	Westinghouse T1.C	Hand slipper & magnetic slipper	Brush/EE	38	1912	1931/32	Same design as 30 to 43 series.

Fleet No.	Type	Trucks	Motors	Controllers	Brakes	Body	Seating	Entered service	Withdrawn	Notes
70 -79	DD top covered, open balc. 4-wh	Brill 21E Single truck	DK 30B 2 x 40 hp	EE DB1 K3B	Hand slipper & magnetic slipper	English Electric	36/22	1920	1932	
80 - 85	DD encl. 4-wh	Preston 21E Single truck	DK 30B 2 x 40 hp	EE DB1 K3B	Hand slipper & magnetic slipper	English Electric	42/22	1925	1932	80 last car on system, route 17.
86 - 89	DD encl. 4-wh	Preston 21E Single truck	DK 30B 2 x 40 hp	EE DB1 K33B	Hand slipper & magnetic slipper	English Electric	42/22 [42/20 in '29]	1926	1932	89 transverse leather seats, and 50 hp H/sp motors 1929.
90 - 92	DD encl. 4-wh	Brill 21E Single truck	Brush 1202 2 x 35 hp	Brush 3A	Hand slipper & magnetic slipper	English Electric	42/22	1926	1932	
93	DD encl. 4-wh	Brill 21E Single truck	MV 107 2 x 65 hp H/spd Worm drive	MV OK9B	Hand slipper & magnetic slipper	Rochdale CT	42/20	1927	1932	EE top cover. Transverse seats.
94	DD encl. 4-wh	Brill 21E Single truck	MV 102 DR 2 x 50 hp	MV OK9B	Hand slipper & magnetic slipper	Rochdale CT	42/20?	1928	1932	EE top cover. Transverse seats.
-	Water car 4-wh	Brush AA ? Single truck	Brush 1002 2 x 25 hp?	Westinghouse T1.C	Hand slipper & magnetic slipper	Brush/EE	-	1912		

Notes

BTH British Thomson-Houston
comb. Combination cars, with central saloon and seats on platforms at each end.
CT Corporation Tramways
DK Dick Kerr

EE English Electric
ER&TCW The Electric Railway and Tramway Carriage Works Ltd.
METC Middleton Electric Traction Company Limited.
MV Metropolitan Vickers.

APPENDIX G
ROCHDALE TRAMWAY DEPOTS

Depot	Location	Opened	Closed	Traction	Operator	Notes
Steam tram depot	Entwistle Road	07.05.83	11.05.05	Steam 3' 6"	MBROT	
Steam tram depot	York Street, Heywood	20.12.04	20.9.05	Steam 3' 6"	HCT	
Steam tram depot	Littleborough ??			Steam 3' 6"	MBROT?	Marked on 'Atlas' (not shown in WGSH).
Steam tram depot	Royton	?	?	Steam 3' 6"	MBROT	
Temporary shed	Bridgefold, Spotland Bridge	?	18.07.04 ?	Electric	RCT	
Temporary shed	Bury Road/Bridge Street	?	?	Electric	RCT	
Bacup	Rochdale Road	?.11.11 ?	14.05.32 ?	Electric	RCT	
Rochdale Tram Depot (east)	Mellor Street	15.07.04	12.11.32	Electric	RCT	Used as bus garage until November 1991 Offices opened 23.06.05
Rochdale Tram Depot (west)	Mellor Street	1920?	12.11.32	Electric	RCT	Used for munitions during First World War.

APPENDIX H
FINANCIAL DATA 1903 – 1933.

Year ended 31st March	No. of passenger cars	Route mileage Single track	Double track	Total track	Car Miles	No. Passengers	Units Per Car mile	Units used	Traffic revenue £	Total revenue £	Working expenses £	Interest (net) £	Sinking Fund £	Rents £	Income Tax £	Balance £
1902					130,879	878,223				5,456						
1903					190,890	1,156,301				6,980						
1904					386,547	2,837,110				14,974						
1905					962,352	7,612,524				42,033						
1906					1,119,757	9,480,293	1.690	1,896,278	53,830	54,138	29,505	10,621	6,734	3,613	772	2,893
1907	59	11-1710	8-1694	20-1644	1,166,632	9,943,740				56,557						
1908	59	11-1710	8-1694	20-1644	1,248,362	10,247,338	1,785	2,077,320	56,731	57,271	31,853	11,328	9,388	3,876	1,015	-189
1909	59	11-1710	8-1694	20-1644	1,275,351	10,428,065	1,798	2,124,487	57,341	57,889	32,954	11,046	9,387	4,134	726	-357
1910	59	11-1710	8-1694	20-1644	1,402,532	11,360,871	1,739	2,261,384	62,393	63,000	34,356	11,091	9,397	5,509	703	1,944
1911	59	13-1610	10-100	23-1710	1,589,866	12,711,114	1,508	2,250,037	72,203	73,002	37,368	11,380	9,447	7,626	695	6,486
1912	69	16-1200	11-1187	28-627	1,749,967	13,740,152	1,553	2,566,554	79,567	80,345	41,998	10,587	9,454	9,328	700	8,224
1913	69	16-1200	11-1187	28-627	1,788,030	14,584,777	1,546	2,610,994	81,926	83,176	44,429	10,326	9,456	9,455	1,020	8,490
1914	69	16-1200	11-1187	28-627	1,772,546	14,286,607	1,694	2,836,062	81,995	83,402	46,892	10,081	9,455	9,444	2,038	4,284
1915	69	16-1200	11-1187	28-627	1,698,504	14,632,646	1,729	2,777,673	86,644	87,909	51,387	10,396	9,398	9,254	3,865	3,609
1916	69	16-1200	11-1187	28-627	1,647,046	15,119,798	1,857	2,887,035	89,466	90,812	54,039	10,110	9,576	8,851	6,464	1,773
1917	69	16-1200	11-1187	28-627	1,639,815	17,582,301	1,957	3,025,678	106,783	108,472	65,087	10,167	9,575	9,586	5,706	8,351
1918	69	16-1200	11-1187	28-627	1,533,513	18,721,524	1,816	2,785,548	116,252	118,033	80,574	10,105	9,566	9,934	7,492	662
1919	69	16-1200	11-1187	28-627	1,854,672	19,726,158	2,034	3,597,583	159,210	161,457	125,960	10,480	9,583	10,043	8,073	-2,682
1920	69	16-680	11-1054	27-1734	1,869,424	21,192,223	2,109	3,768,262	184,396	186,855	154,387	12,092	9,507	10,383	9,821	-9,335
1921	79	16-680	11-1054	27-1734	1,825,691	19,919,351	2,010	3,509,833	174,616	176,970	153,266	14,873	7,700	8,977	11,284	-19,130
1922	79	16-680	11-1054	27-1734	1,937,083	20,369,139	1,865	3,450,431	172,124	174,550	122,295	14,639	8,608	10,454	12,112	6,442
1923	79	16-420	11-1314	27-1734	1,937,307	19,882,607	1,805	3,343,483	163,041	165,359	117,767	13,009	8,608	10,302	6,138	9,535
1924	79	16-420	11-1314	27-1734	2,020,896	23,908,447	1,777	3,440,825	161,674	164,160	119,213	11,159	8,608	10,331	7,781	7,068
1925	79	16-420	11-1652	28-312	2,245,514	26,437,854	1,844	3,964,177	175,293	178,027	129,603	11,528	9,922	11,535	8,329	7,109
1926	88	17-980	12-584	29-1564	2,242,129	25,870,494	1,854	3,974,617	173,605	177,483	137,378	11,122	8,670	8,048	11,961	304
1927	88	17-980	12-584	29-1564	2,416,557	27,045,462	1,890	4,376,321	173,634	177,757	135,934	11,609	8,928	5,726	11,762	3,797
1928	88	17-914	12-738	29-1652	2,569,593?	25,695,793	1,917	4,452,736	160,383	164,644	135,062	11,384	9,290	11,253	7,785	-10,040
1929	83	17-914	12-738	29-1652	2,333,708	24,948,463	1,934	4,316,310	146,150	150,867	125,799	12,862	9,334	10,440	4,476	-12,044
1930	81	16-1431	13-221	29-1652	2,076,386	20,927,629	1,967	3,885,612	115,586	125,516	116,438	13,530	10,216	9,059	2,278	-5,196
1931	64	16-1431	13-221	29-1652	1,422,103	12,619,716	2,130	2,820,339	74,390	79,257	79,216	12,776	10,216	8,403	6,355	-14,314
1932	46	16-1431	13-221	29-1652	359,018	3,496,111	2,086	694,421	19,599	22,346	26,189	12,353	10,216	5,841	4,000	-16,127
1933	0	16-1431	13-221	29-1652												

APPENDIX J

DATA FOR ROCHDALE CORPORATION TRAMWAYS

Table 1. Statistical data for peak year of operation, 1927/28.

Item	Data	Notes
Route length, single track	16.51 miles	
Route length, double track	12.06 miles	
Total route length	28.57 miles	
Equivalent single track length	40.63 miles	
Sidings and depots, single track equivalent	1.20 miles	
Total single track length	41.83 miles	
Running powers route length	13.74 miles	
Number of cars – up to 40 seats	32	Combination cars
Number of cars – 41 to 60 seats	34	
Number of cars – 61 to 80 seats	22	
Total number of cars	88	
Total seating capacity	4,548	
Average number of seats per car	51.68	
Number of passengers carried	27,252,491	
Number of car miles run	2,429,140	
Number of car hours worked	303,919	
Number of car miles per car hour	8.00	
Maximum authorised line voltage	550 V dc	
Number of traction units consumed	4,376321	
Number of traction units per car mile	1.89	
Average fare paid per passenger journey	1.53 d	
Average fare per mile, ordinary	1.30 d	
Average fare per mile, workmen	0.65 d	
Revenue per car mile	17.50 d	
Revenue per route mile	5,909 d	£24 12s 5d
Working expenditure per car mile	13.72 d	
Operating ratio	77.96%	Total working expenditure divided by total income x 100.

189

Table 2. Track mileage by local authority, 1927/28.

Authority	Single track	Double track	Total Route miles	Total equivalent single track miles
Rochdale Corporation	9.65	8.79	18.44	27.23
Bacup Corporation	1.07	0.51	1.58	2.09
Littleborough U.D.C.	2.05	0.79	2.84	3.63
Milnrow U.D.C.	1.18	0.60	1.78	2.38
Whitworth U.D.C.	2.56	1.37	3.93	5.30
Total	16.51	12.06	28.57	40.63

Table 3. Tram and bus performance, 1926/27 to 1930/31.

Item	1926/27		1927/28		1928/29		1929/30		1930/31		1931/32	
	Tram	Bus	Tram	Bus	Tram	Bus	Tram	Bus	Tram	Bus	Tram	Bus
Passengers carried	20,544,387	1,621,224	27,045,462	3,216,136	25,695,793	5,878,549	24,948,463	7,137,023	20,927,629	9,901,465	12,619,716	19,142,076
Total receipts, £	177,482	13,986	177,756	33,062	164,644	70,154	150,867	81,779	125,516	100,244	79,257	148,173
Surplus (deficit), £	304	2,231	3,796	6,955	(10,040)	16,822	(12,044)	16,217	(5,196)	35,783	(14,314)	43,625
Revenue per veh. mile, d	18.9	12.0	17.6	12.1	15.8	12.3	15.5	12.5	14.6	13.1	12.6	13.0
Pass. per veh. mile	11.5	6.6	11.2	5.7	10.6	4.3	10.7	4.5	10.1	5.4	8.9	7.0
No. of trams/buses	88	10	88	25	83	35	81	33	64	54	46	79

APPENDIX K
TRAMWAY SYSTEMS IN THE NORTH WEST

Ref. No	Location	County	Tramway	Traction	Gauge	Open	Closed
1	Accrington	Lancs	Accrington Corporation Steam Tramways Company	Steam	4' 0"	1886	1907
2	Accrington	Lancs	Accrington Corporation Tramways	Electric	4' 0"	1907	1932
3	Ashton-underLyne	Lancs(GM)	Manchester Carriage & Tramways Company	Horse	4' 8½"	1881	1903
4	Ashton-underLyne	Lancs(GM)	Oldham, Ashton & Hyde	Electric	4' 8½"	1899	1921*
5	Ashton-underLyne	Lancs(GM)	Ashton-underLyne Tramways	Electric	4' 8½"	1902	1938
6	Barrow-in-Furness	Lancs(Cum)	Barrow in Furness Tramways Company	Steam	4' 0"	1885	1903
7	Barrow-in-Furness	Lancs(Cum)	Barrow-in-Furness Corporation	Electric	4' 0"	1904	1932
8	Birkenhead	Chesh(M)	Birkenhead Street Railway Company	Horse	5' 2"/4' 8½"	1860	1901?
9	Birkenhead	Chesh(M)	Hoylake and Birkenhead Rail & Tramway Company	Horse	4' 8½"	1873	1879
10	Birkenhead	Chesh(M)	Wirral Tramway Company	Horse	4' 8½"	1877?	?
11	Birkenhead	Chesh(M)	Birkenhead Corporation Tramways	Electric	4' 8½"	1901	1937
12	Birkenhead	M	Wirral Metropolitan Borough Tramway	Electric	4' 8½"	1995	open
13	Blackburn	Lancs	Blackburn & Over Darwen Tramways Company	Steam	4' 0"	1881	1900*
14	Blackburn	Lancs	Blackburn Corporation Tramways	Horse	4' 8½"	1887	1901?
15	Blackburn	Lancs	Blackburn Corporation Tramways	Steam	4' 8½"	1887	1902?
16	Blackburn	Lancs	Blackburn Corporation Tramways	Electric	4' 8½"	1899	1949
17	Blackpool	Lancs	Blackpool Corporation Tramways	Horse	4' 8½"	1885	1899?
18	Blackpool	Lancs	Blackpool Corporation Tramways	Electric+	4' 8½"	1885	open
19	Blackpool	Lancs	Blackpool & Fleetwood Tramroad Company	Electric	4' 8½"	1898	1920*
20	Bolton	Lancs (GM)	Bolton Corporation Tramways	Horse	4' 8½"	1880	1900
21	Bolton	Lancs (GM)	Bolton Corporation Tramways	Electric	4' 8½"	1899	1947
22	Burnley	Lancs	Burnley & District Tramway Company	Horse	4' 8½"	1881	?
23	Burnley	Lancs	Burnley & District Tramway Company	Steam	4' 8½"	1881	1901*
24	Burnley	Lancs	Burnley Corporation Tramways	Electric	4' 8½"	1901	1935
25	Bury	Lancs (GM)	Bury Corporation Tramways	Electric	4' 8½"	1903	1949
26	Carlisle	Cumb (Cum)	City of Carlisle Electric Tramways Company	Electric	3' 6"	1900	1931
27	Chester	Chesh	Chester Tramways Company	Horse	4' 8½"	1870	1902
28	Chester	Chesh	Chester Corporation Tramways	Electric	3' 6"	1903	1930
29	Colne & Trawden	Lancs	Colne & Trawden Light Railway Company	Electric	4' 0"	1903	1934
30	Darwen	Lancs	Blackburn & Over Darwen Tramways Company	Steam	4' 0"	1881	1899*
31	Darwen	Lancs	Darwen Corporation Tramways	Steam	4' 0"	1899	1900
32	Darwen	Lancs	Darwen Corporation Tramways	Electric	4' 0"	1900	1946
33	Farnworth	Lancs (GM)	Bolton Corporation Tramways	Horse	4' 8½"	1880	1900
34	Farnworth	Lancs (GM)	Farnworth Urban District Council Tramways	Electric	4' 8½"	1902	1906*
35	Heywood	Lancs (GM)	Manchester Bury Rochdale & Oldham Steam Tramway	Steam	3' 6"	1884	1904*

Ref. No	Location	County	Tramway	Traction	Gauge	Open	Closed
36	Heywood	Lancs (GM)	Heywood Corporation Tramways	Steam	3' 6"	1904	1905
37	Lancaster	Lancs	Lancaster & District Tramways Company	Horse	4' 8½"	1890	1921
38	Lancaster	Lancs	Lancaster Corporation Tramways	Electric	4' 8½"	1903	1930
39	Liverpool	Lancs (M)	Old Swan Tramway	Horse	4' 8½"	1861	1862?
40	Liverpool	Lancs (M)	Liverpool Tramways Company	Horse	4' 8½"	1869	1897*
41	Liverpool	Lancs (M)	Liverpool & Prescot Light Railway	Electric	4' 8½"	1902	1919*
42	Liverpool	Lancs (M)	Liverpool Corporation Tramways	Horse	4' 8½"	1897	1903
43	Liverpool	Lancs (M)	Liverpool Corporation Tramways	Electric	4' 8½"	1898	1957
44	Lytham St Annes	Lancs	Blackpool St Annes & Lytham Tramway Company	Gas	4' 8½"	1896	1903
45	Lytham St Annes	Lancs	Blackpool St Annes & Lytham Tramway Company	Horse	4' 8½"	1900	1902
46	Lytham St Annes	Lancs	Lytham St Annes Corporation Tramways	Electric	4' 8½"	1903	1937
47	Manchester	Lancs (GM)	Manchester Carriage & Tramways Company	Horse	4' 8½"	1877	1903
48	Manchester	Lancs (GM)	Manchester Corporation Tramways	Electric	4' 8½"	1901	1949
49	Manchester	Lancs (GM)	Greater Manchester Metro Ltd/Serco Metrolink Ltd **	Electric	4' 8½"	1992	open
50	Middleton	Lancs (GM)	Middleton Electric Traction Company	Electric	4' 8½"	1902	1925*
51	Morecambe	Lancs	Morecambe Tramways Company	Horse	4' 8½"	1887	1909*
52	Morecambe	Lancs	Morecambe Tramways Company	Petrol	4' 8½"	1912	1924
53	Morecambe	Lancs	Morecambe Corporation Tramways	Horse	4' 8½"	1909	1926
54	Nelson	Lancs	Burnley & District Tramways	Steam	4' 8½"	1881	1901*
55	Nelson	Lancs	Nelson Corporation Tramways	Electric	4' 0"	1903	1933*
56	Nelson	Lancs	Burnley Colne & Nelson Joint Transport Committee	Electric	4' 0"	1933	1934
57	Oldham	Lancs (GM)	Manchester Carriage & Tramways Company	Horse	4' 8½"	1880	1901
58	Oldham	Lancs (GM)	Manchester Bury Rochdale & Oldham Steam Tramway	Steam	4' 8½"	1885	1902
59	Oldham	Lancs (GM)	Oldham Ashton-under-Lyne & Hyde Electric Tramways	Electric	4' 8½"	1899	1921*
60	Oldham	Lancs (GM)	Oldham Corporation Tramways	Electric	4' 8½"	1900	1946
61	Preston	Lancs	Preston Tramways Company	Horse	3' 6"	1879	1903
62	Preston	Lancs	Preston Corporation Tramways	Electric	4' 8½"	1904	1934
63	Rawtenstall	Lancs	Rossendale Valley Tramways	Steam	4' 0"	1889	1908*
64	Rawtenstall	Lancs	Rawtenstall Corporation	Steam	4' 0"	1908	1909
65	Rawtenstall	Lancs	Rawtenstall Corporation	Electric	4' 0"	1908	1932
66	**Rochdale**	**Lancs (GM)**	**Manchester Bury Rochdale & Oldham Steam Tramway**	**Steam**	**3' 6"**	**1883**	**1904***
67	**Rochdale**	**Lancs (GM)**	**Rochdale Corporation Tramways**	**Steam**	**3' 6"**	**1904**	**1905**
68	**Rochdale**	**Lancs (GM)**	**Middleton Electric Traction Company**	**Electric**	**4' 8½"**	**1902**	**1925***
69	**Rochdale**	**Lancs (GM)**	**Rochdale Corporation Tramways**	**Electric**	**4' 8½"**	**1902**	**1932**
70	St Helens	Lancs (M)	St Helens & District Tramways Company	Horse	4' 8½"	1881	1890?
71	St Helens	Lancs (M)	St Helens & District Tramways Company	Steam	4' 8½"	1890	1901?
72	St Helens	Lancs (M)	New St Helens & District Tramways Company	Electric	4' 8½"	1899	1919*
73	St Helens	Lancs (M)	St Helens Corporation Tramways	Electric	4' 8½"	1919	1936
74	Salford	Lancs (GM)	John Greenwood	Horse	c.5' 0"?	1861	1872?

Ref. No	Location	County	Tramway	Traction	Gauge	Open	Closed
75	Salford	Lancs (GM)	Manchester Carriage & Tramways Company	Horse	4' 8½"	1877	1901*
76	Salford	Lancs (GM)	Salford Corporation Tramways	Horse	4' 8½"	1901	1903
77	Salford	Lancs (GM)	Salford Corporation Tramways	Electric	4' 8½"	1901	1947
78	South Lancashire#	Lancs (GM)	South Lancashire Electric Traction & Power Company	Electric	4' 8½"	1902	1906*
79	South Lancashire#	Lancs (GM)	Lancashire United Tramways	Electric	4' 8½"	1906	1933
80	Southport	Lancs (M)	Southport Tramways Company	Horse	4' 8½"	1873	1902
81	Southport	Lancs (M)	Birkdale & Southport Tramways Company	Horse	4' 8½"	1883	1900
82	Southport	Lancs (M)	Southport Corporation Tramways	Electric	4' 8½"	1900	1934
83	Stalybridge	Lancs (GM)	Stalybridge, Hyde, Mossley and Dukinfield Tramways and Electricity Board	Electric	4' 8½"	1903	1945
84	Stockport	Chesh(GM)	Manchester Carriage & Tramways Company	Horse	4' 8½"	1880	1902?
85	Stockport	Chesh(GM)	Stockport & Hazel Grove Carriage & Tramway Company	Horse	4' 8½"	1890	1905*
86	Stockport	Chesh(GM)	Stockport Corporation Tramways	Electric	4' 8½"	1901	1951
87	Trafford Park	Lancs (GM)	British Gas Traction Company	Gas	4' 8½"	1897	1908
88	Trafford Park	Lancs (GM)	British Gas Traction Company	Electric	4' 8½"	1903	1905*
89	Wallasey	Chesh(M)	Wallasey Tramways Company	Horse	4' 8½"	1879	1902*
90	Wallasey	Chesh(M)	Wallasey Corporation Tramways	Electric	4' 8½"	1902	1933
91	Warrington	Lancs(Ches)	Warrington Corporation Tramways	Electric	4' 8½"	1902	1935
92	Waterloo & Great Crosby	Lancs (M)	Liverpool Overhead Railway Company	Electric	4' 8½"	1900	1925
93	Wigan	Lancs (GM)	Wigan Tramways Company	Horse	3' 6"	1880	1885
94	Wigan	Lancs (GM)	Wigan Tramways Company	Steam	3' 6"	1882	1893*
95	Wigan	Lancs (GM)	Wigan & District Tramways Company	Steam	3' 6"	1893	1902*
96	Wigan	Lancs (GM)	Wigan Corporation Tramways	Electric	3' 6"	1901	1925
97	Wigan	Lancs (GM)	Wigan Corporation Tramways	Electric	4' 8½"	1923	1931

*   taken over by another tramway.
+   conduit current collection 1885-1899.
#   Atherton, Ashton in Makerfield, Hindley, Leigh, Tyldesley, etc.
** Stagecoach from 17.07.07

County codes (County shown at time of opening with current county in brackets).
Chesh   - Cheshire.
Cum   - Cumberland.
Cumb   - Cumbria.
Lancs   - Lancashire.
GM - Greater Manchester.
M   - Merseyside.
NB: Many takeovers and changes of company names occurred, particularly in the earlier years of tramways. Also operating franchises, powers and joint working were commonplace in some areas. The operator shown is the major or predominant operator.

APPENDIX L
CHRONOLOGY

	1777	Coach to London commenced running; five days journey.
	1788	Fare to Manchester by the York Royal Mail Stage Coach 5/-.
	1788	Canal from Sowerby Bridge to Rochdale opened.
	1790	'High Flyer' first local stage coach from Rochdale to Manchester began running.
21 December	1804	Rochdale Canal opened, cost nearly £500,000.
	1810	Drake Street opened, named after Vicar of Rochdale.
September	1830	Liverpool and Manchester Railway opened.
June	1832	Rochdale made Parliamentary Borough.
19 June	1835	Stage coach overturned in Blackwater Street. Several persons seriously injured.
4 July	1836	Act of Parliament to enable the construction of the Manchester and Leeds Railway received Royal Assent.
4 June	1839	Manchester and Leeds railway opened as far as Littleborough.
September	1840	Summit Tunnel, begun in February 1838, completed. 41 fatal accidents occurred during construction. Tunnel is 2,986 yards long. (Year of Queen Victoria's wedding).
1 March	1841	Manchester and Leeds Railway opened throughout.
	1846	Town became a Municipal Borough.
23 April	1856	Paddle steamer and boats placed on Hollingworth Lake.
13 September	1856	Daily Railway service to Manchester, 13 trains; to Leeds 10; to Liverpool 8.
	1858	Railway excursions run to to Blackpool and Southport, return fare 1s 6d.
16 September	1861	Buses commenced running to Oldham to bring passengers into communication with the new route to the south.
7 June	1862	Shawforth Branch Railway Bill approved; it was opposed by the Fieldens who declared that the scheme would be for years, it might be for ever, a constant drain on the income of the Yorkshire and Lancashire Railway Co..
2 November	1863	Railway through Milnrow to Oldham opened for passenger traffic.
1 March	1865	L & Y began cheap train service to Manchester ; single third class fare 8d, return 1s.
31 July	1865	Construction of Shawforth Railway commenced by turning a sod near Foxholes.
	1865	Norden Coach Company formed, capital £700 in £1 shares.
26 November	1866	Horses attached to the Whitworth 'bus bolted. In Whitworth Road the vehicle collided with a lamp post; a man killed falling from the top of the 'bus.
	1868	The Esplanade opened.
1 October	1868	Smithy Bridge Railway Station opened.
	1869	Movement on foot to construct branch railway to Norden.
1 November	1870	Railway opened as far as Facit.
27 September	1871	Town Hall opened.
15 May	1872	Public meeting of residents at Merefield and Sudden to urge L & Y Railway Co. to provide a station at New Barn Lane.
12 May	1872	Introduction of the Block System on the railway between the town and Manchester; eight block stations provided.
24 October	1874	Town Council reject a proposal to make a tramway between the Coal Siding and the gasworks.

October	1875	'Bluepits' railway station re-named 'Castleton'.
May	1876	Rochdale Carriage Company Ltd. formed.
November	1876	Castleton new railway station opened.
25 December	1876	An omnibus began to run daily between the town and Oldham; fare inside 10d, outside 7d.
12 May	1877	An omnibus began to run daily between to Littleborough; fare inside 5d, outside 4d.
27 June	1881	Hudson's coach from York to Liverpool commenced running through the town; withdrawn 1 August.
	1881	1881 Tramways Company formed. £10 shares.
6 October	1881	Mr. S.S. Platt C.E. appointed Borough Surveyor.
1 December	1881.	Railway extension from Facit to Bacup opened.
27 July	1882	Tramways construction begun by Alderman Tweedale removing two paving stones at the junction of Oldham Road and Drake Street.
7 May	1883	Steam Tram depot opened on Entwistle Road by Manchester, Bury, Rochdale & Oldham Steam Tramways Company.
		Tramways opened to the public. The first car started from the Wellington Hotel for Buersill, and returning proceeded to Littleborough.
November	1883	Tramway as far as Ending opened.
30 March	1884	Trams first run from Rochdale to Bury.
30 May	1884	Tramway to Bury opened throughout.
11 July	1884	Tramway extension from Ending to Whitworth opened.
1 March	1885	Tramway opened to Royton.
3 March	1885	Tram accident at the Dusty Miller Inn, Sudden. A car broke away from the engine and ran down Manchester Road at considerable (from Castleton)speed. Several persons injured.
3 April	1885	Steam tramway to Facit opened throughout.
May	1885	Mr J.S. Ayton appointed General Manager of Tramway Company.
1 August	1885	Tramway extension from Royton to Oldham opened.
24 May	1886	Tramway waiting room, South Parade, opened.
May	1886	Mr E Rothwell appointed Tramways Manager.
24 May	1887	Heywood 'bus, which for many years ran from Old Market Place to the neighbouring borough, ceased running.
29 October	1887	Tramway Co.'s shares, £10 paid up, were quoted at 20s per share.
October	1887	Tramways winding up petition presented to court. £500,000 had been expended on the undertaking; debts owing by the company, £160,000.
September	1888	Tramways reconstruction scheme announced. New company formed, £1 shares.
October	1888	Manchester, Bury, Rochdale & Oldham Steam Tramways Company taken over by Bury, Rochdale & Oldham Tramways Company.
1 April	1889	The town became a County Borough.
28 April	1889	Rochdale New Railway Station opened. The site of the extensions cost £70,000.
April	1889	Tramcars to Littleborough at this time started from Cheetham Street.
November	1894	Scheme for making a railway to Norden announced; abandoned owing to want of financial support.
March	1895	Norden Railway Bill for the construction of a line, 1 mile 5 furlongs in length, from Facit Branch line, before Parliament.
27 February	1897	Motor car first passed through the town.
24 December	1897	Electric lighting installation, Edenfield Road, Norden, inaugurated.
6 February	1898	Mr E Rothwell, Tramways Manager, died.

195

February 1898	Mr J Brindle, secretary of the Tram Co., appointed Manager.
2 June 1898	Town Council adopted a resolution in favour of taking over the undertaking of the Tramway Company within the Borough in 1902. Tramways undertaking cost over £500,000 to complete. (Refers to steam tramways??).
March 1900	Rochdale Borough extended to include Castleton Urban District Council, population 6,990.
1900	Rochdale Corporation Act 1900. (Acquired the Tramways Undertaking).
11 August 1900	Runaway steam tram at Royton.
25 October 1900	Electricity Works opened in Dane Street. Manager and Engineer: Mr C C Atchison (Oct 1900-Nov 1917) Mr F H Rudd (January 1918 -)
1901	Municipalisation of tramways. Tracklaying begins for electric tramway.
15 May 1901	Mr John Brindle, Tramway Manager, and his family thrown into Hollingworth Lake when landau overturned.
8 March 1902	Trial run of tram on thecastleton to Middleton tramway.
28 March 1902	Inauguration of the Middleton to Sudden tramways by private company.
22 May 1902	Rochdale electric tramways opened - Manchester Road to Bury Road (Cemetery). Borough Electrical Engineer, Mr C C Aitcheson, appointed to manage tramways.
17 June 1902	Tram route to Norden via Spotland and Edenfield Road opened.
25 June 1902	Announced that sub-way through railway station to be closed to all except railway officials and passengers.
21 July 1902	Tram route to Spotland (Rooley Moor Road) opened.
1902	Tramway Company's powers expire.
1902	Rates increased to 7/7 in the £. Ratepayers complained bitterly about high rates and urged need for economy.
1903	Councillor Wilson Dunning appointed Chairman of Tramways Committee.
7 July 1903	Horse omnibus accident (Bacup bus), driver killed and three persons injured.
May 1903	Rochdale Council authorises capital expenditure for reconstruction of steam tramway tracks and conversion to standard gauge, covering of River Roach in town centre (Rochdale Bridge to Wellington Bridge) to provide central tram terminus, and construction of tramway depot at Mellor Street with construction of new road between Mellor Street and Spotland Bridge.
May 1903	River covering from Yorkshire Street to the Wellington Bridge was started. Completed July 1904. This was the first section of the River Roach to be covered.
December 1903	Rochdale Council and old Tramways Company still not come to terms about purchase price of company.
1904	Rochdale Corporation Tramway Order confirmed by the Tramways Orders Confirmation (No.1) Act.
1904	Mellor Street opened.
2 January 1904	Announced that Rochale's identification mark for motor cars was 'DK'. Reported that 9 motors and 8 motorcycles had been registered and 23 persons had applied for driving licences.
July 1904	Mr J S D Moffatt appointed General Manager.
10 July 1904	Rochdale Corporation purchase Manchester, Bury, Rochdale and Oldham Tramway routes within Rochdale.
16 July 1904	The tramway arbitration award was £159,075, exclusive of £3,600 still in dispute.
12 August 1904	Major Druitt, Railways Inspectorate, inspects new tram line in Mellor Street and tests river covering. New depot opened.
20 August 1904	Circular tram route opened after inspection by Major Druitt from town centre via Drake Street, Oldham Road, High Level Road, Tweedale Street, Manchester Road, and Drake Street.
2 September 1904	Tram route opened along Oldham Road to Kings Road.

196

4 October	Tram routes opened from Kings Road to Thornham (Oldham Road, Firgrove (Milnrow Road) and Sudden via Manchester Road or Drake Street.
1904	
1 November 1904	Tram route extended from Thornham Summit to Royton and Oldham. Joint tram service with Oldham Corporation between Hathershaw and Norden.
23 November 1904	Tram route opened from Cheetham Street to Healey.
17 January 1905	Trial run made on reconstructed tracks in Yorkshire Street from St James's Church to Heybrook.
24 January 1905	Through tram service opened between Spotland and Heybrook.
11 May 1905	Last steam tram runs, on Littleborough route.
11 May 1905	Steam tram depot closed. Subsequently demolished and site used to provide public baths.
1905	Tramways completed within the Borough of Rochdale..
1905	Steam tram depots in Rochdale, Royton and Bury sold at auction for £500. At the arbitration proceedings the authorities valued these depots at £15,861, while the private company placed the valuation at £26,887. The sale was one of the sensations of the year.
July 1906	Rochdale Corporation Tramways Order confirmed by the Tramways Orders Confirmation Act.
1906	Rochdale, Bury and Oldham Tramways made a further payment to shareholders.
7 December 1906	The new Maclure Road opened to vehicular traffic.
December 1906	Arctic weather - heavy snowstorm stops trams running for a time.
	1907 It took 7 hours to go by electric tram from Rochdale to Liverpool and cost 2/7d.
4 June 1907	Tram car runs away down Drake Street.
25 September 1907	Mr R. A. L. Hutchinson fined for striking a tram conductor with a whip.
April 1909	River covering from Yorkshire Street to the west side of the Newgate started. Completed July 1910.
26 July 1909	The last meeting of the shareholders of the Bury, Rochdale and Oldham Tramways Company held. Shareholders received £1 12s 1 3/5d for each £1 share.
1910	New street through to Newgate completed. Spotland trams run through to town centre.
1911	Bolton's illuminated tram came to Rochdale.
3 August 1911	At the 'Rushbearing' holiday a train strike forces holidaymakers to find other forms of transport to seaside. "Undaunted, many holidaymakers determined to get to the seaside left the town in brakes, wagonettes an even furniture vans. Others went by tram, walking the distances between the trams of the various towns. Fortunately the strike was of short duration and the trippers were able to come back in greater comfort." (New Annals).
1914	Joint tram service with Oldham ceases.
14 February 1914	Tram car ran away down John Street, crashing into the Pioneers' store at the bottom; 20 persons injured.
15 January 1915	An illuminated tramcar, bearing appeals for recruits, toured the main tramway routes.
27 January 1915	Tramway collision, resulting in injury to three persons, occurred near the Gale Inn, Whitworth Road.
18 March 1915	Railway accident, Smithy Bridge; four killed and many injured. Great snowstorm blowing.
18 March 1915	Great blizzard; snow fell for a period of 19 hours. Tram traffic was rendered impossible. One of the worst storms on record.
24 November 1915	Railway engine plunged down into new Barn Lane; driver and fireman injured.
1915/1916	£1,744 profit from tramways transferred to rate fund.
12 May 1916	Runaway tramcar, Drake Street; several injured.
2 November 1916	Tram car runs away downhill at Shawforth; wrecked; dozen passengers injured.
20 July 1918	Thunderstorm, accompanied by extremely heavy rainfall, causing much damage by flooding, particularly at Littleborough, Smallbridge and Milnrow. Train and tram traffic disorganised.
11 March 1919	Mr George Webster, tramways manager, received O.B.E.
17 August 1919	Tram smash at Shawforth; several passengers injured.

July	1920	Permanent way men of the tramways came out on strike.
4 July	1920	A Milnrow char-a-banc overturned in Derbyshire Peak district, several Milnrow and Newhey passengers being injured.
April	1921	Application to run bus service from Rochdale to Wardle and Hollingworth Lake refused.
14 December	1921	A tram conductor was crushed between two trams on the Broadway and died on the 15th.
	1921	Population of Rochdale 92,700 (1921 Census).
9 February	1922	Tram car ran away down John Street and, overturning, crashed into the Pioneers' shop at the bottom. Eighteen injured, among them Mr F. H. Rudd, Borough Electrical Engineer. A similar accident occurred at the same spot on 14th February 1914.
June	1922	River covering from Newgate to Theatre Street started. Completed June 1923.
October	1923	River covering from Wellington Bridge to Weir Street started. Completed July 1925. Officially opened by Mayor on 30 January 1926.
	1924	A Bill passed in Parliament giving powers to Rochdale Council to run motorbuses in the town and districts.
	1924	River covering to Weir Street completed.
	1925	Rochdale Corporation Act. (Granted powers to run motor omnibuses).
2 February	1925	Tramcar posting boxes inaugurated.
6 April	1925	Third John Street tram smash. Tram out of control dashes downhill and overturned at the bottom; 24 persons injured, 11 detained at the Infirmary.
1 August	1925	Rochdale Corporation takes over northern portion of Middleton Tramways route through Castleton to Sudden.
30 January	1926	River covering Wellington Bridge to Weir Street opened. Cost of covering Weir Street to Theatre Street £78,000 approx.
	1926	Milnrow Road railway arch widening completed.
3 May	1926	General strike called and lasted for 9 days; trains, buses and trams all stopped but gas and electricity keep going.
24 December	1927	Heavy fall of snow; trams held up.
18 October	1930	First tram route abandonement: Littleborough and Summit.
15 December	1930	"Electric House", the Corporation Electricity Department's new showrooms formally opened by Councillor L W Taylor JP.
12 January	1931	Mr R. S. Pilcher, Manchester Transport Manager, lectures on 'Trams v. Buses' at the Reform Club.
12 November	1932	Rochdale electric tramways closed; last route Rochdale to Manchester.
12 November	1932	Rochdale electric tramways depot closed. Subsequently converted for use as bus garage.

January	1983	Light rail route to Rochdale proposed in Feasibility Study.
January	1984	Greater Manchester Council accepts Rail Study Group recommendation for Rail Strategy including light rail to Rochdale after consultation with District Councils.
November	1987	Parliamentary Bill deposited for conversion of Oldham/Rochdale railway line to light rail.
November	1989	Parliamentary Bill deposited for extension on street between Rochdale railway station and Rochdale town centre.
April	1990	Royal Assent obtained for conversion of Oldham/Rochdale railway line to light rail.
October	1991	Royal Assent obtained for Rochdale town centre extension.
July	2001	GMPTE issues bid documentation to four consortia bidding for Phase 3.(includes Rochdale line):
		Greater Manchester Rapid Transit Company (AMEC Project Investments, Bombardier Transportation, First Group plc.)
		Greater Manchester Tramways Ltd.(Stagecoach Group Holdings plc, Alstom Holdings SA, John Mowlem & Company plc, Edmund Nuttall Ltd, Virgin Group Ltd.)
		Maintram (Bechtel Enterprises(UK)Ltd, Amey Ventures Ltd, Group 4 Falck Global Solutions Ltd, MTR Corporation Ltd, Semaly SA.)
		Manchester Tram Company (Serco, SNC Lavalin).
4 January	2002	Bids submitted by four consortia.
10 December	2002	Alistair Darling, Secretary of State for Transport, announces approval for £520 million government funding for £820 million Phase 3 contract.
19 December	2002	GMPTE announces two shortlisted bidders for Phase 3 Greater Manchester Tramways and Manchester Tram Company
17 July	2004	Alistair Darling, Secretary of State for Transport, announces withdrawal of government funding for Phase 3 contract.
16 December	2004	Secretary of State for Transport re-instates £520m package for Metrolink extensions including Oldham-Rochdale.
30 June	2005	Rail Minister Derek Twigg announces £102m upgrade for existing Metrolink system.
6 July	2006	Douglas Alexander, Secretary of State for Transport, announces conditional approval for Phase 3a extensions including Oldham to Rochdale Station but not the extension to the Town Centre.
27 July	2007	Transport Innovation Fund (TIF) bid submitted to Government including Metrolink extension from Rochdale Station to the Town Centre, and congestion charging.
	2009?	Oldham-Rochdale line closes to allow conversion works to begin?
	2010?	Construction of light rail in Rochdale begins??
	2012?	Trams run again in Rochdale??

APPENDIX M
ABBREVIATIONS

A.M.I.C.E.	Associate member of the Institution of Civil Engineers
A.M.I.E.E.	Associate member of the Institution of Electrical Engineers
A.M.I.M.E.	Associate Member of the Institute of Mining Engineers
B.E.T.	British Electric Traction Ltd.
BCT	Bury Corporation Tramways
BR	British Railways (took over all railways on 1 January 1948).
BRO	The Bury, Rochdale and Oldham Steam Tramway Company
BTH	British Thomson-Houston
CT	Corporation Tramways
d	Pence (12 old pennies = 5 new pence)
DK	Dick Kerr
EE	English Electric
ER&TCW	The Electric Railway and Tramway Carriage Works Ltd.
GMPTA	Greater Manchester Passenger Transport Authority
GMPTE	Greater Manchester Passenger Transport Executive
HCT	Heywood Corporation Tramways
L & Y	Lancashire and Yorkshire (became part of London & North Western Railway on 1 January 1922).
LHAS	Littleborough Historical and Archaeological Society
LMS	London Midland & Scottish Railway (took over L&NWR on 1 January 1923).
LRTA	Light Rail Transit Association
M & L	Manchester and Leeds Railway (became Lancashire & Yorkshire Railway on 9 July 1847).
MCT	Manchester Corporation Tramways
M.Inst.C.E.	Member of the Institution of Civil Engineers
MBRO	Manchester, Bury, Rochdale and Oldham Steam Tramways Company Limited
METC	Middleton Electric Traction Company Limited.
MoT	Ministry of Transport
MTMS	Manchester Transport Museum Society
MV	Metropolitan Vickers.
OCT	Oldham Corporation Tramways
PTE	Passenger Transport Executive
RCT	Rochdale Corporation Tramways
RVT	Rossendale Valley Tramways
s	Shilling. (= 12 pence. = 5 new pence)
SELNEC	South East Lancashire North East Cheshire.
TIF	Transport Innovation Fund
T.I.M.	Ticket Issuing Machines Ltd.
TMS	Tramway Museum Society
UDC	Urban District Council

APPENDIX N

BIBLIOGRAPHY

1. 'Tramway Traction - Résumé of Paper'. S. S. Platt. Rochdale Literary and Scientific Society. 18 March 1898. (Reprinted from Rochdale Observer, 23 March 1898).

2. 'Annals of Rochdale'. Robert D. Mattley. Aldine Press. Rochdale. 1899.

3. 'Rochdale Corporation Tramways Official Guide and Illustrated Map of the Electric Tramway Routes'. Edwards & Bryning. Rochdale. 1906

4. 'Jubilee 1856-1906' Edwards & Bryning. Rochdale. 1906.

5. 'Where to go by Car'. John Lingard. 1908.

6. 'Rules and Regulations for Officers and Servants and Tramway Bye-Laws and Regulations'. Rochdale Corporation Tramways. 1915.

7. 'Where to go by Tram'. John Lingard. 1924. (Re-printed by Manchester Transport Historical Collection. Rochdale. c.1966).

8. 'Rules and Regulations for Officers and Servants and Tramway Bye-Laws and Regulations'. Rochdale Corporation Tramways. 1926.

9. 'Tramways and Light Railways (Street and Road) and Trackless Trolley Undertakings'. (Returns for 1927/28). H.M.S.O. London. 1928.

10. 'New Annals of Rochdale'. T.T.Heywood. Rochdale Times. Rochdale. 1931.

11. 'History of the Steam Tram'. Dr.H.A.Whitcombe. Journal of the Institution of Locomotive Engineers, Vol.XXVII, No.137, May-June 1937. (Reprinted by Adam Gordon 2000).

12. 'Municipal Transport in Lancashire'. R. Stuart Pilcher. Proc. Conference on Transport in Lancashire. Manchester. July 1938.

13. 'The Story of Rochdale Transport' C. T. Humpidge. Paper to Rochdale Education Guild. Rochdale Art Gallery. 16 March 1946. (unpublished).

14. '50 Years of Municipal Transport Operation 1902-1952'. Commemorative Brochure. Rochdale Corporation Passenger Transport. 1952.

15. 'Tickets of the Road Transport Services linking Ashton-under-Lyne, Oldham and Rochdale'. W.H.Bett and Roger Atkinson. Ticket and Fare Collection Society. London. 1955.

16. 'Rochdale Retrospect' A Centenary History of Rochdale. Rebe P. Taylor. Ernest Taylor, Ed. Rochdale Corporation. 1956.

17. 'Great British Tramway Networks'. Wingate H.Bett and J.C.Gillham. LRTL. London. 1957.

18. 'History of Rochdale Corporation Tramways and Transport'. Anon. 12 March 1959. (unpublished) (Rochdale Observer archives).

19. 'Transport in Rochdale and District'. T B Maund. The Omnibus Society. 1959.

20. 'Buses in Rochdale and District 1931 - 1946'. F.P.Groves. Buses Illustrated Nos. 125, August 1965, 127 October 1965, 129 December 1965, 131 February 1966, 133April 1966. Ian Allan. Shepperton. 1965/66.

21. 'Railways and Mineral Tramways of Rossendale'. B. Roberts. The Oakwood Press. 1974.

22. 'The Brush Electrical Engineering Company Limited & its Tramcars'. J.H.Price. TLRS. 1976. (Walter Gratwicke Memorial Lecture 1975).

23. 'The Tramways of South-east Lancashire.' W H Bett and J C Gilham; J H Price (Ed). Light Railway Transport League. London. 1976 (?).

24. 'Middleton Tramways'. A K Kirby. Manchester Transport Museum Society. Castleton, Rochdale. 1976.

25. ' Rochdale Corporation Tramways - 1'. H.G.Dibdin.Tramway Review Vol.12 No. 93. Spring 1978. LRTL.

26. 'Rochdale Corporation Tramways - 2'. H.G.Dibdin. Tramway Review Vol.12 No. 94. Summer 1978. LRTL.

27. 'Rochdale Corporation Tramways - 3'. H.G.Dibdin. Tramway Review Vol.12 No. 95. Autumn 1978. LRTL.

28. 'The Manchester Bury Rochdale & Oldham Steam Tramway.' W G S Hyde. Transport Publishing Company. Glossop. 1979.

29. 'Rochdale – a postscript.' H.G.Dibdin. Tramway Review Vol.13 No. 98. Summer 1979. LRTL.

30. 'Trans-Pennine Heritage. Hills, People and Transport'. Keith Parry. David and Charles. Newton Abbot. 1981.

31. 'Roads and Rails of Manchester'. J.Joyce. Ian Allan. Shepperton. 1982.

32. 'Rochdale's Tramways.' Clifford Taylor. Manchester Transport Museum Society. Heaton Park. Manchester. 1987.

33. 'The Bacup Branch Rochdale Facit Bacup.' Branch Lines of the L.&Y.R. No.7. The Lancashire & Yorkshire Railway Society. Sutton-in-Craven. 1989.

34. 'Trams in Trouble'. Brian Hinchcliffe. Pennine Publications Ltd. Sheffield. 1990.

35. 'The Directory of British Tramways.' Keith Turner. Patrick Stephens Limited. Yeovil. 1996.

36. 'English Electric Tramcar Album'. Geoff Lumb. Ian Allan. Shepperton. 1998.

37. 'Old Ordnance Survey Maps. Rochdale (South) 1908. Lancashire Sheet 89.05' Alan Godfrey Maps. Consett. 1999.

38. 'Castleton - A History'. James J.Connolly. for Springhill Hospice. Rochdale. July 1999.

39. 'The Directory of British Tram Depots'. Keith Turner, Shirley Smith & Paul Smith. Oxford Publishing Company. Hersham. 2001.

40. 'Old Ordnance Survey Maps. Rochdale (West) 1908. Lancashire Sheet 88.04' Alan Godfrey Maps. Consett. 2002.

41. 'Old Ordnance Survey Maps. Rochdale 1908. Lancashire Sheet 89.01' Alan Godfrey Maps. Consett. 2002.

42. 'National atlas showing canals, railways and street tramways, Volume 2p, Rochdale and Oldham. G.L.Crowther. Preston. 2002.

43. 'The Tram Depots of Oldham and Rochdale'. T Clarkson. Colamda. Huddersfield. 2003.

44. 'From the Mersey to the Pennines by Tram'. T.B.Maund. Archive, Issue 42 June 2004 (Part 1), Issue 43 September 2004 (Part 2).

45. 'British Tramway Accidents'. Frank E. Wilson; Ed. G. B. Claydon. Adam Gordon. 2006.

Also:

Annual Reports and Accounts of The Tramways Committee, County Borough of Rochdale (1907 – 1933).

Rochdale Corporation Tramways. Minutes of Sub-Committee. 15 March 1909 to 28th January 1914, and 25th March 1914 to 29th August 1932.

Rochdale Observer archives.